C000151996

SCALE for SALE

Advance praise for *SCALE for SALE*:

"*SCALE for SALE* is highly practical and absolutely picks up the points that need to be considered to scale up and then sell a company. It asks all the right questions of the reader and can be used like a reference manual or a go-to guide as well as being an invaluable source of insight and information".

Dr Paul Beven, Serial Entrepreneur, Director & Co-Founder of The Healix Group.

"*SCALE for SALE* should be a must read for every business school teaching entrepreneurship and for anyone considering a start-up or looking to scale-up and then plan an exit. Mark's personal experience from his start-ups make the critical points memorable. It is the most pragmatic and candid description of how to build an organization and dare I say inspiring!"

Jas Awla, Entrepreneur, Head of Strategy & Partnerships, MIB, USA.

"The tone of the book is extremely engaging, the conversational style of the writing is perfect for this kind of book, the last chapter is as readable as the first. The scope of *SCALE for SALE* is ambitious – going from start-up via scale up to exit in less than 350 pages, yet the energy and interest is kept throughout".

Dr Maria Wishart, Research Fellow, Enterprise Research Centre, Warwick Business School, Warwick University.

"*SCALE for SALE* is an inspiring, interesting read and is full of useful tips you can immediately apply and implement in your business."

Robert Archer, Commercial Director, Asset Protection Group LTD.

"*SCALE for SALE* is a wonderful insight for entrepreneurs and an enjoyable read into what it takes to develop, grow and then sell a company - As I read through, I think about the young people I've helped over the years and how much of this text would help them - It is an excellent, engaging narrative and a must read for anyone thinking of a career as an entrepreneur".

Mike Bright OBE, Former CEO & Mentor for the Prince's Trust.

"*SCALE for SALE* is an engaging read packed with practical advice, real-world examples and valuable insights. It should certainly be on the reading list of all entrepreneurs thinking about their scale-up journey."

Maroun Mourad, President, Global Underwriting at Verisk Inc., and author of 'The Insurance Management Playbook'.

"When in the middle of putting the building blocks to your start-up operation in place it's not easy for entrepreneurs to visualise too far ahead. How are you going to scale your business? What do you envisage for your exit in 5, 10 or 15 years down the line? Visualising the bigger picture and planning your way from start-up to scale-up to exit is alien and complex to most, yet critical for success. *SCALE for SALE* is extremely useful in this regard. The book offers a peek into the future journey of a start-up highlighting important points that need to be considered, providing tried and tested approaches to tackling typical roadblocks, challenges, and bumps in the road. It is essential reading for a scale-up journey."

Siddharth Bhaskar, Founder, Adept Thinking LTD and author of 'Hindu Philosophy for an Inquisitive Mind'.

"…a tremendous tour de force…focused on scaling and business building. I like the writing style, the practical nature of the book and the exercises and stories. It will be a great reference source for early-stage entrepreneurs. The breadth of business building topics has been covered tightly and cohesively."

Paul O'Dea, Managing Director, Select Strategies LTD and author of 'The Growth Roadmap', 'The Business Battlecard' and 'Select Selling'.

This publication is designed to provide accurate and authoritative information regarding the subject matter covered. It is sold with the understanding that the publisher is not engaged in rendering legal, accounting, or other professional services. If legal advice or other professional assistance is required, the services of a competent professional person should be sought.

No responsibility or liability is assumed by the Publisher for any injury, damage or financial loss sustained to persons or property from the use of this information, personal or otherwise, either directly or indirectly. While every effort has been made to ensure reliability and accuracy of the information within, all liability, negligence or otherwise, from any use, misuse, or abuse of the operation of any methods, strategies, instructions, or ideas contained in the material herein, is the sole responsibility of the reader.

All information is generalized, presented for informational purposes only and presented "as is" without warranty or guarantee of any kind.

The moral right of the author has been asserted.

First published in the UK by Blue Ocean Analytics LTD 2021.

ISBN 9798749418767

Copyright 2021 by Mark Harrison - All rights reserved.

www.scale-for-sale.com

SCALE
for SALE

How to Build a Business
and Sell it for Millions

MARK HARRISON

This book is dedicated to Alison, Abby, Josh and Jonny.

CONTENTS

Synopsis

"Are you sure we should be selling the Golden Goose?" Asked Peter, a non-executive director, and shareholder. The board had just received a revised offer for our business - we would become millionaires! Just over a decade later, it was déjà vu. I was now presiding over another high growth, high margin business. A giant American corporation interested in acquiring our company had put a proposal on the table. *"That is a life-changing amount of money Mark but is this the time to be selling?"* asked Mike, a retired former blue-chip CEO, now a non-executive advisor and mentor.

Building a thriving business often involves some luck as well as requiring hard work, focus and determination. It also means getting some of the simple but critical things right. Few people have successfully repeated the process. I have. Though I am no genius, had a modest upbringing and went to a state comprehensive school. By reading this book, you will discover that anyone choosing to be an entrepreneur can become a multi-millionaire with the right mindset, know-how, and approach.

This book encapsulates some of the key learnings from my experience through various ventures, not all successful. I show you methods I found work to propel a business from the start-up phase through scaling up, preparing for sale, and then eventually how to approach your exit. In other words, how to progress from an initial fledgling firm through to putting that multi-million-pound cheque in the bank.

Written by somebody who has been there, done it and had repeated success, this book focuses on those who have started a new company and are now ready to scale. It is also, I hope, helpful to all those budding entrepreneurs out there, undecided about the next step and thirsting for inspiration.

My background

I live in Hertfordshire, England with my wife and three children. I can usually be found either hacking a ball around a local golf course or walking my dog Bailey in the beautiful Hertfordshire countryside.

I spent the first ten years of my career in the corporate financial world, initially in technical product development roles, and then in managerial positions. I always had a burning desire from a young age to do my own thing, to be my own boss and run my own company. Following a couple of false starts with failed technology start-ups, 'ValueInsurance.com' and 'MyNest' in the 1990s, I finally had my opportunity in July 2001. I led a management buy-out of Geological Information Systems (GIS) and the assets of a UK insurance analytics business, Intermediary Systems, from the Marsh & McLennan Group (NYSE: MMC).

The new business (ISL) grew at a rapid pace, reaching over £1 Million net profit within three years. This was a remarkable success and several of the ISL products reached a high level of customer penetration in the UK Property & Casualty (P&C) Insurance market. The company was agile, creative, and innovative. Pioneering new products were developed that influenced insurance risk pricing in the UK. For example, a risk mapping and analytics software platform was developed, called 'RiskPoint', winning an industry award for 'Risk Management Initiative of the Year'. This assessed property risk across a range of geographic risk factors by address for every house in the UK. ISL was subsequently acquired by Experian Plc [NYSE: EXPN] in 2004 for millions of pounds.

In 2008, during the backdrop of the financial crisis, I started another company 'Business Insight' from a blank sheet of paper. From the initial start-up this company was scaled successfully and grew into being a leading provider of software, data, and analytical services to the UK & Irish P&C

Insurance market. I achieved my second successful exit when this business was sold to Verisk Analytics Inc [NYSE: VRSK], a $31 billion-dollar American Corporation, in February 2018.

In the subsequent couple of years after the sale I worked at Verisk as the General Manager for Europe (Underwriting). In 2020 I decided to take time out on a personal sabbatical. Time to take a step back and then pursue a new challenge and an interest in writing a book about business. '*SCALE for SALE*' is my first book, based on my own life experiences and backed up with research. It is aimed at entrepreneurs and business owners searching for advice and inspiration on how to scale and then sell a business.

I am passionate about the value entrepreneurship adds to society. I'd love to be able to help other entrepreneurs reach their goals and benefit from my experiences and knowledge. If you need any support or advice in approaching the scale-up or the preparation for the sale of your business, please drop me a note at (Mark.Harrison@scale-for-sale.com).

Introduction

"Welcome to the world of Risk and Reward", said an investor to me on signing a shareholder agreement and my taking that first step into the new and unfamiliar territory as an entrepreneur. It was 2001, and I was thirty-three years of age. After ten years in the relative comfort and safety of a corporate environment, I was now on my own. It was an exciting time; the sense of freedom and anticipation of the challenge ahead was intoxicating! I had been searching for an opportunity for years to cut loose, free from the corporate world, bureaucracy, free to do my own thing and the moment had arrived.

Running your own company is a great adventure and one that I would highly recommend. There are currently 582 million entrepreneurs worldwide[1], a staggering number.

Though a global survey of business owners in 2020 revealed the main drivers to start a company vary from country-to-country, a universal fact remains that entrepreneurs are vital to the growth and future of all economies.

Table 1: Motivations to pursue a career as an entrepreneur.

Motivations (strongly agree)	% USA	% UK	% Canada	% Australia	% China	% Germany
To make a difference in the world	66%	49%	67%	52%	40%	44%
To build great wealth or a very high income.	69%	52%	64%	65%	48%	32%
To continue a family tradition	31%	6%	44%	23%	41%	69%
A way to earn a living because jobs are scarce	41%	64%	63%	41%	66%	43%

Source: Global Entrepreneurship Monitor 2020

Entrepreneurship plays a crucial role in society, bringing new ideas and innovations to market, new ways of working, creating new jobs, not to mention generating wealth and growth in an economy.

Globally, entrepreneurship has been on the increase and the number of new start-ups has been going up. Many people are enticed into launching a new venture, to be their own boss and to pursue their passion; and the numbers continue to increase year on year. Large numbers follow a career as an entrepreneur to add value to society, to pursue a purpose, fulfil a need and to make a difference. In the UK, over the last decade, there has been a 35% increase in new businesses registered[2].

In the USA, a growing number of people are considering entrepreneurship as a career option and over half of the working population would like to set up their own company[3]. Recent opinion polls in the UK[4] shows this number to be even higher in the younger generations, with a startling 83% of respondents in the 18 to 24-year age group stating their aspiration to start their own firm and become entrepreneurs.

A career as an entrepreneur is now 'cool' and has also become glamorized in recent times by TV programmes such as 'The Apprentice' and 'Dragons Den' in the UK, and 'Shark Tank' in the USA.

It may seem fashionable to the youth today though it is not an easy career path. Building a profitable venture requires significant time, hard work, resources, energy, and dedication. Many people start out on their entrepreneurial journey full of optimism, enthusiasm, and hope – yet without any knowledge or experience in the business of managing or running a company. It takes courage to go down the entrepreneurial path, yet most of what is taught in schools or universities does not prep you adequately for what is required.

The failure rate of start-ups is exceedingly high. Statistically, a third of UK businesses go bust within three years, and less than half survive five years of trading. In the USA, the pattern is very similar[5]. The figures are even more brutal in the technology space, with around 70% of start-ups failing – many within around 20 months of first raising financing[6]. In the UK, only 4% of companies typically reach the milestone of £1 million turnover[7] and even fewer get to the threshold of £1 million annual net profits.

<u>Fewer still exit via a trade sale and then repeat the process. I have, to Experian and to Verisk, though I am no genius.</u>

There have certainly been setbacks and lots of bumps in the road on my journey, though I believe that anyone can be successful with the correct mindset, approach, and focus. Unquestionably there are vital points to appreciate, simple things to get right, blind alleys to avoid and things to look out for.

I have experienced success and failure through the ventures I have been involved in. I have also made plenty of mistakes and, over time, have found ways that have worked for me to overcome obstacles, and that has led to repeated success. I wanted to share some of this knowledge and experience to help others and give some insight into scaling a business. If I can do it, so can you. So, during the first pandemic 'lockdown' of 2020, I decided to embark on a project to write a business book. My initial thoughts were: Where do I add value to those with a 'scale-able start-up'? What anecdotal material from my career experiences could I share that might be useful? What areas should I focus on to avoid reinventing the wheel?

Where are there gaps in the literature that I might fill with suitable material to produce something thought-provoking and compelling for the reader?

Following some initial research, I noticed many useful books available focusing on starting a company from scratch, plenty encouraging entrepreneurial ideas, and an abundance covering business skills from accounting to sales and marketing. Beyond getting the business up and running, the scale-up and growth phase seems underserved – or at least that is where more help might be useful. Consequently, the 'start-up to scale-up' phase is where I intend to focus, for entrepreneurs up and running with a viable business but wanting to embark on the next steps to fast growth.

By sharing my experiences and things that have happened along the way on my journey, I hope to add value. I will give my candid views on what has worked for me, covering some of the lessons learned through the pitfalls and crises, detailing how they have been overcome. And including valuable nuggets I have picked up from other people that have helped me along the way. We will look at the essential elements to get right in taking a company from that initial start-up phase through to fast growth, sustainable business. Then how to prepare for and approach your exit.

If you are already up and running with your business idea, well done! It is a big step on a journey where you will learn a lot about yourself and one from which you will hopefully get a lot of fulfilment from and a sense of freedom and accomplishment as you progress along the way. Perhaps you are about to embark on a scale up to the next level and looking for insight into what it takes to reach a higher level of turnover and profit to attract acquirers. How do you get into that small percentage of companies that sell for millions of pounds?

If you have already established your start-up and are now planning to scale, this will be essential reading for you.

OK, let's get started. What you need to do from the beginning is to lay solid foundations, put in place plans, have a clear competitive strategy, create a team structure to support growth and attract great talent to join you on the journey. And this all starts with you and your mindset.

So, first things first, it all begins with the dream, a vision, a goal. This is where the adventure commences and why your self-belief, ambition, values, and vision for where you are headed are critical.

References /Further reading

1. www.smallbizgenius.net/by-the-numbers/entrepreneur-statistics/
2. *House of Commons Briefing Paper No 06152 16 Dec 2019*
3. https://smeloans.co.uk/blog/64-percent-of-britains-workforce-want-to-start-a-business/
4. www.inc.com/leigh-buchanan/us-entrepreneurship-reaches-record-highs.html
5. Kelly L: 'Entrepreneurs ready to rebuild' Sunday Times 3/1/2021
6. *U.S Bureau of Labor Statistics* https://www.bls.gov/bdm/entrepreneurship/bdm_chart3.htm
7. https://www.cbinsights.com/research/startup-failure-post-mortem
8. https://www.cityam.com/why-most-businesses-never-reach-1m-turnover/

PART 1: LAYING SOLID FOUNDATIONS

SCALE for SALE

CHAPTER 1: IT'S ALL ABOUT THE FOUNDERS

"If I have the BELIEF that I can do it, I shall surely acquire the capacity to do it, even if I may not have it at the beginning"

– *Mahatma Gandhi*

Choosing a career as an entrepreneur and deciding to leave a comfortable well-paid job to go it alone is not an easy decision to have taken. It takes guts, courage, tenacity, dogged determination, and self-belief.

When you started on your business you were probably doing a variety of jobs, maybe you developed the product offering, sold it into that first customer and perhaps even also fulfilled the order. Out of necessity you need to be versatile at the start, multi-skilled, capable, and willing to do a variety of jobs – whatever it takes to get the operation off the ground.

Once that has been achieved, moving onto the next stage is another significant challenge.

There is nothing that compares to the feelings of freedom, inspiration and limitless energy when running your own business, though if you don't scale it you are unlikely to reap huge rewards.

Scaling up from an initial start-up or a small business is not straight forward and a path that many entrepreneurs never take.

1.1 What is the one thing that prevents most founders from being able to 'scale-up'?

Some people are happy to be integral to their business, comfortable providing a product or service, working long hours, so long as they are working for themselves. They work hard, are good at what they do and maybe even content making a reasonable living.

That is an achievement and is fine if you want a lifestyle business.

What happens though when you are ill? What if you want to take some time out or eventually want to sell up? If you go under a bus the business goes with you! You are working in the business, not on the business. And that is where a lot of entrepreneurs go wrong.

I have seen this many times and was guilty myself, in my younger days, of being reluctant to let go. To handover product development to other people, to step back and look at what needed to be in place for growth.

To ensure your business is not completely reliant on your skills, talent, contacts, and knowledge, you need to scale up.

Guess what, without scaling up and making the business self-sustaining you will struggle to ever sell it and you will not be able to be free of it to do anything else. Such as - to pursue hobbies or take special holidays to far flung places in the world that you have always wanted to visit. Certainly not for life changing amounts of cash!

To move to the next stage to scale-up you need to adapt, remain agile, and have a leadership mindset. Looking to work on the business rather than being fundamental within it.

Many entrepreneurs are not able to transition to a more 'hands-off' role. The firm remains completely dependent on the owner or main couple of shareholders. This inhibits growth and ultimately it becomes a difficult business to develop further and, at some point, sell on to realise the value within it.

Being able, willing, and conscious of the need to change with the requirements of the business and the market is vital to growth.

1.2 How scalable is your business?

Of course, not all businesses are easily scalable, even in the technology space.

Scaling up means increasing the revenues and growing the profit margin, not just growing the cost base. For example, management consultancies and companies that are heavily people dependent are the least scalable. Scaling these businesses involves hiring more and more talent, and that is expensive. Revenues are often largely generated through human-based projects that you need to keep on winning. You have a growing fixed cost base. And the pressure to preserve a high utilization rate for all your staff to ensure revenues continue to build. These businesses are challenging to scale and often difficult to sell on.

A lot of the value of the company is vested in the people, their skills, and capabilities, as they are the main asset.

Capital dependent companies such as insurance or mortgage companies are more scalable though they have limitations, for example, due to their balance sheet and solvency restrictions. The more scalable types of company are ideas-based companies with intellectual property (IP) that can be protected. For example, companies that can provide a product or service via a software app with the capability to distribute to and reach customers across the whole world via the Internet.

Software and analytics modelling technology firms are capital light, and examples of highly scalable companies. They are 'intangible' asset-based businesses where the core assets are things such as intellectual property, computer programs, data models, and the know-how and deep domain expertise of the team. With the right proposition and powered by the internet the rate of growth can increase exponentially. We have seen a few examples in the business to consumer market, or 'B to C' market where firms can become huge. There are well known examples in recent times, such as

Facebook, Netflix and Amazon that have scaled to become some of the biggest companies (by market value) in the world.

In the book 'Capitalism Without Capital' Haskel and Westlake[1] argue that in the rise in the value of technology, or intangible asset-based companies, scalability is the most pertinent factor. The core intangible assets of the firm, such as IP, brand, and the creative capability within the company, have no constraints and can be used again and again without getting used up or deteriorating.

This may explain some of the reasoning why companies such as Instagram and WhatsApp, with massive potential have been acquired for eye watering amounts before they were scaled. Instagram had only 13 employees and zero revenue when it was acquired by Facebook for $1 billion in 2012. In a 2018 Bloomberg Intelligence report[2], Instagram was estimated to have reached 1 billion users. In the same report a Bloomberg analyst estimated the photo sharing platform to be worth around $100 billion, and it continues to grow.

Many technology start-ups have business models that revolve around high volumes of transactions with low margins, particularly in the B to C market. The emphasis is on providing a useful service and gaining market share. It is all about rapid growth, early mover advantage and trying to gain a dominant market position. It has been referred to as 'blitzscaling' where companies scale and build out their offering ultra-fast to be first to reach global markets. Monetisation and profit are usually not a consideration in the early growth stages of such companies.

They burn through cash fast as they try to scale quickly. They are often reliant on continuous funding rounds of weighty investment from private equity and venture capital firms to maintain the 'runway' and growth trajectory.

Many fail, running out of cash and disappearing before the next stage of funding. A small number get acquired, and an even smaller number succeed in scaling to be huge, such as Uber, Airbnb, and Slack. These are the tiny minority.

Even those that have received substantial initial backing early on have only a 1% chance of achieving Unicorn status (valuation of $1 billion)[3], according to an industry study. So, the rewards may be high, but the risk of failure is significant.

Would a focus on profitable growth at an earlier stage in the scale-up journey increase the chances of success? In my view, yes, probably.

The business to business or 'B-to-B' market is perhaps not as large in terms of number of customers though the revenues involved can still be considerable for software and analytics type companies. For many such companies, once the initial upfront investment has been made in building the software application, or in creating a product such as a predictive data model or algorithm, the incremental cost of providing the software to a new client or customer is negligible.

I have found this to be the case in the insurance analytics or 'Insurtech' space, where I have worked for the last 25 years, supplying products to large blue-chip insurance companies. It is a niche area with lower volumes, lucrative fees per transaction, strong recurring revenues, and much higher margin business.

'Build it once, sell it many times' is the mantra often quoted.

It is also the reason why this type of company is often able to attain rapid growth and to produce net profit margins of over 50%.

Business angels and investors in my businesses have often referred to this type of company as a 'Golden Goose'. This sort of business is extremely scalable, very cash generative, and importantly, commands a high price on exit.

1.3 What sources of funding are available to help you scale?

Scaling up your company is going to involve further investment and perhaps significant external funding. The first question that you as an entrepreneur need to resolve is:

How much will you need?

You need to work this out and by when before you start approaching different sources of financing. The strength of your existing business and the speed of your scale-up plans will help to define your requirements. Regardless of the amount, you will still need to have a well thought out business plan, a credible founding team and a good narrative that engages investors. You also need a credible financial model and detailed cashflow forecast. This will guide you as to how much is required to keep your scale-up moving forward, and crucially, at what points in your plan capital is needed to ensure the runway does not evaporate.

You will need a solid business plan to attract investors and to give them confidence that you know what you are doing. Investors will want to understand what you are going to do with the funds, whether your plan is believable and what is likely to be in it for them.

Having an existing track record is also a factor in attracting funding. If you have been successful before people will be quicker to lend you money, given a sound idea and a plan. Whereas if you are a new entrepreneur you may have to work a lot harder to convince people of your ability to execute a scale-up plan. It can sometimes take up to two or three years to attract significant funding.

If you don't have a strong existing track record of running businesses start networking early when you begin your company. Contact potential future investors, get them educated about the business and opportunity, build some trust, and start to nurture relationships long before you require the funding.

The good news is that there is an abundance of financing options available to entrepreneurs now compared to when I first started as a business owner. Picking the right option really depends how much you need and where you are on the scale-up journey.

OK, what are the common routes to finding additional funds?

At what point does a particular funding option become relevant in an entrepreneur's journey?

What sources of additional scale-up funding are you considering?

The first option to contemplate is usually your own money. You may have already invested significantly to get your business up and running, and you may not have the means to invest further. This may be the first time you have considered looking externally for additional investment. Certainly, anyone considering investing in your company will want to see that you have already 'put your money where your mouth is'. How can you expect other people to invest in the further expansion of your business if you don't have plenty of 'skin' in the game?

Not bringing in external investors keeps things simple, though founders are sometimes reluctant to invest more of their own money. This involves taking more risk.

The next option to consider is for you to approach friends and family for additional funding. If the money you require is not significant then this might be a possibility to consider. Scaling a company usually involves more money than the seed money required to get initial business ideas off the ground.

This is not an option I have considered in the past as I like to keep family life and business separate. It is a personal choice, though may be the only option for some. In the past,

I have not sought to ask family to invest. I have not wanted the additional stress of things potentially going wrong, and then having to explain to relatives what happened to their savings.

The next stop on the funding journey would be to consider business angels or crowdfunding websites to access seed capital and what is called pre-series A funding. This is appropriate for companies looking to scale from the initial start-up phase, that have at least a tested proof of concept product, and ideally have customers on board. Government grants are also available and accessible at this stage, as is help and funding from accelerators.

The next stage of funding after that is termed series A, when companies have established some foundations to the business, and is usually the first time that venture capital funds or family offices become relevant as a source of capital. The average series A funding raised in 2019-2020 was $15.6M.

Following the series A, further rounds of funding by VC's, Private Equity or Family offices are referred to as series B, series C, and series D. The company is frequently either bought via a trade sale along this route or sometimes progresses to an Initial Public Offering (IPO) where the shares are traded on a public stock exchange. A summary of the different funding options with the main pros and cons for each are shown in Table 2 below. For more detail and a deeper dive into all the different funding options available, please read the appendix at the end of this chapter or refer to the further reading section.

One thing to mention is you should seek professional advice on the legal regulations, hoops you must jump through, and criteria you must adhere to relating to different types of fundraising, this can vary by country.

Whatever path you choose to source additional funding try to find a firm or individuals with contacts and expertise in your niche, so that they also bring additional value to the table to support you in the next phase of growth. What options are you going to consider? When are you going to make the move to scale your business?

Table 2: A summary of funding options available to help scale your start-up.

	Options for funding to consider	Pros	Cons
1	Self - Bootstrapping	Keep control, saves time otherwise spent fundraising, forces you to be frugal.	Slow to grow when self financing.
2	Friends/Family	Cheaper than banks/flexibility.	Strains on personal relationships, may not add any value other than money.
3	Crowdfunding (Kickstarter)	Can be fast once campaign initiated. Sometimes only option available, don't have to pay back or give-up equity in your new company.	Funds available often small to test out a concept or idea. Have to put in time to set-up and run a fundraising campaign.
4	Bank loans	Don't give up equity, you remain in full control.	Very difficult to access unless secured against your personal assets (e.g. home).
5	Government Grants/Loans/Tax incentives	Grants often non repayable, anyone in theory can apply for grants/loans.	Time to apply, criteria to satisfy.
6	Business Angels	Act as mentor/advisor, bring experience, industry contacts.	Time required to establish a relationship, Amounts limited.
7	Business Incubators	Access to mentors, networks, office space, training, help with funding.	Many ask for equity, quality of offering can vary significantly.
8	Crowdfunding (Equity)	Can be fast (when campaign initiated), way of testing appeal of product idea, investors can become customers (B to C)	Give equity away, Time and cost involved to set-up and run marketing campaign, If target not achieved any money received is returned, reputational damage if campaign fails to raise funding.
9	Business Accelerators	Acquire skills, access expertise, wider network, help with further external funding, best for first time founders and those looking for further external funding.	Give equity away, finding the right programme for your needs can be difficult, competition for places on best schemes.
10	Family Office Funding	Access to networks at a higher level to help find strategic partners and customers, Act as mentors, Often quicker decision making, Family wealth is frequently self-made so tend to be flexible and more alligned with entrepreneur mindset.	Give up equity, More difficult to reach, Do sometimes provide seed or early stage funding but usually interested in later stage businesses that are already established (Series A, Series B financing).
11	Venture Capital	Access to larger funding for high risk ventures, business expertise, guidance and support. Access to networks and provision of business support to scale your operation.	Give up equity and dilution of ownership. Give up some if not all control of the business, Can be time consuming to raise funding as they will want to get to know the founders, They will want to do extensive due diligence which takes up your time. Aggressive drive for growth.
12	Private Equity	Access to larger funding as they have deep pockets. Business expertise and support. Access to wider business networks to help scale the business.	Give up equity. Will usually buy a controlling stake in the business. Have tended to invest in later stage, more established businesses rather than providing seed and start-up capital. Aggressive push for growth.

1.4 I mortgaged my house in the middle of a crisis. What are you willing to do to scale your business?

When I started Business Insight in 2008 it was just a few months before the global financial crisis. Starting a new venture during a recession can be tough. We had to endure a difficult and tricky trading period selling our products into financial companies that were looking to cut expenses and curb their spending. It was a testing time and the focus to begin with was survival rather than fast growth.

In 2001, my first taste of running my own business, via a management buy-out, was during the time of the Dotcom crash. The banks and venture capitalists would not lend us a bean, even though we had an experienced team, solid, proven products, and a detailed, comprehensive business plan. I have since found out over the years the only time the banks are happy to talk to you and want to lend you money is when you have plenty in the coffers already and don't need it!

Gathering the necessary funds was tough, involving outside investment from wealthy private investors, re-mortgaging my house and basically putting every penny on the line. I had a young family to provide for at the time, so it was an immense risk to take and one that gave me a few sleepless nights. I guess I was lucky as I was still young and confident of getting a job back in the corporate world if things did not work out. For me, it was a risk worth taking and the opportunity I was searching for.

I think it becomes more difficult to make similar choices as you get older, with more responsibilities, a larger mortgage, and a nice salary to leave behind. It is also tough 'rocking the boat' if you have established your own business, and are now considering further investment, and taking a risk to move things to the next level.

Understanding what the end goal is and what you want to achieve can help clarify your decision making.

Do you have a clear idea of when you would like to exit your business?

Are you building to generate a large dividend income stream?

Do you want to progress towards an IPO (Initial Public Offering) or sell to a much larger corporate company in a trade sale?

Knowing where you are headed is important. You can then work back from there and appreciate what you need to achieve by when to meet your goals. You can plan the details and have a better understanding of what you need to have in place. And the necessary funding required.

How much more of your own money are you willing to invest? If you approach outside investors, how much funding do you need and how much of your business are you willing to sell?

What do investors look for when considering putting money into a company? Will you be able to convince investors to fund the scale up of your business?

Have you given any thought to what level of risk you are prepared to take to scale your company?
What will you do?

Do you have what it takes to scale and move your business to the next level?

In his book 'Angel'[14], Jason Calacanis, successful technology entrepreneur, business angel and early investor in Uber, reveals his key ingredient when picking potential winners from thousands of technology start-ups.

"I don't need to know if your idea is going to succeed, I need to know if you are",

"People aren't everything, they are the only thing."

This suggests that many angel investors look at the people first and the business idea second. This is something you should keep in mind when you are looking to raise funds for your company. If it is a new concept or technology idea it is sometimes too difficult for investors to pick out which will be the big winners. Consequently, the decision to invest will usually be weighted towards the impression of the founder, and the track record of the management team.

In 2000, Masayoshi Son of Softbank invested $20 million in Alibaba, an internet start-up founded by Jack Ma[15]. It is one of the most successful investments of all time as Softbank's $20 million was turned into $100 billion. Unbelievably, when Ma pitched to Softbank for the investment, he had no business plan, zero revenues and was not technical.

Son is quoted as saying:

"His eyes were very strong; I could tell he had charisma and leadership".

In other words, the whole decision to invest $20 million was based entirely on the founder.

My belief is that for success, you still need a compelling proposition that solves a problem or addresses some customer pain. A poor business idea isn't going to change by bringing in someone brilliant at executing a plan. Though arguably, if they are very competent, they would probably quickly pivot the business anyway. On the other hand, a great idea without a founder with the right mindset, as well as the ability and skills to execute is likely to fail, no matter how good the business concept is.

Most entrepreneurs are extremely competitive people. They thrive on competition, enjoy the battle of bringing out new offerings and going head-to-head with others in the market. They love winning. This is true for myself and for many other successful entrepreneurs I have met. Besides this and a great idea or initial product offering it takes a lot more to scale a company and grow it into a multi-million-pound venture.

In Donald Krause's book 'The Art of War for Executives'[16] his analysis of Sun Tzu's 2500-year-old Chinese text revealed that battles are won by those with a major competitive advantage, but it is not the determining factor in achieving success.

People do the fighting and win the battles.

The most important person is the guy calling the shots, deciding the strategy, and marshalling the troops – the general or in a business context, the founder.

<u>Investors, business partners and early adopter customers will assess you first before deciding to work with your company.</u>

The next question you might ask is:

What qualities do you need to convince them to pick you?

What are the common traits of phenomenally successful entrepreneurs?

In the next chapter we will explore what investors look for in the founder when considering investing in a business.

References /Further reading:

1. Haskel J, Westlake S: *'Capitalism Without Capital' The Rise of the Intangible Economy'* Princeton University Press 2018
2. https://www.ejinsight.com/eji/article/id/1941253/20180911-unicorn-probability-of-vc-startups-at-about-1-study-suggests
3. https://www.bloomberg.com/news/articles/2018-06-25/value-of-facebook-s-instagram-estimated-to-top-100-billion
4. Understanding Private Equity (PE) (investopedia.com)
5. www.pwc.com – Private Equity Deals Insights: 2021 outlook
6. https://www.gov.uk/guidance/innovation-get-details-about-innovate-uk-funding-competitions#smart
7. https://entrepreneurhandbook.co.uk/grants-loans/
8. Bone Jonathan, Allen Olivia, Haley Christopher: *BUSINESS INCUBATORS AND ACCELERATORS: THE NATIONAL PICTURE*, BEIS Research Paper Number 7 April 2017
9. https://www.gov.uk/government/publications/business-incubators-and-accelerators-the-national-picture
10. Bone J, Lahr H, Haley C, Gonzalez-Uribe J: THE IMPACT OF BUSINESS ACCELERATORS AND INCUBATORS IN THE UK, BEIS Research Paper Number 2019\009
11. https://www.nesta.org.uk/blog/the-current-shape-of-crowdfunding-platforms-in-the-uk-1
12. https://p2pmarketdata.com/crowdfunding-statistics-worldwide/
13. https://p2pmarketdata.com/crowdfunding-for-startups/
14. Calacanis, Jason. *Angel: How to Invest in Technology Startups- Timeless Advice from an Angel Investor Who Turned $100,000 into $100,000,000.* Harper Business
15. What are VCs looking for? Future of Fintech, Raconteur.net 20/12/20
16. Krause, Donald G. *Sun Tzu THE ART OF WAR FOR EXECUTIVES.* Nicholas Brealey Publishing
17. www.investopedia.com/articles/personal-finance/102015/series-b-c-funding-what-it-all-means-and-how-it-works.asp
18. Sifted.eu/articles/family-office-funding-startups/

19. www.investopedia.com/articles/personal-finance/102015/
20. www.startups.com/library/expert-advice/crowdfunding-pros-cons
21. Sullivan T: Blitzscaling, Entrepreneurship Magazine April 2016, Harvard Business Review.

Key takeaways

• Transition to work on the business not just be integral within it. If you wish to scale this is a necessary early step.

• Not all businesses are scalable. Companies that can licence IP such as software with significant recurring revenues are the most scalable. 'Build it once, sell it many times'.

• What additional funding do you need to scale up? You need to work this out before determining the most appropriate route for finance.

• Business Angels and Venture Capital Firms are the most established forms of funding to fuel the scaling up of start-ups.

• Accelerators and Crowdfunding platforms are newer, growing sources of finance and help for start-ups. These are becoming important avenues for entrepreneurs to pursue for funding and support for expansion of their companies.

• The downside to sourcing external funding is relinquishing some equity in your company. So, you need to decide what your plan is. What do you want from your business? What level are you scaling to and what is your exit plan? How much risk are you prepared to take to scale your company to the next level?

• The quality of the founder is the one constant factor across successful businesses.

• Investors, business partners and early adopter customers will assess you first before deciding to work with your company.

HOMEWORK

Now over to you. If you are going to scale your business, you first need to answer a few questions and to be honest with yourself. You need to know what the end goal is, what you want from your business, and get your story together to enthuse others to join you on the journey.

1. *What do you want from your business? What are your personal life goals and aspirations (e.g., Financial independence, larger house, Ferrari or better life/work balance and more time with the kids)?*

2. *What is your exit plan and ideal timeline? When do you envisage exiting the business? Do you have a preferred route in mind (perhaps you know companies that would be interested if via a trade sale, sale to management or employees or an IPO)?*

3. *How much additional funding do you need to scale up and when do you need it? What sources can you reach out to now for funding and which require more research? How much equity are you willing to concede in return for adequate funding?*

Please think about these questions and answer them as best you can now. They could form part of your revised business plan as well as shape some of the options to consider on your 'scale-up' journey. The worksheets in each chapter can be downloaded from the website www.scale-for-sale.com, the password is START-TO-SCALE.

APPENDIX:

An overview of different funding options available to help scale your business.

An overview of funding options to help scale your business.

Self-funding

The first option entrepreneurs usually consider is their own money. Some companies self-fund their start-up and then fuel further expansion through cashflow or through various ways to squeeze their cost base down without any external funding. You are lucky if you can do this. This is often referred to as 'bootstrapping' and essentially relates self-funding to pulling yourself up by your own bootstraps. Example ways to bootstrap the business would be things such as getting the staff to take equity and work for no salary for a while, not taking as much office space, negotiating preferential deals with suppliers so initial costs are zero. This should be the first option to consider.

When I started Business Insight, we took a small, serviced office on a preferential deal, paid nothing for office furniture, got several people to work below market rates in exchange for equity, and paid zero to suppliers upfront. We squeezed our cost base right down until we got things moving, so did not require as much external funding. This may not be possible for some businesses.

Prior to selling my previous company Business Insight the shareholders considered further expansion into Europe as an option and this would have involved significant additional investment. The business was stable and generating substantial dividends, and as a board we decided we were not prepared to risk the investment.

The big advantage to self-funding is that you keep complete control of the business and continue to make all the decisions without consulting a board of shareholders. You also don't dilute your shareholding.

Friends & Family

The next option to consider is for you to approach friends and family for additional funding. It is one sometimes taken by founders to start-up a company when the sums involved are relatively small. Scaling a company often involves a lot more money than the initial seed money to scale and establish the business. Selecting this option can put a strain on personal relationships and you are unlikely to receive any business benefit other than money.

Business Angels

Business Angels are high net worth individuals and private investors in start-ups and early-stage companies. They are often experienced businesspeople who have had success either running their own company or as senior executives in the corporate world.

They will generally invest a sum of capital, in the range £10,000-£250,000, in return for equity in the company.

In addition, angel investors also bring experience, contacts, and market knowledge with them. They often will act as mentors and advisors to a founder. Angel investors are normally found from the founder's own industry network, or from family and friends. There are also registered networks of Business Angels that can be accessed to search for suitable people who you can work with.

A couple of things to contemplate when searching for a Business Angel are:

How much are you prepared to dilute your shareholding? And what is your company worth now?

How much equity would you need to give up in exchange for the additional funding?

When do you need the funding?

If it is someone from outside your network, they are going to want to get to know you before handing over any money.

It could take 6 to 12 months to get the funding, so factor that into your plans.

The right Business Angel can bring a lot more to the table than just money. Try to find someone that can bring relevant experience and contacts with them, and that can help you plug the knowledge gap in how to scale a business. This could add significant value to the company and a lot more than simply cash funding. Ideally you want someone who understands your market, has useful client or supplier contacts and who can open a few doors for you. Someone with experience of business and who can help to coach you in areas where your knowledge is thin could be invaluable.

When you do raise finance be careful how much your shareholding is watered down. Do not cede control of the company. I was naïve when bringing in external finance in my first company. Business Angels took 52% of the equity in return for funding; in effect we surrendered control of the firm. This was not such a smart move though we were lucky the investors were reasonable people.

A top tip is making sure you put in place a shareholder agreement with protections included, covering the interests of the minority shareholders, not just the majority ones. This ensured as a management team that we maintained the same level of influence and voice in the business.

When putting a shareholder agreement together make sure you have considered all the scenarios that you might find unpalatable. Cover scenarios where other shareholders might try to drive things through against your wishes. Such as hiring people you don't endorse or want on board, dictating the dividend policy or remuneration policy, spending on projects without your consent, or wishing to sell the business without your agreement. Ensure you have protections in place. And if you can't get them to agree, look for the funding elsewhere.

Government grants, loans & tax incentives

In the UK, there are several government tax relief schemes to encourage Angel and Venture Capital investment in start-ups such as the Seed Enterprise Investment Scheme (SEIS), the Enterprise Investment Scheme (EIS) and the Investor Relief Scheme (IRS). The tax relief available for the funds invested in start-ups can reduce the capital at risk for investors significantly. These are major incentives that help to encourage the flow of investment funds into the start-up area. You should ask your accountant or finance person to contact the local tax authorities to find out the current criteria at the time for the relevant scheme (e.g., SEIS) and about any certification you may require. This will help you to attract more interest from investors. Some may insist you need to have one of the tax relief schemes in place before they invest.

There are also many government grants and loans available for start-ups, and to support the scale-up of small and medium sized companies in the UK, and across Europe[6].

One of the recent schemes launched at the time of writing this at the end of April 2020, called the Future Fund, provides government loans to UK-based companies ranging from £125,000 to £5 million. This provides funding for companies looking to accelerate their growth plans, though it is subject to at least equal match funding from private investors. There are also a few other criteria that must be met, such as at least £250,000 must have already been invested in equity funding, and at least half of the business must be based in the UK. These schemes are worth investigating and examining the fine detail to find out if any match your requirements.

I have also heard of significant government support being given to technology start-ups in Europe. For example, if you open an office in one of the major University towns in Poland, such as Krakow, Warsaw, Poznan, or in Bratislava in Slovakia, there are significant tax breaks and grants available to encourage firms to locate there.

In the UK, this support is available through local and national schemes[7], often to encourage entrepreneurs to locate in certain areas, to help fuel job creation and growth in the economy. For example, there are local area business development grants available in many areas, often in partnership with local Universities, providing grants and support to local businesses to help them grow.

The downside is that getting grants can sometimes be difficult, and you are often competing against many other companies for a limited amount of funding. The application process can also be time consuming and there are sometimes stringent criteria that must be met. Lastly, the grants usually only cover part of the money you need, and you normally must match the funds awarded with your own money.

Bank loans

Banks are one avenue to try for funding though they will normally want personal guarantees from the founders if the business is still in start-up mode, and does not have a solid income stream, sustainable profits, and recurring revenues. Bankers don't like high risk, and it is not uncommon to have some collateral they can take, such as your house, should you default on any loan advanced. Start-ups are high risk ventures, as borne out by the level of failure rate. In the UK, banks are often reluctant to lend to early-stage start-ups or companies that are not yet established.

Business Accelerators and Incubators

Business incubators and accelerators are organisations that provide support and help to early-stage and start-up companies. Around £20M-£30M of public funding is allocated to incubators and accelerators in the UK. Their purpose is to try to improve the survival rates of start-up ventures through providing support and sharing knowledge, and expertise. And hopefully guaranteeing the same mistakes don't keep getting repeated time and time again. They tend to provide office space, mentorship, training & business support services, access to investors and sometimes direct funding. According to a government funded study[8,9] in 2017 there were over 200 incubators and 170 accelerators across the whole of the UK at the time. A larger proportion of accelerators are in London though incubators are more evenly spread throughout the UK.

Incubator programmes are typically run by universities and academic organisations, and non-profit organisations, though some are also run by commercial companies. They tend to focus on early-stage ventures and according to the study the main services provided are office space, networking and access to investors, and mentoring. The active incubators in the UK provide funding to around 7000 early-stage businesses at any one time. They are normally publicly funded and charges for services are either free or via a membership fee to cover office rent. Only 14% of incubators provide any direct funding to entrepreneurs.

Accelerators are a more recent phenomenon and have grown rapidly over the last 10 years. They support over 3600 new businesses each year in the UK with an intensive package of support, mentoring and training over typically a 6-month period. Many accelerator programmes tend to be increasingly funded by large corporates who also provide direct funding in return for equity. In the government study, in 2017 it was found that the average investment was £39K and the average equity taken in return for direct investment and services 7%.

The accelerator programmes are more appropriate for the first-time entrepreneur and those lacking scale-up experience. A database of the majority of those operating in the UK can be found via the link in the references at the end of this chapter[10]. You will need to think long and hard about whether what is offered represents good value. Not all the programmes available ask for equity in your company. For example, Microsoft Ventures offers a 16-week programme for 46 companies a year that they term are 'later-stage' or ready to be scaled-up. They don't ask for equity in the business and start-ups are able to attend workshops, get access to one-to-one mentors, use office space, and have access to Microsoft's customer and partner network.

In a government study into the impact of accelerators in 2019[11] the majority attending the programmes considered their participation worthwhile; 64% of entrepreneurs stated their involvement as significant or vital to their success. The businesses taking part experienced higher rates of growth and attracted higher levels of funding. The main benefits highlighted by attendees of the accelerator schemes in the study were access to investors, access to peers, help forming teams, direct funding, media exposure and mentorship. These were all benefits likely to have an impact of higher and faster rates of growth.

However, the study itself couldn't quantify the added value of attending a scheme as the accelerators are highly selective and only pick the best from those applying. The companies chosen would probably have experienced higher rates of growth than average whether they had attended the programme or not.

There are also some very specialist accelerator programmes such as 'Cyber London' which is a hub exclusively for start-ups focused on the rapidly growing area of cyber security. This is a 13-week intensive programme where start-ups working in this area can work alongside other entrepreneurs in the same field and have access to the hub's unique network and expertise, whilst they focus on business and product development. The accelerator also provides a small amount of direct funding. In return they ask for 3% of the equity in the company. In other schemes they ask for a lot more of the equity.

You will need to assess each scheme on what is offered versus what you must give up in equity, and whether it is a good deal or not. On the one hand for a young, inexperienced team, having access to professionals that have been on the journey before, that can provide extra funding, contacts, advice, guidance, and open a few doors to customers, can be invaluable. And could be the difference between success and failure. It could help to create a bigger venture than might have otherwise been possible and it could lead to a better deal being negotiated on exit.

On the other hand, as with private equity and venture capital firms, they will be motivated to get a return on their investment within a certain period, usually between 4 to 7 years. This will drive them towards an exit suiting their own interests, not necessarily aligned with those of the founders.

Crowdfunding

Crowdfunding is a way of raising finance to fund a project or venture by asking many people for a small amount of money. It enables entrepreneurs to raise funding by harnessing the power of the internet to reach a wide-ranging group of investors. The concept originated in Ireland in the 1700s. Small donations from many wealthy donors were used to create a fund to provide loans to poor rural families. The first crowdfunding example on the internet is believed to have been in 1997 when the UK rock band Marillion funded their US tour through many, small on-line donations from their US fans. The global crowdfunding market has grown significantly since and was valued at over $304 billion USD in 2018 across 171 different countries[12].

One type of crowdfunding is idea stage fundraising where entrepreneurs post up specifications for a proposed project or product and ask for donations from the public to bring it to fruition. An example would be a platform called 'Kickstarter' which is designed to help get creative projects off the ground. It is an all or nothing funding model. So, if the target amount required is not met then the entrepreneur gets nothing. This type of funding is really for those right at the start of their journey rather than those looking to scale-up.

More relevant to scale up scenarios, equity crowdfunding is a mechanism that allows wide-ranging groups of individuals to invest in private start-up and small companies in return for equity. If your business is a B-to-C market proposition, then this is one funding option worth looking into. The public are more likely to understand the idea and problem you are trying to solve, and as a result more likely to invest. On the other hand, for a B-to-B idea they may have more difficulty in understanding the business model, the likely size of the opportunity and hence whether it might be one to invest in. B-to-C campaigns to raise funds have tended to be more successful for this reason.

Equity crowdfunding has emerged as a major funding source for Entrepreneurs over the last 10 years and currently accounts for around 16%-20% of all seed and venture capital funding for start-ups.

Equity crowdfunding for start-ups offers individuals the opportunity to invest small amounts and have a chance to own a small stake in unlisted companies that might be the next Uber or Facebook. This area is growing quickly, and the World Bank is projecting the size of funds invested in equity crowdfunding to reach $90 billion USD per annum by 2025. China, USA, and the UK are the countries where crowdfunding is the most popular.

In the USA, over one in five people have participated in crowdfunding. There were 65 crowdfunding platforms in the UK at the end of 2017[13], about a third of these offer equity crowdfunding. Seedrs is the most popular and is the biggest crowdfunding platform in Europe. Crowdcube and Syndicate Room are other popular platforms for investors in the UK. Across Europe FundedByME, Companisto and Invesdor are popular platforms to raise funding.

For entrepreneurs, the platforms charge a single, one-off fee if the campaign is successful, typically around 5%-6% of the amount raised. In return guidance is provided to the entrepreneur on how to build a pitch video, pitch deck and other content to support the fundraising campaign. The platforms will also do all the advertising and marketing of the pitch. Seedrs claim that a fundraising campaign typically lasts 30 days though you would also need to factor in the time for preparation of all the sales and supporting materials.

Platforms such as Seedrs and Crowdcube have large retail investor bases with several hundred thousand registered investors and raising up to a £1 million can be done relatively easily, although bigger amounts have been raised previously. One example is a crowdfunding campaign run by Crowdcube in 2017 for Monzo, the digital challenger bank, which raised £2.5 million from 6500 investors. This was part of a £22 million scale-up fundraising exercise.

Crowdfunding is certainly one avenue that has emerged in recent years as an option for entrepreneurs to source scale-up funding and is a useful, feasible way for businesses to raise money. The downside is that it can be an expensive way to raise funds and you are giving away equity in your company without any other benefit apart from the funds raised. You are not getting the industry experience, access to contacts and vast knowledge that business angels can also bring to the table.

Family Offices

Family offices (FO) are private wealth management service companies that look after the one, Single Family Office (SFO) or a small number of ultra-high net worth families, Multiple Family Office (MFO). They manage the financial investment side for the ultra-affluent and there had been an increasing trend in recent years to invest in high-growth, high risk businesses. There are around 3000 family offices, both SFO and MFO, in the United States.

On the positive side FOs are backed by people usually experienced in building and growing businesses. So, they are often more patient in the development of the company and often aligned with the entrepreneur mindset. They also tend to be well connected and can help in sourcing customers and in finding other partners to expand the firm further.

To get in contact with them start by looking in the press at who has been investing in your sector in different businesses. You could also ask local venture capital firms what families are receptive to investing in your area.

Venture Capital

Venture Capital firms (VCF) provide financing to start-ups and small businesses with the potential to scale (and to become much larger companies). The source of the funding is usually from financial institutions, investment banks and wealthy investors. They tend to prefer more established start-ups requiring at least £1 Million in additional funding, rather than smaller amounts of early-stage seed money. It can also take time, perhaps six months or so, to raise money initially from this source. The VCF's will not just handover significant sums of money without doing some due diligence on the business, getting to know the founders, and understanding the potential for the company more fully.

Technology is a major area of focus for VCF's. They look for businesses that are highly scalable, and that offer extraordinary growth potential. By investing in a wide spectrum of start-up companies they cast the net wide in the hope that a tiny minority will scale rapidly, covering the cost of the whole fund. And that just one or two might achieve 'Unicorn' status.

In addition to financial support, they can provide guidance, contacts and help to start-ups. They will take a large chunk of the equity, want to have influence in how the business is run and will push hard for growth. They will also want a seat on the board and can negotiate complicated terms. For example, in addition to equity they may ask for preferential shares, a capital structure with a mix of preferential shares plus convertible notes. They may also ask for anti-dilution rights to ensure they can maintain their share of the business in later funding rounds.

Each round of additional funding will see your shareholding further diluted. Although of course, if you progress through the different rounds of funding, which is referred to as 'Series A', 'Series B', 'Series C' etc, the size and value of the business will be substantial.

Private Equity

Private Equity (PE) firms raise funds of private capital from institutional investors and high net worth individuals to acquire majority equity stakes in mature, established companies or in buyouts of distressed public companies.

PE firms own many large businesses and well-known brands across many different industry sectors, from exceptionally large retail brands through to financial services and software companies. At the end of 2019 there were $3.9 trillion of assets under PE ownership[4]. Even though we had a global pandemic in 2020, according to a report by PWC[5] in the United States there were 4,100 deals by Mid-November, an increase of 5% in the USA compared to all of 2019.

PE organisations develop and grow the businesses within their portfolio of companies they own and sell them or list them on a stock exchange to make a profit.

When turning around distressed public companies PE firms will first acquire all the shares and delist the stock. They tend to use a significant amount of debt or borrowed money to finance the deal which is known as a leveraged buy-out. The debt is secured against the assets of the target company. The PE firm would then be involved in changing the management and finding ways to improve the financial performance. They will then wait for the business to grow for a few years before selling it on or relisting it at a sizeable profit.

PE firms will tend to have a smaller number of companies in their portfolio than a VCF and will normally take a majority, controlling stake in the business. They are looking to find operations with unlocked growth potential or value that they can expand either by adding other assets or resources to it.

They tend to be actively involved in the running of the business, providing advisory services, enhancing, or changing around the management and helping to position the business for growth. Most PE firms are very hands on with the investments they make and will meet frequently with management.

In recent years PE firms have also invested in young technology companies with high growth potential. So, depending on the stage you are at it may be worth considering. They can, for example, provide the capital to buy-out shareholders looking to retire whilst allowing other members of the management team to stay fully or partially invested.

This can be a solution if you have been successful in establishing the business to a certain level, e.g., £3M-£5M turnover, want to stay with the business, yet are not ready for a trade sale or to be integrated into a large corporate company. Typically, in this scenario, a PE firm may look to sell on the company after 3 to 5 years. I do know individuals in senior management roles at several PE owned companies, who have retained a minority stake in the business through several rounds of different PE owners, and made significant money each time. If you don't want to depart for a beach, the golf course and retirement, this might be an avenue to explore.

Try to find a firm with contacts and expertise in your niche, so that they also bring additional value to the table to support you in the next phase of growth.

CHAPTER 2: WHAT DO INVESTORS LOOK FOR IN A FOUNDER

'Watch your thoughts, for they become words. Watch your words, for they become actions. Watch your actions, for they become habits. Watch your habits, for they become your character. And watch your character, for it becomes your destiny.'

– *Margaret Thatcher*

What are the vital personal attributes investors look for in a founder when trying to pick a winner amongst a sea of entrepreneurs pushing their ideas? Not everyone has what it takes to scale a business, adapt their skillset, and be versatile with the demands on their time constantly changing.

What does a founder need to have in his make-up and demeanour to have a good chance of success?

What are the character traits and the typical DNA common across successful technology entrepreneurs?

What are the things that set them apart from the rest?

What does it take to scale up a business and sell it for millions?

2.1 What attributes do you need as a founder to 'scale-up', and crucially, what do investors look for?

I have summarized the main attributes that I believe are essential in table 3 below.

Which of these do you have? And which do you need to develop further?

Table 3: A SUMMARY OF THE KEY ATTRIBUTES INVESTORS LOOK FOR IN A FOUNDER
• Focus
• Belief
• Resilience
• Vision
• Courage
• Purpose & Passion
• Integrity & Honesty

2.1.1 Focus

First and foremost, you need focus! Having a positive attitude, high energy, and a can-do mindset focused on goals not obstacles in your path is critical to starting and then scaling a company. Fortunately, I learnt quite early in my career before branching out on my own that a lack of focus or not having clear objectives can be a recipe for failure. Back in the late 1990s, I had a role as a Product Development Director and reported into the Managing Director, let's call him James. I was part of a management team focused on building up a new analytics and data science business through investment in new technologies, acquisition, and organic growth.

This was an exciting period, during the DOT COM era, when I was involved in various global risk modelling projects, acquiring a lot of valuable experience, contacts, and knowledge in a fast-paced expanding area. We were building analytics software for financial services companies, some of the work was completely new and ground-breaking, and there was a lot of interest from customers in the market.

Every Monday morning James would call me into his office and tell me about his latest idea. This was going to be the next big thing in our market and so I needed to stop what I was doing to focus on how we could bring this to fruition. He would instruct me to look at the available resources, add it to the plan and ensure it was done. James was very enthusiastic and passionate about his latest idea, though the idea seemed to change on an almost weekly basis. His focus changed frequently, as did the direction he gave me on where the resources should best be deployed. At one point I had so many different plates spinning in the air that bringing projects to completion proved to be almost impossible as the resources were spread far too thinly.

Some of the ideas James had were great but the lack of focus slowed things down impacting the product release timelines and ultimately sales revenues. James was subsequently asked to move on. It may have been different with more focus on the best opportunities, offering the best returns, and the easiest, quickest wins. To scale a company successfully you need focus, discipline, and relentless determination.

2.1.2 Belief

There is a lot written about the power of positive thinking and self-belief. In the Global Entrepreneurship Monitor 2020[1], a study of start-ups and entrepreneurs across 50 countries, the question was posed:

'Are entrepreneurs born or made?'

Local culture, market conditions, and focused government policies are all key in nurturing a favourable environment to create opportunities to fuel entrepreneurship. However, the one consistent theme and attribute required of entrepreneurs is the importance of self-belief, the confidence to act and to grasp openings when they present themselves.

The significance of YOUR self-belief can't be understated. It all starts with YOU; your attitude, your ideas, your thoughts and belief in your company and ability. This is under your control. I think there is a lot in the power of 'self-belief' linked with the desire to achieve. I believe we all have the capability within us to accomplish great things. I have met a lot of successful business owners and founders over the years; some have gone on to be billionaires.

<u>The winners have unshakable belief in their vision, are prepared to take a risk and are focused on goals rather than obstacles.</u>

Many people however are limited by their own self-doubt which might be deep rooted going all the way back to their childhood, school, university, or family environment. What their teachers at school might have said to them, how they were categorized at school, university or initially at work, or how they might have fared in school exams when they were growing up.

You only need to think of the 11+ exam undertaken by 11-year-old children in certain parts of the UK as a good case in point. This attempts to stream children into those considered intelligent enough to go to grammar school and those who go to a secondary modern school, perceived to be of a lower academic standard. Some might argue the test itself is, or at least in the past has been, unfair. Children, from wealthy backgrounds are heavily tutored in exam technique to ensure they pass, and the exam used to be biased towards those good at english rather than those with mathematics talent.

Whether or not it is a fair test of intellect for those aged 11, what lasting damage does it do to the confidence, self-worth and belief of children failing to pass the test at such an early stage in their development? Those who don't make the cut are left with the stigma of failure that often dampens their confidence and self-belief for the rest of their lives, limiting their potential.

My own parents, who failed the 11+, both felt disenfranchised by the school system at a young age and that mindset stayed with them throughout their working lives. How can you make a judgement about someone aged 11? It seems crazy that we still have this system in place in parts of the UK.

It is also interesting how what some people say to you, for example, a teacher or parent, can impact your own views at an early age about your own capabilities, and often this stays with you.

A slightly amusing story for me happened one day in a woodwork class at school in Yorkshire when I was a teenager. My woodwork teacher, Mr. Marley, walked around the class and started grading the work that each pupil in the group had been doing over the previous few weeks. After inspecting the wooden box, I had made with dovetail joints, he glanced at me and said:

'Harrison, are you any good at mathematics?', to which I replied,

'Yes, sir, quite good' and he responded with

'Thank goodness for that, you are rubbish at woodwork'.

That stayed with me and I have tended to lack the belief and confidence in doing anything practical or 'Do-It-Yourself' related ever since. My wife thinks I use this story as an excuse to avoid doing as much 'Do-It-Yourself' as I might otherwise have gotten involved in over the years.

I have shared this with others on numerous occasions and have heard a lot of comparable stories. A friend Phil, from Wigan, told me his schoolteacher had ridiculed his exam results one year in front of the whole class and said a monkey would have done better. He laughs about it now, though it is still vivid in his memory, over thirty years later.

Seriously though, what other people say to you, particularly when you are growing up, can and does impact thinking, confidence, and self-belief. You need to see past this, believe in yourself, look around you for positive stories of others that have been successful for encouragement. Have the courage to act and follow your dreams.

Whilst drafting this book I have spoken with a few people about the power of 'belief', and there was a certain amount of scepticism expressed by some. Perhaps you are the same, so let me convince you otherwise with an example.

Years ago, I read the story of a boy who struggled at school and was in the lowest of six classes for mathematics. The boy lacked confidence, he was an introvert, and did not think he was intelligent or capable of doing well in his education. Then a family friend showed him a mathematics technique, not commonly taught in schools. The technique, translated from some ancient sanskrit scriptures, is one of several rediscovered ancient maths methods in a book published in the 1960's by Swami Bharati Krishna Tirtha[2]. This knowledge enabled the boy to develop an incredible skill. He was quickly able to do ultra-rapid multiplication without the need of a calculator.

The boy could soon do something most of the adult population could not do; multiply large numbers together rapidly, and just write out the answer as a string of digits from right to left. Can you do this? Can you appreciate what this would do for the youngster's self-belief and confidence?

This energised the boy, giving him a huge confidence boost. He then had belief in his own abilities. He went from the bottom class in maths to the top, making him realise he could succeed at school in other subjects. Anything was possible.

It changed his life.

The technique is in the appendix at the end of this chapter if you are curious to find out how to do this yourself.

The power of belief is incredible. All it takes is the right mindset, and something to instil belief and confidence.

You can achieve anything you want to in life with belief.

The speech given by Steve Jobs[3] to Stanford University graduates in 2005 left a lasting impression on me and I think made the point very well about having the self-belief to follow your dreams and find something that you love to do.

"Your time is limited, so don't waste it living someone else's life. Don't be trapped by dogma – which is living with the results of other peoples' thinking. Don't let the noise of others' opinions drown out your own inner voice".

Believe in yourself, visualize and focus on your goals and don't allow your own thoughts or others to limit your own ability to succeed.

Self-belief is key in challenging times in overcoming problems and focusing on the end goal. Some of the best innovation has been during times of adversity when alternative ways of doing things have been devised or invented.

In 1665 at the time of the Great Plague in England social distancing orders were introduced to attempt to curb the spread of the bubonic plague. Isaac Newton[4] aged just 23 at the time, left Cambridge University as a student and self-isolated in the countryside for 18 months. Many of his critical insights and major contributions to science and mathematics were discovered during that time. In later life he referred to this period as his 'Annus Mirabilis' or his amazing year. No doubt there will be some amazing new ideas, start-ups and innovations emerging that will be launched by today's entrepreneurs when the current 2020 crisis has eased, and the World Economy starts to get back to normal.

2.1.3 Resilience

There are always problems, issues, hurdles to overcome, and challenging times as an entrepreneur. It is never easy. You need to be single-minded, have the hunger and desire to go it alone, to enjoy the freedom and challenge of doing your own thing but also accepting all the risks and the responsibility that goes with it. Most of all though you need to be resilient, to put up with setbacks, failures, and disappointment. And to keep plugging away, not give up easily when the going gets tough, and things become problematic. To painstakingly carry on towards your goals with relentless determination.

Resilience is a crucial attribute for an entrepreneur. I don't think you are just born with resilience. I think you are shaped by your experiences in life. Belief, determination, and the desire to succeed will help you to bounce back from failures and to build a more resilient capacity. It is rare to find a successful entrepreneur that has not had to overcome some failures or major setbacks on their journey or during their lives. When we fail, we learn, and we also develop resilience to cope with the mental side of the ups and downs of running a business. It is important to have the capacity to be able to bounce back when you fall short. How you respond to adversity can be what defines the successful from the also-rans.

Throughout your life, every time you overcome hardship, you evolve your means of coping and your resilience. I have certainly had my failures and trying times. Experiences make you stronger and more determined to move forward. Treat each failure as a learning experience, an opportunity for personal growth and improvement. Be self-aware and always look for ways' things could have been done better. Uncover your weaknesses and then go and fix them. Think of it as being part of your entrepreneurial journey, a bump in the road perhaps. But while you are learning, you are still making progress. Turn the negatives into positives.

The key thing is to keep moving forward.

If you do fail, ask questions: What did you learn? What skills are you missing? What will you do different in the future?
Then park it and move on.

I think you can also gain inspiration and learn a lot from other people's stories. Whether from how they responded to personal adversity or business failure or maybe how they overcame a significant hurdle. Hearing inspirational stories from others that have been able to cope with tough situations and bounce back can help to reframe your own situation and put things into perspective.

One such inspiring story I heard from a young guy called Henry Fraser[5]. I attended a talk he gave to pupils and parents at Berkhamsted School, in Hertfordshire, a couple of years ago. Henry was a talented rugby player and had been part of the academy team at the Saracens Rugby Club, and probably destined for a career as a professional rugby player. Then in 2009, whilst he was on holiday in Portugal with his friends' he had a terrible accident which left him paralysed from the shoulders down. He was aged just 17 at the time.

In his talk, Henry said that he chose not to feel sorry for himself, to be positive, and to get on and do something with his life. He had a keen interest in art and so learnt how to hold a paintbrush in his mouth to enable himself to paint. He now produces amazing, awe-inspiring artwork. He has also become an accomplished author and is a successful motivational speaker.

Another inspirational story I heard watching a TED talk in 2012 given by Giles Duley[6]. Giles is a professional photographer and packed in his job as a fashion photographer to travel the World. He wanted to document the lives and stories of diverse groups of ordinary people coping with hardship, poverty, and adversity. Giles visited villages in Burma where they lived in squalor, lacking basic amenities and medicines. He also lived with impoverished people on the streets of Ukraine to photograph the hardship faced every day by homeless children. Then whilst photographing a patrol in Afghanistan, Giles stepped on an improvised explosive device (IED). He lost several of his limbs. So, as he put it in his talk, he became part of the story.

The stories of the people and the hardship that he had documented inspired him to get through his own trauma. He chose to carry on with his photography and continues to bring stories that need reporting to the attention of the media. He is a remarkable individual. Giles made the point that losing your limbs does not end your life. You can have what seems to be a disability but not be disabled. You can also do anything if you put your mind to it and believe in it. And we can all help and inspire each other with our own stories and experiences to support one another through hard times.

These are just two examples of extraordinary, inspirational individuals, how they have responded to extreme adversity and what being resilient really means. Examples of the stories of remarkable people such as Henry and Giles can give strength to us all. When we hit low points, fail at something, or hit difficult times, it is stories and examples of other people's resilience that can give us support. It can help to think of your setback, failure, or hardship in a different way, in a new light, and not be defeated.

Fear of failure and not at least taking a risk or trying new things is the ultimate failure. That guarantees you certainly will not move forward.

Do not be left wondering at the end of your life what might have been.

2.1.4 Vision

Do you have a clear idea of how and why your business will scale and make money? What is going to be your unique value proposition and why will customers choose you over competitors? Can you visualize the product or service, how the company will look at scale and operate? And articulate this effectively to others? Having the capability to spot gaps in the market, then visualize solutions and communicate this to enthuse others is an archetypal trait of phenomenally successful entrepreneurs.

Thinking back to the late 1990s, during the development of the internet and the Dotcom era, new tech start-ups were springing up on an almost weekly basis. There was a lot of hype and media attention in the new technology. It was fast-moving, exciting, intoxicating and all budding, wannabe entrepreneurs, including myself, were exploring how they could get onto the bandwagon.

At the time, I was working within a large insurance group helping to build a new analytics and data science capability. I was lucky; it allowed me to assimilate a lot of knowledge and experience very quickly and to meet internet pioneers, business founders and a lot of useful contacts in the technology space. Two meetings remain vivid in the memory though from different ends of the spectrum, the visionary technology entrepreneur, and the businessman with an idea but no clear awareness of how the service might operate in the future. Both helped to shape my thinking, though for different reasons.

The first was a meeting set up through a consultancy working for us at the time, ECSOFT, in Washington DC in the United States with Michael Saylor, the founder of a business intelligence software company called MicroStrategy. I had been flown out to his office with a colleague and Michael was very generous to give us some of his time with his vision of how data, analytics and the internet revolution were going to change the world. He eulogized about the internet, the likely impact on the future and every part of society. He also explained in-depth why data and analytics were going to be much more significant in the next decade, particularly in better understanding and predicting customer requirements. He was ahead of the curve and certainly had the vision, foresight, and a deep understanding of how this was going to all fit together. I sat there, astounded, and absorbed it all. Everything he said came true.

It is easy to look back and say you did not have to be a genius to know that was going to happen, but it was not that clear to most people or me.

MicroStrategy now has a market capitalization over $1 billion, so Mr. Saylor made the most of his vision. For me, it was a light bulb moment. Michael had done a great sales job, though I did not want to buy his software. I wanted to create my own business. Change through technology was on its way and I realized after the meeting that data and analytics was the area I had to get into with my own company and that I needed to find or create an opportunity. For every entrepreneur you need to find an area that you know well, preferably a niche market where you can create and build something of sustainable value. You also need to find something that can make a healthy margin (more on this in a later chapter).

The second meeting that remains vivid in my memory during the late 1990s was with an internet start-up called 'easier.com'. The start-up was planning to be an on-line estate agency, like several we have now such as Zoopla and Rightmove. At the time, I had taken my idea ('MyNest.co.uk') and outline plan for an on-line data-driven website for buying and selling property to a few venture capital firms and had received short shrift. I thought it would be interesting to have a chat with the founder of easier.com and see if there was anything of mutual benefit. Easier.com had raised several million in the initial funding round. The founder did not seem to have a unique value proposition or idea how buying or selling property over the internet might operate in the future. The plan seemed to be all marketing focused and about building an on-line brand for property as quickly as they could, with expensive TV advertising being a major component.

The idea I pitched was to provide something unique to the market at the time based on my knowledge of what data and models were available. I thought prospective buyers could be attracted to the website to find out an estimate of a property's value, to understand the flood risk of property they may be interested in buying or any other risks relevant to purchasing a property. On-line reports of relevant information to assist the home moving decision are now commonplace, though back then there wasn't anything available.

It was disappointing for me when the founder said they had no interest, and he could not see any value. He seemed to lack the vision in how an on-line service might operate differently, and how the new proposition might add value to complement a physical estate agency service. He chose to spend the bulk of the money they had on TV advertising to build the brand first.

It was no surprise that easier.com burnt through all their funding quite quickly and soon disappeared, along with many other internet start-ups around that time who were trying to gain first-mover status. They used up a lot of money to build a brand rapidly but without managing their cash flow properly. They seemed to be focused on using expensive old media, such as TV advertising, to promote their services rather than on how the new channel might revolutionise an industry, for example through new services powered by data and analytics.

The vision of how the new proposition and service would deliver value was not fully developed and perhaps some companies were too early into the market. Many seemed to lack any solid foundations or have a workable, proven, profitable business model in place first. Few of them had any revenues and virtually none made a profit, yet some of the valuations on the stock market at the time were ridiculous, it literally was like the children's story *'the emperor's new clothes'*.

Having a clear vision is important. Make sure you can articulate your vision of what is unique about your proposition, what problem you are solving and why people will buy from you. And how can it be monetised. Weave this into a story that differentiates you and that connects emotionally with your audience when you pitch for investment.

2.1.5 Courage

The courage to act, not confidence, is fundamental. Being super confident is not the key to success, it is the courage to grasp any opportunities that fall your way, to take a risk and follow your dreams. A lot of the time as an entrepreneur you will be taking a step into the unknown doing new things.

If you wait to be confident you may never move forward.

Whatever your background, or upbringing, it is courage not confidence that is important in the entrepreneurial world.

One thing I am sure about is you don't need to be a genius to start, run and grow a business successfully and what happened at school is irrelevant. I lacked self-confidence when I left school and my results were average. I went to one of the largest state comprehensive schools in the country, bullying was endemic, and you were labelled a 'swot' or nerd if you were interested in learning. What I have had is courage to follow my dreams and have always been laser-focused on achieving my goals.

Sure, you need common sense, to work hard, a positive attitude and focus. Though having the belief that you can do it and the courage to act are more important.

I take a lot of inspiration from stories of other entrepreneurs, both past and present that have been successful, particularly those that have overcome seemingly impossible obstacles or difficulties to achieve their dreams.

One such inspiring, amazing story, I heard one day from one of the non-executive Directors and friends in my business, Tony McCallum. He told me he had to go up to Whitby to unveil a commemorative plaque in honour of one of his ancestors, an entrepreneur from the 1800s. I was curious to find out more as I knew that Tony had been to a top private school and he was well connected. I had assumed his ancestors to be landed gentry.

His ancestor, George Elliot[7], it turns out, had a humble beginning, being the son of a colliery worker and started work as a labourer in the local coal mine in the North of England, when he was just 9 years old. The working classes at the time were mainly illiterate as state funded education was not available. The young George Elliot worked long hours underground, and then used what little money he had spare to get himself educated via evening classes.

It is difficult to imagine working long, exhausting hours underground at such a young age. And then having the courage, energy, and determination to attend classes in the evenings. George got himself educated. Eventually, he made the level of mining engineer. He then worked his way up through the ranks until he was a manager and then owner of the local coal mine. He didn't stop there and became a major entrepreneur and business leader of his day, acquiring several other coal mines and expanding into other business areas.

Remarkably, George bought a wire cable manufacturing company that supplied the first Transatlantic telegraph cable across the Atlantic in 1865 which shortened communication links between Europe and America from weeks to hours. He also became a member of Parliament and one of the richest men in the North of England.

What I found interesting about the life of George Elliot is that he had purpose. He wanted to make a difference and never forgot his humble beginnings, campaigning tirelessly for better working conditions for all colliery workers. He was very influential in improving workers' rights and in getting new legislation pushed through. He was also a major philanthropist of the time and contributed towards many worthy causes in the North of England. Tony told me he set-up a trust fund for his off-spring to ensure his future descendants were educated, and so would have similar opportunities to him in life - this was still running seventy years after his death.

A more contemporary example is the story of Jan Koum[8], the founder of WhatsApp. Jan had humble beginnings growing up in a small village outside of Kiev in Ukraine. He moved to California with his mother and grandfather aged 16 whilst his father remained behind in Ukraine for work. He spoke little English to begin with and his family lived on welfare benefits, and in government funded housing. He also used to have to get up early to catch the bus to school as his family did not have access to a car.

Fifteen years later, aged 31, Jan quit his job at Yahoo! to start his own business. Driven by his own desire to keep in regular contact with his father and his experience of phone lines in Ukraine, which were routinely tapped, he started WhatsApp. He had a vision, a purpose, and the determination to create a new messaging application that was free from adverts, secure and that provided a better experience for users. In February 2014 WhatsApp was acquired by Facebook for $19 billion.

Both examples, of past and present, are brilliant illustrations of what can be achieved through self-belief, the courage to act, determination, and sheer hard work.

Overcoming what must have seemed like insurmountable obstacles to achieve career and life goals. How to scale a business and use a purpose, focus and determination to drive you. You are only limited by your own thoughts, aspirations, and desire. This demonstrates that when you want something badly enough and focus you can achieve whatever you want and are limited only by your own imagination.

Do not limit your goals, dream big and set the bar high!

Attitude and energy are also vital, it all starts with you. You should strive to be the best you can possibly be, to exceed client expectations in supplying your products and services and your company to be the best in class in its area of focus.

<u>Aim to be the dominant supplier in your niche area, play to win and view the encounter with competitors as a game of continual improvement.</u>

You should never stop looking for ways to win more business, provide a better product or service, out innovate, and outstrip competitors. Constantly be searching for ways to grow your business.

2.1.6 Purpose & Passion

Do you have purpose and passion about what you do? Do you have 'fire in your belly' driving you towards your vision? Are you able to motivate others? Money alone will not drive a higher performance towards your goals.

You must be able to inspire your team, enthuse about what you do and attract new talent to join you on the journey. Are you passionate about the business? Is this going to work? What is the mission of the company and why will people keep buying from you? What do you and your company stand for? What is the culture of your firm? What value do you add to the local community and wider society?

As the founder and a leader of the business you should have the answers to these questions. You need to be convincing, genuine and your answers should enthuse and energise others. Why should you expect anyone to follow you on the journey if you don't have the energy, conviction and positive, can do attitude that your venture is going to work. How do you tap into this energy and inspire your team?

The simple answer, in part anyway, is to find purpose in what you do. In the Global Entrepreneurship Monitor 2019-2020, more than 40% of entrepreneurs in 35 out of 50 countries taking part in the survey cite a main motivation to starting a business being to make a difference in the world. Having a purpose to motivate and galvanise a team, to connect emotionally with customers, to drive a higher performance, has become essential. What is the purpose of your business?

Do you know what you want from your life? What are your goals? What do you want to achieve? And what do you want from your business? Do you want financial independence for yourself and your family? or enough money to lead a lavish lifestyle? or to spend half your life on the golf course, do whatever you want or buy whatever you want? Is it more about the challenge? or are you driven by having the freedom of being your own boss, having the independence, the responsibility and getting fulfilment from creating something from scratch and expanding it to dominate the market?

Do you also have a wider purpose and want to put something back into the community? If you were to die tomorrow what do you think people would say at your funeral and what would you want them to say about how you lived your life? Are you passionate about fulfilling a need in society? Are you on a mission to leave a legacy and make the world a better place? If you are, fantastic! let's face it most people start out in business mainly for selfish reasons, I certainly did. I think it is important to have a view and some understanding of what you want to achieve in your life, and what you want from your business.

What purpose does your business serve for you, your team, your customers, and wider society?

Be clear on this and it will help to motivate and energise you.

It can't all just be about making a pot of money for yourself, not if you want a sustainable purpose and one that makes sense to a team following you. Having a purpose motivates and brings people together, making them feel more connected.

<u>The most successful entrepreneurs want to serve and add value to society.</u>

<u>To make a difference.</u>

One interesting analogy about three bricklayers is supposedly based on a true story during the building of St Paul's Cathedral in London after the Great Fire in 1666. The architect, Sir Christopher Wren, approached the three men as they worked on the initial foundations of the new building and asked each bricklayer in turn what they were doing. The first said he was laying bricks to earn some money to feed his family, the second said he was building a wall and the third said he was building a Cathedral and a place for people to worship. Clearly, the third bricklayer, saw the bigger picture and purpose in what he was doing.

Having a purpose gives people meaning and helps to motivate them to a higher performance. Work is a significant part of life and if you can find purpose in what you do it ceases to feel like a daily grind. You will feel more energized, empowered and it will motivate you to go much further and take larger steps forward, progressing to goals that you might otherwise have dismissed as unobtainable.

Another personal story relates to a great friend of mine, Jonty Gaines, who left the financial services industry to teach Mathematics at a secondary school in Yorkshire. He was an extremely bright, talented, and engaging individual, and could have done anything in life. He found that teaching was his passion and what he loved to do. Helping children and young adults fulfil their potential was his purpose in life and he was the most energized and motivated person I have ever met. Always going the extra mile, he would phone myself and others up in industry to help his students find work placements. He took an interest in people, advising his pupils and providing help on their academic and career development long after they had left school.

Sadly, Jonty died in his forties. At his funeral over three hundred people attended and many of his past students had stories of how he had inspired, motivated, and helped them reach life goals they never thought they would attain. Having a purpose can make a difference both to how you approach what you do, how others view you and how you motivate others in your mission as the leader of the business.

Fulfilling my personal goals has been a significant source of motivation for me. However, I have always been mindful of having a purpose for the business and communicating that to the team. The companies I worked in all contributed towards making the pricing of insurance more accurate and cover more affordable. Insurance plays an important role in society protecting people, homes, and livelihoods, providing a safety net when things go wrong.

Financial remuneration linked to performance is essential to incentivize a team. Nevertheless, if you want to drive sustainable high performance, you need a common purpose and a business vision. Something meaningful that people identify with as a shared goal and a contribution towards society.

In the businesses that I have been involved in we provided computer data models to UK insurers to better understand a range of different natural hazard risks, such as whether your house is at risk of being flooded, or damaged through subsidence, or a severe storm. We also provided software tools, data models and information to insurance companies to help better manage, understand, and price risk. The products helped insurance companies to gain a deeper understanding of geographic risk and to improve the accuracy of insurance premium pricing. They also helped to ensure that risk cover could be provided to a wider spectrum of society as they were able to differentiate risk to a much finer level of granularity.

Given that the business reached 90% market share on several product lines we certainly would have influenced the pricing of UK property insurance, contributing towards a deeper understanding, and fairer pricing of risk.

With the more accurate, more granular risk models we provided, many people found they were now able to buy affordable insurance cover when previously they had found it to be more expensive or less easily obtainable. For example, prior to the adoption of our products in the market insurance companies often assessed flood risk by postal code which often covers a wide area in rural locations. So, often people living at the top of a hill in rural areas would have their house deemed to be at risk of flooding when clearly the risk was negligible or zero.

The solution we provided to insurers assessed the risk for each individual house in the UK, millions of data records, which at the time was new to the market and so had an instant impact on the accuracy of pricing property risk.

We also provided price comparison solutions and services to help new insurance start-ups to enter the market and to compete with much larger established companies. The same data was used to underpin the British Insurance Premium Price Indices for home and car insurance published monthly by the AA. This increased competition and coverage ensuring wider availability of different types of insurance cover and ultimately lower and more affordable prices for consumers, even though at one point the government regulatory authorities were considering restricting the supply (more on this later). We believed our products provided a useful purpose that contributed towards a more financially secure and healthier society and we communicated this regularly to our team to help drive the business forward.

What is your purpose? Why are you in business? What value do you add to the community at large? How do you serve your customers and how do you improve or make society better? Finding a way to add value, helping other people, and making a difference in the world will give you a sustainable goal to aim for and sharpen your focus. It will also help to create an emotional connection between your team and the purpose to drive higher performance and provide a deeper sense of fulfilment from your business.

2.1.7 Integrity & honesty (values)

Closely related to this are your values. What principles do you, your company, and your brand stand for? Define these, set the culture in the business, and live by them. Be authentic, set the example and make sure that you walk the walk. If your vision is to be the best supplier and most trusted advisor to clients in the market how should you act? How should you behave? Right from day one when you start your company you need to adopt the behaviours and habits so that it becomes natural, normal, and part of the DNA of your company.

Building a brand and gaining the trust of customers across the market takes time. If you want longevity in your market, to become a trusted supplier or achieve advisor status with customers, you need to build a solid reputation and credibility, and you need to design this into your plan from the start for the long term. Investors as well as your suppliers and customers want to trade with people with integrity and honesty. They want to know they can trust you and that they will be treated fairly. Behave with integrity, treat everyone with respect and honestly. Live these values, do the best you can and strive for excellence.

Whatever you do, don't bad mouth the competition to customers. You should not put them down, be disrespectful or bad mouth their products.

Remember, LIVE, and BREATHE your company values in the market, with your customers, your competitors, your suppliers and with your employees.

Set the bar high and keep it there. Do not just pay lip service, you will soon be found out!

In the past there have been some colourful characters in the industry competing against us. One sticks in the memory with a lesson on what not to do. Let's call him Paul (not his real name). Paul worked for a large blue-chip company and had led the development of their insurance risk product portfolio. Paul was passionate about the products he had developed, his company had a well-known brand, and they had a strong offering for the U.K. Insurance market at the time.

Paul's company had recently launched a new product, a geographic risk database and underwriting software platform, to help price insurance property risk. We were pitching against one another for a £1 million contract to supply insurance underwriting solutions into a new market entrant to help them accelerate their underwriting capability. I won the business. When the client informed Paul that he had been unsuccessful he could not hide his disappointment and told the client they had made a big mistake and were 'idiots'. Unfortunately for Paul's company this was not an isolated incident and Paul became well known for his behaviour in the market, berating customers if they did not agree with his point of view.

The client told me this story and that they would not be inviting Paul to pitch for any more business in the future. He had burnt all his bridges with them. If you are passionate about your product and genuinely believe in your solution it can be bitterly disappointing when a client does not agree and buys something else.

Remember the war is not won over a single battle and there will be other opportunities if you treat the setback as a chance to learn and improve.

You want longevity in the market. A good reputation takes a long time to build and can be very quickly damaged by a few 'off-the-cuff' comments. And, unfortunately, bad news travels fast. Ensure you and your team live the company values across the market, safeguard your reputation and your brand.

2.2 How can a founder maintain motivation, energy levels and keep performance levels high in the team?

OK, so we have covered attitude, mindset, and the typical attributes a founder needs for success. You also need to be clear about the WHY you are in business, what you want from a 'scale-up' and how your life goals relate to this. I have highlighted this and the importance of finding purpose in what you do. As an entrepreneur, you also need to manage the ups and downs, often rollercoaster ride of a growing enterprise, be adaptable to doing new things all the time, yet maintain your motivation, energy, and enthusiasm. Not only at the start of the journey but also as you scale and develop the business. This can be difficult to do and sustaining your drive and energy levels can be a massive challenge.

So, what can help you to re-energise, to maintain your enthusiasm, motivation and to perform at peak levels for prolonged periods?

As the business grows and expands, it will have diverse needs, require different skills from you, from other people, and need more resources. It will be daunting and stressful at times. It will also be exciting, intoxicating, exhilarating, and rewarding in many ways. It is impossible to be highly motivated and full of energy all the time, everyone goes through peaks and troughs. Times when you are feeling a bit low, when things aren't going exactly to plan and times when energy levels are down.

One thing that I have found useful to do is to -

Remember to have fun!

Celebrate successes with your team and enjoy life.

You could break your business plan down into several shorter-term milestones. Push hard towards each milestone, then have some downtime and enjoyment with the team. Food and nice wine have always been my favourites, maybe take your team out for dinner, or maybe an outing for a curry and a beer? It could be a trip to the theatre, whatever works.

You will feel a real sense of accomplishment and fulfilment when you hit targets in your plan and milestones on your journey. I would urge you to set achievable but stretch goals and link them to a reward.

These moments will go by in a flash, so celebrate them and the successes with your team along the way. It is important to have some valuable time out to relax and reflect with your team at the accomplishment of a major milestone, winning a big contract or successfully completing a large project.

When we hit the £1 million turnover point at Business Insight, we took our team for a day out to watch horse racing at Ascot, a team dinner and then an overnight stay in a pleasant hotel. It was a wonderful day out and still sticks vividly in my memory.

We had similar outings as we hit and celebrated further milestones along the way. This is a suitable time to take stock of where you are, re-set and re-energise. It can enable you to de-stress, take a step back before focusing on the next part of the plan. It is also a valuable time to reflect on what is working well and to give people recognition where it is due.

Recharging your batteries and spending time with your team is also important for mental well-being. It helps in fostering a stronger bond and understanding within your team. Whatever it is, make sure you do it, enjoy, and relish the moment, congratulate, and thank all the team for their input.

Then enthuse to them all about the next phase in the journey.

<u>And keep moving forward.</u>

References / Further reading

1. Global Entrepreneurship Monitor 2019-2020. Global Entrepreneurship Research Association, London Business School.
2. Tirtha Krishna Bharati 'Vedic Mathematics' 1965 Motilal Banarsidacs Publishers, Delhi.
3. https://news.stanford.edu/2005/06/14/jobs-061505/
4. https://www.britannica.com/biography/Isaac-Newton
3. https://henryfraserart.com/
4. https://www.ted.com/talks/giles_duley_when_a_reporter_becomes_the_story/transcript?language=en
5. https://en.wikipedia.org/wiki/Sir_George_Elliot,_1st_Baronet
6. https://en.wikipedia.org/wiki/Jan_Koum
7. Hill Napolean: 'Think and Grow Rich' 1937 Ebury Publishing

Key takeaways

• Investors look at the quality and ability of the founders as a major factor in deciding to fund a business.

• A positive, can do mind-set is critical for a successful founder. Focus on goals not obstacles. Follow your dreams and the 'fire in your belly', try to put your fears to one side.

• Believe in yourself, visualize your goals and don't allow your own thoughts or others to limit your ability to succeed.

• Resilience and courage are vital. The courage to act, not confidence is essential to growing a company.

• Find purpose in what you do, financial rewards and money alone will not drive high performance from your team towards your goals.

• Find a higher purpose to serve others and you will unlock higher performance from your team in pursuit of a shared, meaningful goal.

• Integrity and honesty are important founder character traits for longevity in the market.

• Define the values you, your business, and your brand stand for.

• Live by the values, set an example to your team. Reputation is everything if you want to be a trusted partner and supplier in the market.

• Breakdown your plan into key milestones and make sure that you celebrate these with your team. Remember to have fun. Then prepare for the next leg of the journey.

HOMEWORK

Now over to you. If you are going to scale your business, you first need to answer a few questions and to be honest with yourself. You need to know what is the vision? What is the purpose of the business? And what are the values? As in the previous chapter you need get your story together. Use this to enthuse others to join you on the journey.

1. *Why are you in business? What purpose does your business serve? How do you help and add value for your customers?*

2. *What is your vision for the company? Where would you ideally (and realistically) like to be in 2-, 5-, and 10-years' time? What do you want to achieve and be able to look back on with a sense of pride and accomplishment?*

3. *What are the core values of your company? When clients or suppliers are asked about your business in the future what do you want them to say about your company and your brand?*

SCALE for SALE

APPENDIX: An example of inspiring belief: How to multiply two 5-digit numbers together in under a couple of minutes without using a calculator or computer.

HOW TO MULTIPLY TWO FIVE DIGIT NUMBERS
TOGETHER IN UNDER TWO MINUTES USING THE VEDIC
MATHS APPROACH

If you multiply 43,210 by 12,340 the answer is 533,211,400. How quickly do you think you could work this out without the use of a calculator? The technique outlined below is one of many translated in the 1950s by a monk Swami Bharati Krishna Tirtha from ancient Sanskrit scriptures. Try out the method below and you will be amazed, with practice, how quickly you can calculate the answer with other numbers.

Start by writing the two numbers down you wish to multiply together and begin working from left to right, moving along one column at a time as shown in the working example below. The arrows signify cross-multiplication between the numbers. Think of each step as collecting all the numbers relevant to that column. First the units, then all the digits in the 10's column, then the 100's and so on.

EXAMPLE FIVE DIGIT MULTIPLICATION USING THE APPROACH										WORKING RIGHT TO LEFT
FROM THE BOOK				4	3	2	1	0		The arrows signify cross multiplication
Vedic Mathematics				1	2	3	4	0	x	0 x 0 = 0
BY Swami Bharati Krishna Tirtha								0		**0**
				4	3	2	1	0		(0x4) + (0 x 1)= 0
				1	2	3	4	0	x	
							0	0		**0**
				4	3	2	1	0		(2x0)+(3x0)+(1x4) = 4
				1	2	3	4	0	x	
						4	0	0		**4**
				4	3	2	1	0		(0x3) + (0x2)+ (2x4)+(3x1) =11
				1	2	3	4	0	x	
					1	4	0	0		**1** (carry 1)
				4	3	2	1	0		(0x4) + (0x1) + (4x3) + (1x2) + (2x3) + 1 = 21
				1	2	3	4	0	x	
				1	1	4	0	0		**1** (carry 2)
				4	3	2	1	0		(4x4) + (1x1) + (3x3) + (2x2) + 2 = 32
				1	2	3	4	0	x	
		2	1	1	4	0	0			**2** (carry 3)
				4	3	2	1	0		(3x4) + (2x1) + (2x3) + 3 = 23
				1	2	3	4	0	x	
		3	2	1	1	4	0	0		**3** (carry 2)
				4	3	2	1	0		(2x4) + (1x3) + 2 = 13
				1	2	3	4	0	x	
	3	3	2	1	1	4	0	0		**3** (carry 1)
				4	3	2	1	0		(1x4) + 1 = 5
				1	2	3	4	0	x	
5	3	3	2	1	1	4	0	0		**5**

SCALE for SALE

CHAPTER 3: HOW CAN YOU IMPROVE YOUR CHANCES OF SCALING NOT FAILING?

'Success consists of going from failure to failure without loss of enthusiasm'

– *Sir Winston Churchill*

The ability to change direction rapidly and to pivot the business quickly when required is a significant advantage that small technology start-ups have over much bigger corporate competitors.

In large multi-national corporations, there needs to be a certain level of governance, reporting and administration. The bureaucracy can be very time consuming, stifling and can act like a millstone slowing things right down when trying to create new products, open new markets and innovate. The lack of entrepreneurial talent in large corporates can also inhibit their ability to spot opportunities and move quickly enough to take advantage when they appear. Executives are not incentivized to take risks - to put their reputation and career on the line. Legacy systems, old technologies, outdated skillsets, and inefficient processes are often the norm.

Routinely likened to huge oil tankers, it takes time and effort for large corporates to change direction.

3.1 What two characteristics common to all start-ups must be embraced in the quest for growth?

The simple answer is speed and agility. Start-ups can move fast and change focus rapidly, this enables them to remain agile, to fail fast when going down a blind alley and to pivot the business if required until a path for growth has been found. Make sure you keep agility and flexibility at the forefront of your mind when designing and then scaling your business. Certainly, in your product plans, development, agreements, and any commitments you sign up to.

By agile, I am referring to the principles around the ways of working that unlock value, keep the business nimble, increase employee engagement, enable a more efficient use of resources, and permit a faster route to market. Those advocated by agile development and project management methodologies of collaboration between stakeholders and developers, flexibility, iterative progress, simplicity, and constant attention to technical excellence. As a start-up, you begin agile. You start working in small, cross functional teams. You need to empower your people and make them accountable to get things done. This ability to react swiftly to customer feedback and to adapt quickly to changing technologies, and market demands, are major advantages.

Remaining agile is important when searching for the optimal track to scaling up and finding fast growth. When you are trying to scale a company, developing, and trialling new products, searching for the path to a sturdy base in the market can be elusive. It is not easy, and often not a straight road. There will be bumps in the road and you will sometimes need to change direction quickly.

Having to react to changing customer needs and requirements is part of the learning experience as you tune your offering, home in on the best opportunities and discover what is going to drive your future growth. It is important to learn from setbacks and failure, it is also key to cut your losses when you must, but never give up. Do not let bumps in the road dampen your enthusiasm to keep trying or to keep moving forward. It is often said about the Great Gold Rush in California in the 1850s that the people who made the most money were the people selling the shovels and supplies. The merchants selling the supplies made all the money[1].

A famous example is Levi Strauss[2], a 24-year-old Bavarian, who left New York in 1853 for California to prospect for gold. Instead of following the herd he set up a wholesale business selling materials to miners. Sometimes the easiest way to make money is the obvious one and may involve taking a step back and not doing exactly what others are running towards.

YouTube is perhaps one of the most famous and successful business pivots and is an interesting example of what can be possible. When it was initially built YouTube started out as an online video dating service. Users would upload short videos of themselves and then browse videos of others to search for their ideal partner. The slogan for the site was 'Tune in, hook up'. This was not remarkably successful, though when the business was pivoted into a wider video sharing platform it took off. Google acquired the business for $1.65 billion in October 2006.

I was associated with an internet insurance start-up called 'ValueInsurance.com' towards the end of the 1990s. We had the idea of an automated, data-driven, on-line virtual insurance company providing property and motor insurance products to the masses quickly, over the internet, at the click of a button. At the time, no such service existed though it was clear to most people that this was a requirement that would be filled by someone in the future. We had a partnership lined up with a leading insurance software supplier to provide software, IT and to distribute the product. We also had a strong team in place; an Underwriting Manager, David Whitaker, from one of the top insurers, a former Finance Director of RSA Insurance, John Sidwell, a former Chairman of Guy Carpenter, Tony McCallum, a senior guy from IBM and me (focused on data and analytics).

The ideas and the plan were solid though things unravelled and fell apart before any contract or monies were committed. There were a few dominant personalities in the team with different views on how the company should be run.

The blend in the team did not gel as I had hoped, and a deal with a key partner company also fell apart. With hindsight it was probably a blessing, I think, as we were too early to market. The insurance industry is traditionally slow to change, particularly when adopting new technology, even now over twenty years later, insurers are still talking about 'digital transformation'. It took a while for people to get comfortable buying insurance over the internet, and timing the market with innovative, new products is essential.

With hindsight, 'ValueInsurance.com' was too early to bring to market and may have failed anyway. We knew the idea was a winner as was proven by a company called Swiftcover.com, which came along about five years later with a similar plan, executed flawlessly and grabbed a large slice of the market. Again, I learnt quite a bit from the experience and moved on.

On a positive note, I found out quickly that 'ValueInsurance.com' and the other business idea for 'MyNest.co.uk' were not going to happen for me at that time. If you are going to fail, fail fast, learn, and move on but never give up on the dream.

You must at least try. Have the courage to take a risk and have a go.

A lot of people wait to feel confident enough to try something new, and the fact is that a lot of the time as an entrepreneur you will be trying new things or taking a step into the unknown. Failure is not a bad thing, and most people who have experienced a productive life will have failed at some things. You should consider failure as part of the learning process and improve towards being the best you can be.

Learn what you can from your mistakes and what went wrong or what is missing from your idea, plan, skillset, experience. Never stop trying, if you don't at least try you will never find out what works and what doesn't. And you won't move forward.

You will be left with that nagging doubt in your mind, what if I had tried, maybe it could have worked.

Remember, obstacles and brick walls to achieving goals are there for a reason, to stop all the other people.

From the initial failures and false starts on my entrepreneurial journey, I did widen my network, and learn some useful lessons.

I also met some valuable contacts. Some helped me, years later, to finally take the plunge into the entrepreneurial world and gain the traction I had been searching for.

3.2 What is frequently the main reason start-ups fail and the one thing, alongside being agile, you must do?

You should put the customer at the heart of everything you do – you must stay customer centric. Customer requirements give direction to agility. To remain acutely customer centric, you need to remain agile. When you try out new things try to see them through the client lens. Look at things from the customer perspective and keep trying to design your products, services and whole offering around servicing your clients in the most efficient and effective way you can from day one. The customer should be front and centre in all your thinking.

Running out of cash, or 'runway' as it sometimes referred to, is maybe the reason most often referred to when start-ups fail. In a survey of start-ups across 21 countries in the EU[3] cashflow was highlighted as being one of the biggest challenges. But it isn't the underlying causal factor. In the EU[4], the main issue cited for a start-up failing is down to the founder not validating their product with clients or having an early adopter on board prior to launch in the market. This reason also came top in a recent survey of failed start-up businesses in the USA by CBInsights[5] with 42% of founders pointing to a lack of market need by customers for their offering. The main reasons highlighted by surveys in the EU and the USA can be seen in table 4 below -. Amongst some of the other top ten causes for failure were 'ignoring customers', 'user unfriendly product', 'poor marketing' and 'got outcompeted'. If you don't stay close to the customer, deliver what they want and evolve your offering, you will fail to scale.

Table 4: Results from an analysis of past business failures

	Main reasons given for businesses failing in the USA and EU
1	No market need
2	Ran out of cash
3	Not the right team
4	User unfriendly products
5	Outcompeted
6	Pricing/cost issues
7	Product without clear business model
8	Product mistimed
9	Poor marketing
10	Ignore customers
11	Poor leadership (EU not mentioned in US list)
12	Inability to raise capital (EU not mentioned in US list)

Sources: CBInsights.com, EU-Startups.com

OK, so how you might ask do I stay close? Well, you need to capture information from customers about their requirements, what they are currently spending budget on and where their emerging needs are. You also need to listen to all customer suggestions and comments about your products, what they like and where they think improvements could be made. Ask them the question why? Why do they buy your product and from you as opposed to anyone else? Just as important, if someone leaves for a competitor, ask them the same questions.

You need to be capturing any information from client interactions about competing products, whether that is over the telephone, in trade shows, conferences, sale pitches or account review meetings. Collect the data and use this, and business analytics to drive your decisioning. This is one of the key differentials between the top 20% best performing companies and the rest. One of the best ways to capture this information is with a customer relationship management system and make sure that your team all commit to entering data from every client interaction from the start.

You don't have to spend a lot of money to get software that does the job and efficiently captures the information you need. You should track your sales and all the information from client interactions. Keep on top of the evolving requirements of your customer base. We used software called 'Pipedrive', but there are other packages. Capture the data, listen to customers, track your performance, and ensure that you provide great service. Make sure your products continue to meet client needs, that you understand when and how the market changes. Ensure future development is client focused.

Often in large organisations, particularly in technology, you have the developer who thinks he knows best and how the product should look and work. This is often without any customer input, steer, or guidance. I have experienced this in the corporate world and seen lots of examples of products where the technical lead or developer builds what he wants but not what the client wishes to buy. It may be built using the latest technology but will not be optimized for the client workflow. It will be what the technical lead thinks the client should buy rather than the reality of what is required. I have personally seen millions of pounds poured down the drain in such scenarios. If you experience this in your company point out who the company is serving and where the revenue comes from. If there is not a quick change in approach move the person on.

Unless you have the vision of Steve Jobs, changing the world with something completely different and new, I would advise working with your client base very closely. Get a deep understanding of where the client pain is and how you can develop your current offering much wider and deeper. Follow their guidance on the problems they want solved and where they will spend their budget. Prototype, test with them and develop at pace. Move rapidly to fulfil the needs and gain a solid foothold in the market.

You should always be aiming to provide exceptional service, monitor this in the business and never stop looking for ways to improve. In the companies I have been involved in the customer was always first and we took pride in our ability to respond quickly to serve customers and to respond to any changes in the market. Whether that meant going into the office on a bank holiday to work on an urgent tender or working through the night until the early hours of the morning, we would get the job done.

To get ahead of your competitors you should go the extra mile and ensure the job gets done to the best of your ability. Provide an excellent product with exceptional service, build up credibility and trust with your client base, always treat people fairly and act with integrity. Put all this at the heart of what you do, and clients will stay with you and keep coming back. In addition, they will need compelling arguments to go elsewhere, you will have a stronger pipeline of repeat business and customers to cross sell to. You will also create an excellent reputation in your industry and will have a solid foundation for growth.

The customer should be front and centre in all your thinking. Provide exceptional service and never stop looking for ways to improve.

3.3 What major benefits will an agile approach bring to the make-up of your business as it is scaled?

An agile approach will enable you to pivot quickly if you must and react quicker to market needs. The same approach can be applied in other areas of the business. Scaling up involves investment, it may mean committing to weighty contractual agreements with suppliers, buying more kit, hiring more people, or signing leases for new premises. Wherever there is risk try to stay flexible and <u>bring agility to negotiations, control your costs</u>. Ensure you keep on top of your costs and stay close to budget but bring an agile mindset to the negotiating table. We were able to secure exclusive contracts with some of our suppliers for both companies I owned a share in. Importantly we also ensured every time that the downside was protected. If things did not go to plan our costs were always contained.

For example, when not a soul in the insurance industry was interested in river flood risk underwriting, we managed to secure exclusive reseller rights to vital geographic data from the Institute of Hydrology (IOH) (now renamed the Centre for Ecology & Hydrology) relating to UK river flood risk. We were an early entrant to the insurance technology risk modelling market. Initially, we did not have anyone interested in licensing the product, even though it was a useful database. Then following a few severe flood events in the UK over a couple of years the landscape suddenly changed. Insurers now required a solution.

The government also wanted the Environment Agency to make a new national flood risk map for England & Wales and to supply this to the insurance market. One of the hurdles to overcome was the exclusive contract we had in place for one of the components. I received a letter from the IOH requesting we rescind the contract though initially there was no incentive to do so. In subsequent negotiations we found a solution that worked for all parties. We then had exclusive rights to another dataset that we could put into our whole solution. The market was picking up, we had stayed on good terms with our supplier and still maintained our differentiated product that competitors could not replicate at the time.

Always look for a 'win-win' solution in negotiating with suppliers even when protecting your downside and looking for a competitive edge. Look to build long term relationships with suppliers as well as with customers. Get to know the people, what their interests are outside work, where they like going on holiday, be a good listener – build up a rapport. When your suppliers have something new that is relevant for your market you want them knocking on your door first to discuss taking it to market.

We applied the same approach when hiring advisors. We wanted the best we could get but without busting the budget, well at least in the early-stage growth phase. For example, I managed to get a deal with a top London law firm, Farrer & Co, to help in negotiating contracts with blue chip clients. We were able to secure a preferential rate at the start on the understanding that as the business developed, we would push more work their way and would use them on exit.

The introduction to one of the partners at Farrer's came about through my involvement in ValueInsurance.com. We were only a small start-up. So, it certainly helped when entering contractual discussions with large insurers to have a legal firm representing us that had some gravitas in meetings, and that our clients' legal team listened to.

'How did you end up having Farrer's representing you?' was a question asked every time by prospective clients. I knew that Farrer's were one of the oldest legal firms in the city - though it was not until much later that I found out who their most famous client was, Her Majesty Queen Elizabeth II!

3.4 What can help in navigating the different strategic options and paths for the business as you scale?

What I have found out over the years is you can learn a lot from other people. <u>I had a mentor and so should you.</u> They can be hugely beneficial in sharing past experiences, especially those that have been on a similar path and have been successful. And that have lots of challenging business experiences they have overcome that you can tap into for insight. This can be valuable in avoiding blind alleys, helping to decide when to pivot and in sharing their knowledge in the selection of strategic options for the business. You should never stop learning and you should soak up advice and experiences from others like a sponge.

When you hit bumps in the road, have problems, and business issues to overcome having a sounding board or experienced coach or mentor to turn to can be vital. Over the last fifteen years, several mentors have helped guide me, their expertise covering different areas relevant to the business. These included analytics and data modelling, the insurance industry & regulation and general management. I have found this advice and experience invaluable during many challenging times in the past for my businesses.

I would encourage you to find a mentor, schedule a regular call with him or her at least fortnightly and bounce ideas and issues off them. You should also arrange a quarterly meeting over lunch for a more in-depth discussion. I encouraged two of the people involved in the last business to buy shares in the company. It depends, I guess, on how much you think the people will add and if having some 'skin' in the game will sharpen their advice if you hit rough waters. I have certainly found having someone as a sounding board to turn to, someone who understands the business but is not involved on a day-to-day basis, to be invaluable.

My advice would be to find a mentor, someone you get on with, who has extensive experience relevant to your business or field. Someone who is easy to talk to, experienced in coaching and in offering useful advice. If you are working on a 'scalable start-up' with a potentially high growth trajectory, there will be bumps along the way and having someone to guide, coach or give advice at certain times is worth having.

Another useful management tool to help in comparing the different strategic options available to you is the

Business Model Canvas template.

This basically summarises a business plan onto one page. It has been widely used in recent years by start-ups to evaluate and compare different strategic alternatives. It is based on work by Alexander Osterwalder[6,7] and Yves Pigneur who found that the design of a business could be collapsed down to nine key building blocks covering infrastructure, offering, customers and finance.

The nine elements in order are:

1) **Your value proposition,** what do you do for your customers?

2) **What are your key activities**, how do you serve?

3) **What are your key resources**, what do you need to deliver?

4) **Who are your key partners**, who will help you?

5) **What is your relationship with your customers**, how will you interact?

6) **What will be your distribution channels**, how will you reach customers?

7) **What are the different customer segments**, who are you targeting?

8) **On the financial side your costs**, what will it cost?

9) **What will be your revenue streams**, how much will you make?

The hypothetical example for an insurance software business is shown in the exhibit below. You could add to this with numbers estimating the market opportunity, costs relating to different options and the critical supplier contracts you would need to have in place to make it happen.

I think it is useful in being able to encapsulate all the main elements of your business initiative onto one page.

The most crucial element to get right from the outset is the value proposition. Far too often, as evidenced in the survey mentioned at the beginning of this chapter, entrepreneurs have a great idea, or at least they think it is, then pursue their brainchild without fully researching the value proposition or the customer fit in depth. If you aren't solving client pain, meeting a burning need, and creating some improvement to the current market offering why will anyone buy from you.

BUSINESS MODEL CANVAS - HYPOTHETICAL EXAMPLE FOR INSURANCE RISK SOFTWARE

KEY PARTNERS	KEY ACTIVITIES	VALUE PROPOSITION	CUSTOMER RELATIONSHIPS	CUSTOMER SEGMENTS
X, Y, Z Data suppliers	Specialist software development	More accurate insurance pricing	Account managers / personal	Insurance companies
Insurance Software companies	Development of predictive algorithms	Better assessment of risk	Customer support/help desk	Insurance brokers
Group Affiliates	Creation of niche data assets	Improved risk selection	Sales teams	Managing General Agents
	Consulting	Faster, more accurate claims validation. Improved customer		Lloyds Syndicates
Reseller solution providers	**KEY RESOURCES**	experience.	**DISTRIBUTION CHANNELS**	Reinsurance brokers
	Unique data assets	Improved fraud detection	Direct to customer	Reinsurance companies
	People\talent (with deep domain expertise)		Application interfaces\ Industry data distribution hubs	
	Knowhow (Intellectual Property)		Reseller partners\affiliates	

COST STRUCTURE	REVENUE STREAMS
Cost of talent (people)	Software\Data subscriptions (per click usage model and multi year all you use model)
Data \ IT costs (cloud hosting)\ software licensing	Commission from reselling 3rd party solutions
Royalty cost of integrated 3rd party solutions	One-off consulting fees
Office lease	Royalties from reseller solutions providers (reselling our products)

The Business Model Canvas, is released under Creative Commons license (creativecommons.org) from the original source Strategyzer.com

To address this and to carry out a deeper dive into customer expectations Osterwalder designed the Value Proposition Canvas[8] tool. It works in conjunction with the Business Model Canvas, as a prerequisite, comparing the fit between your offering and market requirements. The process forces questioning the product value proposition, encouraging the testing, validation, and assessment of ideas from a customer needs angle first. In short, it promotes a deeper understanding of customer desires, helps to minimise product failure, and makes sure you produce something that people want. The output flows into your Business Model Canvas.

The Business Model Canvas brings clarity. It enables an easier understanding and debating of the options, and it aids faster consideration of different paths for the business to take. Ultimately, it brings speed and focus when considering strategic options with your team and advisors.

When I first started out in business the approach was much more laboured. The writing and refinement of the business plan took a lot of time, and then developing and testing different ideas was much slower than via the business model canvas approach.

To remain agile, and to speed up your strategic planning, I would recommend trying the business model canvas approach. Please work through this in the homework section at the end of this chapter, and then link it with the techniques and ideas in the chapter on refining your competitive strategy.

Hopefully, you will find it useful in clarifying your thoughts, and uncovering new strategic alternatives for your business.

3.5 In the rapidly evolving technology space how can you scale up and stay agile in your decisioning with so much going on?

The pace of change in the technology space has been increasing incredibly fast in recent years. For example, just consider the rate of change in areas such as artificial intelligence and applications for automation of routine processes, predictive analytics, and cloud technology – there is a lot going on. Consider also emerging technologies such as 3D printing or the growth in pervasive computing applications, where microprocessors are embedded in everyday objects allowing them to collect and communicate information (e.g., smart watches, Internet of Things (IOT devices)).

Then there are the recent changes in government data protection regulations such as GDPR (General Data Protection Regulation) in Europe and the California Consumer Privacy Act (CCPA) impacting the use, collection, and storage of personal data.

For a small tech company, it's impossible to be an expert in everything and focus on scaling your business. Nor can you afford to pay for lots of consultants on a sporadic basis for snippets of advice.

How can you stay up to date, widen your knowledge base rapidly and make more informed decisions as you scale?

The simple answer is to nurture a wide network of external experts across all areas of relevance to your business. You could ask the most significant of these to also be mentors that you can tap into, and access advice when you need it. Having more than one mentor can be useful to give a wider pool of knowledge, experiences, and expertise to call on. I had two former senior executives as mentors in my last business. From a product point of view, changing technology, and in terms of changing government regulations, I also sought out advice from several industry experts.

One of these people, Peter Sleight, is a good friend and was a mentor that helped me from a technical and product development perspective. Peter was previously CEO of Pinpoint Analysis, an analytics company, as well as a pioneer of geodemographic modelling and its applications in industry. He is an industry analytics expert and author of several books, including *Targeting Customers: How to Use Geodemographic and Lifestyle Data in Your Business*, a book on the reading list of many university undergraduate geography courses. I have had many an enjoyable pub lunch discussing product development, the future of analytics and current industry topics.

These people are a goldmine of information and knowledge. They are also usually eager to help and to share their experiences. They are happy to give their views on similar paths they have been down in the past. Why things either worked or didn't work for them, and offer advice on similar things you are involved in.

It is rare that you would find one mentor that would be an expert in all areas of your business. Seek out two or three for advice, with diverse spheres of knowledge and experience. If you want to compete with large companies, you need to uncover ways to win, and a way to tap into a deeper knowledge base and understanding of the market. Of course, if they are attending board meetings and giving formal advice then they need to be on contract and to be paid a fair day rate. It will be worth it, and you will find you are making more informed decisions based on deeper knowledge, a greater understanding of the market, and a richer base of experience.

Be a sponge, never stop learning, get the best advice, and keep moving the business forward as it progresses.

References / Further reading

1. https://history.howstuffworks.com/american-history/gold-rush.htm
2. https://www.levistrauss.com/2013/03/14/the-story-of-levi-strauss/
3. Startupmonitor.eu (2018, a survey of start-ups across 21 countries in Europe)
4. https://www.eu-startups.com/2018/09/the-10-most-common-reasons-why-startups-fail/
5. https://www.cbinsights.com/research/startup-failure-reasons-top/
6. *Osterwalder, Alexander (2004). The Business Model Ontology: A Proposition in A Design Science Approach (PDF) (Ph.D. thesis). Lausanne: University of Lausanne. OCLC 717647749*
7. *Osterwalder, Alexander; Pigneur, Yves; Clark, Tim (2010). Business Model Generation: A Handbook For Visionaries, Game Changers, and Challengers. Strategyzer series. Hoboken, NJ: John Wiley & Sons.*
8. Osterwalder, A (2014); Value Proposition design: how to create products and services customers want. Strategyzer Series. John Wiley and Sons.

Key takeaways

• Never stop trying but know when to move on, not having a go is the real failure. Fail fast, learn from mistakes, and move on. Do not let it dampen your belief.

• Stay agile but keep the customer front and centre in all your thinking. Provide exceptional service and never stop looking for ways to improve.

• Put in place a CRM system, capture all data from client interactions and make sure you stay close to emerging market needs.

• Bring agility to negotiations, think outside the box for ways to maximise the deal but protect your downside, particularly in the early days as you scale the company and move toward profitability.

• Look for solutions in negotiations that are also fair and even handed. To scale you need longevity in the market and to do that you need to build trusted relationships with suppliers as well as with your client base.

• Find a mentor. Someone who has been along a similar journey that you can bounce ideas off, use as a sounding board, go to for impartial advice and tap into for their experience and learnings.

• Consider utilizing the Business Canvas model approach in conjunction with the Value Proposition Canvas tool for your planning. It will help to speed up the process of evaluating different strategic options. It supports an agile approach to consideration of strategic alternatives.

• Don't be afraid to seek out mentors across several specialist areas. Be a sponge, never stop learning, get the best advice, and keep moving the business forward as it progresses.

HOMEWORK

Now over to you. *Using the business canvas model template below, fill in the 9 core elements to your plan in the boxes. Produce a different version for each alternative path you are considering. This can be used in discussions with your team to debate and compare different options. As you go through your customer discovery phase it can support finding the most lucrative path to scale up.*

BUSINESS MODEL CANVAS TEMPLATE

KEY PARTNERS | KEY ACTIVITIES | VALUE PROPOSITION | CUSTOMER RELATIONSHIPS | CUSTOMER SEGMENTS

KEY RESOURCES | DISTRIBUTION CHANNELS

COST STRUCTURE | REVENUE STREAMS

The Business Model Canvas, is released under Creative Commons license (creativecommons.org) from the original source Strategyzer.com

CHAPTER 4: HOW DO YOU BUILD AND RETAIN A WINNING TEAM?

'Acquiring the right talent is the most important key to growth. Hiring was - and still is - the most important thing we do'

- Marc Bennioff, Founder, CEO of Salesforce

As an entrepreneur, after the initial product or business idea, the most important task is hiring the right people, putting them in the correct slots and then creating an environment to enable them to succeed. You may have your initial operation up and running, with a couple of friends. You may even have a minimum viable product and some initial customers. This is a brilliant start. To scale, grow quickly and develop into a sustainable business of significant value you need a strong team.

You need to attract and hire great talent and then weave them into an effective, winning team that can execute your vision. The best teams fuel fast growth, working collaboratively towards shared goals. They out-innovate and out-perform rivals, winning becomes second nature. The people you bring on board are a critical part of whether your scale-up will work or fall flat. How do you attract top talent and put together a high-performance team? How do you incentivize and retain them? What are some of the pitfalls to avoid?

4.1 What is vital for success as you assemble your 'scale-up' unit?

The first 10 to 15 people you hire are critical to get right. Are these people up for the fight, to take on much bigger companies and win? Some will form your key leadership team, and all will be important as you scale and grow. According to a survey of failed start-up businesses by CBInsights[1] in 2019, 23% fail due to not hiring the right team. Being able to hire great talent and put together a winning team is vital to successfully scale-up your business. <u>I have always looked for people to hire that are better than me.</u>

If you want to keep improving and do better than you did before hire people that are up for the task, that will contribute but also challenge you. This might seem like a strange thing to say though with the right framework and culture in place it can work well. Some leaders will resist doing this as they may feel insecure, threatened or fear losing control if they hire much smarter people than themselves. This is one of the trade-offs, you need to get over it if you want to build a high performing team. Hire team players with the right attitude, the attributes outlined below and that treat colleagues with respect, it is a strategy that works.

One way to think of whether a person meets your standard is to consider if they fit a benchmark aligned with the 'BATTLE' criteria. Are they competitive, are they a suitable match for YOUR business, are they FIT for 'BATTLE', Do they:

Table 5: The 'BATTLE' Benchmark for talent selection

Believe in and show commitment to the vision for the company.

Adaptability, will they thrive in a rapidly changing scale-up environment?

Trustworthy, do you trust them to do the work and live the company values?

Team, are they team players? Are they selfless and can they focus on shared goals?

Leaders, can they lead, are they self-starters? Can they step-up and take responsibility, will they be an asset in a growing company?

Energised, do they have energy? Are they motivated and tenacious? Will they energise those around them? do they have what it takes to get 'stuff' done?

This is criteria to keep in mind during the interview process and when you bring new people on board during the probationary period. It is useful first pass criteria to apply to each person you consider bringing on board and before you agree to put people on a permanent contract.

How does this fit with your current team?

4.2 What will guarantee you a high-performing outfit?

I have always enjoyed putting winning teams together and this started from a young age. In my last year at Salford University as an undergraduate I was captain of the Rugby League club. We had an average team and in previous seasons had generally lost more games than we had won. If we were to improve, we needed better players and a qualified coach to help create a much stronger, more competitive team.

After a few enquiries I found out that several local colleges in Salford and Manchester were affiliated to our University, and so their students were eligible to play in the team. I enlisted my friend Chris Green, another student who would have made a wonderful salesman, to help sell the vision. We visited every eligible college in the city searching for talent. We enthused about building a team capable of beating much bigger rivals and our ambitious goal of winning the National Student Cup.

We were successful in recruiting a lot of talented players. Some had played a high standard of rugby, for example, one had represented Welsh Schools and two were on the books at local professional clubs Swinton and Warrington. I also managed to recruit a coach after writing to local professional clubs asking for help in training and creating an improved team.

The plan worked, the team was transformed, that season we only lost one match, in the Semi-Final of the National Student Cup against Loughborough University, who had been the best student team at the time. After I left university the team went on to win the cup and were the best student team for a couple of years. Finding top talent and the best people is important and it is certainly worth putting in the extra effort to bring 'A' team people on board.

In a business context it is also essential to ensure you get the right blend of personalities and skills.

<u>Seek out 'A' team players</u>. The best teams usually win.

Not just the best individuals thrown together and there is the distinction.

From the start-up position if you want to scale up and grow rapidly there is going to be a lot of on-going change in your business. Initially it will be a relatively small team. Getting those early hires correct with the right profile is vital.

Find intelligent, ambitious, driven, team players and winners, don't settle for second best. Get your founder purpose and story clear and make it emotionally engaging to create the shared vision.

The emotional story I used to galvanise the Business Insight team was also about the small player taking on bigger rivals and winning against the odds. I told them about an insurance industry conference I went to just before setting up the business. Whilst there I bumped into the CEO of a large established competitor. It was a friendly chat though his parting comment was:

"You know you were just lucky with ISL; I doubt you can do it again".

To which I replied,

"Luck didn't have much to do with it. I guess we'll just have to see what happens with my next venture".

I also referred to another meeting a little time after with the CEO of a large actuarial consulting firm.

He too was dismissive of the new venture and said,

"in the land of the blind the one-eyed man is king",

when referring to the previous achievements of ISL. John Bunch, a colleague and business partner I'd also worked with at ISL, had gone with me to the meeting. John had been responsible for building one of ISL's main products 'Whatif', a product that had managed to attain a 90% market share in the UK P&C Insurance market.

As we left the meeting John said to me:

"Mark, did he really say what I think he said".

"Yes", I replied, *"A bit rude, wasn't he? He thinks we were just lucky being first in the market with some of the products last time around. We will have to prove him wrong."*

We were determined to build even better products that were more accurate and more useful for customers. We were going to take on the much bigger players. And win.

Create your founder story and enthuse about the journey. Search for a way to get the A team players you need on board and put them in the right slots. It is important to get the right people on the bus.

Use your stories and create a shared vision and goal, a sense of belonging to a group all working together, to motivate and galvanise a team ethic.

Then support them to make things happen.

4.3 What are the important traits for people in a winning team?

The profile of the ideal candidates will vary by position slightly across your organization by skillset though they should all share some common traits. It is important to get the blend of personalities right and people that fit with your culture. They should sign up to the shared vision, the values you have set out, and the purpose that you have mapped out for the company. In a start-up operation you ideally should be looking for people who are self-starters, self-motivated, quick to adapt, tenacious individuals that can work well with other people. Find people that are also good problem solvers, strong communicators and that are well organized. You also need leaders, not followers, right across the business, to help scale up a company.

Above all else find people with energy, passion, and integrity. Those with a positive, can do attitude and an optimistic outlook. I would much rather have a competent person, with energy and a fantastic attitude, who is committed to the shared purpose of the team, than a genius with a massive ego that struggles to fit in.

Optimism is important when breaking into new markets. One interesting analogy I heard some time ago involved two salesmen sent by rival shoe manufacturers to investigate opportunities in India. One guy returned and said:

"I can't see much opportunity for our products in India. Most of the people in the streets don't wear shoes".

The other guy returned and had the opposite view for his company saying:

"There is a massive opportunity for us in India, there are huge amounts of people without any shoes".

When I first started working in the insurance market, we were trying to sell a flood risk model by postcode to insurance underwriters to help in premium pricing. Nobody in the insurance market had licensed a model for underwriting property risk at that time. The pessimists in our team were saying there is no market for flood risk models, no insurer has allocated any budget for it. Now of course every property insurer in the market has licensed data to price flood risk, some insurers license several sources of flood data from different suppliers.

Look for optimists to build your business, avoid those that say it can't be done.

Ideally, I would also search for people that are honest, humble, and respectful of others. And that are hardworking and willing to put in a shift. One of the cleverest product development guys I have ever hired in the past, Dr Alan McLachlan, had a post doctorate in neural computing, used to lecture in quantum mechanics at Dublin University and had an enormous amount of industry experience. Yet he was a very humble guy, a superb team player and was always respectful of others in meetings, even when he knew they were talking nonsense.

4.4 How do you ensure you have a balanced group and a foundation for growth?

You need to have diverse skills in the team covering all the essential areas for the business to operate efficiently. This means considering the functional diversity of skills in your crew as well as the blend of personalities. It is an important task for the scale-up leader - Being able to take a step back, think carefully about the requirements. Like putting together a complex jigsaw puzzle, it is vital that you hire the right individuals with complementary skills. Bringing these individuals together and establishing a cohesive, high performing team is a significant step in the entrepreneurial process.

In my companies this meant initially hiring specialist leaders in systems & technology, analytics product development, sales & marketing, and finance as the first guys through the door. Then putting in a functional structure for growth and building out from there. Initially in start-ups the structure is frequently flat with everyone working on the same project, often all reporting into the founder. To grow you need to have a structure in place with people responsible for specific areas and with clear reporting lines.

I know many businesses don't hire a professional sales director, marketing manager, or a qualified accountant to run their finances. Sometimes the founder wears several hats, covering some of these roles and often the accounts or finance function is outsourced. Some companies supplement their full-time staff with consultants and contractors plugging the talent gap in the short term. Just be careful taking short cuts and not doing things properly from the start – it will come back to bite you otherwise.

Ensuring you have accurate financial statements prepared in accordance with locally accepted accounting standards and practice (e.g., in the UK and the Republic of Ireland, at the time of writing, UK GAAP FRS 102[2] are the applicable accounting standards) is important so that issues such as income recognition are accurately considered. You also need to give yourself the best chance of building sales fast and that requires focused, experienced, professionals.

In my view, if you are serious about scaling up you need to be 100% on top of two areas of the business, your sales, and your finances. Having A team players in those roles and having a deep and thorough grasp of these areas is crucial.

Figure 1 below is a typical example of a functional organization for a technology company. This is just one example that I found worked for me, there are other ways to structure the company and the product/industry you are in will influence this. The important point is not to over burden your own area and to take too much on yourself. If you want to grow fast you need help, and to share responsibilities across your top team.

Plan regular board meetings, at least once a month. Get the lead person from each area to report progress against objectives for the year. Get the finance director to prepare a set of monthly management accounts showing progress against budget, and the sales director to prepare a report on sales activity and on the state of the sales pipeline.

The product development/system directors should also prepare a joint monthly report on product development, progress against plan and any customer issues highlighted in the last month. This should go into a reporting pack. Ensure the team is disciplined and tenacious in maintaining these reports, debate them in your board meetings and take any necessary actions.

Raise the bar and keep it there.

FIGURE 1: Example organisational structure

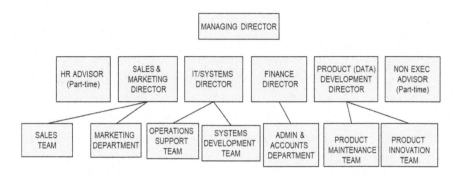

4.5 How can you easily fill areas where skills are initially missing in your business?

When scaling up a small business you will regularly have to wear different hats and cover numerous areas. There are usually many urgent issues competing for your time and you will need quality support and advice across several specialist domains such as legal services, human resources, design (products/marketing) and public relations, amongst others to support your growing business. These are areas that are often threadbare and not well covered in small companies, and it can be obvious to external parties dealing with the firm.

While you would not necessarily hire a full-time human resources manager, or in-house corporate lawyer, it is important to get experienced support. Outsource these areas to part-time consultants or a quality outside firm with a dedicated point person. My advice is to find great consultants you trust to supplement the team.

If you have a vision to be a large business, perhaps the leader in your niche market, then you need to behave and adopt the habits of such a company from day 1. You should project the right professional image and brand to the outside world. From candidates considering joining your fledgling venture to the press or clients considering investing in your products.

If you want people to have the right impression of your outfit as a professional growing company that is going places you need this in place. Ensuring that tasks such as recruitment, talent management and contractual work are handled by experienced, quality people will also take some of the weight off your shoulders and free you up to focus on other parts of your growing business. So that means hiring experienced, quality consultants to represent you and that can project a highly professional view of your firm.

<u>Do not take short cuts, hire the best you can get.</u>

Find people you get on well with and that you trust. Build a long-term relationship and make them part of your team.

We had heavy hitters representing us across all these areas, from a top city lawyer, a veteran PR consultant to a very experienced HR expert who had previously worked for Bret Hoberman (Lastminute.com). We set up these people on retained part-time agreements - it worked well and was worth the investment.

Please do the same - you will not regret spending a penny.

4.6 How can you hire to increase creativity in your organisation?

The best way to increase creativity is to incorporate diversity into your team to bring fresh ideas, new inputs, and to enrich current thinking from as wide an area as possible.

Diversity is important, it should be embraced and taken into consideration when hiring to build a high performing team.

You need to have a framework in place to support this. Everyone should treat the views of everyone else with respect, people should feel at ease in presenting their views, sharing ideas and in contributing. Having people in the line-up from disparate backgrounds, with contrasting ages, cultures, ethnic or religious upbringings and from different countries can bring a wider range of opinions, and diverse perspectives to the table.

It can also deepen the knowledge base and enhance the inventiveness within the company.

When putting together a team how much thought do you give to the types of personality you are hiring? Getting a balance to the blend of various types can make a difference not only to the atmosphere in the office but also to creativity and performance. Hire all introvert 'techies' and who is going to speak to clients? How are they going to brainstorm ideas and 'spark' off one another? How will you discover the route to the best products and how will you sell them in? On the other hand, if you hire all extroverts focused on relationships, you may not get any work done or products completed.

According to the established work by David Merrill & Roger Reid[3] everyone can be classified into one of four different personality types: *'Drivers'* or fact focused extroverts, *'Analyticals'* or fact focused introverts, *'Amiables'* or relationship focused introverts and *'Expressives'* or relationship focused extroverts. Everyone will exhibit a mix of these characteristics though will have one dominant type. Being able to recognize this and the categories that people fit into can enable you to put together more harmonious, productive teams. It can also lead to greater creativity.

Consciously thinking about this and having some understanding of the basic personality types that people naturally fall into can also be useful in other ways. It can give you some insight into how you need to adapt your behaviour to get the best out of individuals in your company.

What approach will certain individuals respond to best? What motivates certain people and how can you get the whole team to gel in the most productive way?

When considering different roles in the company you may wish to contemplate what your ideal candidate in each area might resemble. Certain positions require specific qualities to do well in that area, for example:

In sales roles – you may want people exuding energy, charm, to be people orientated and to have tenacity.

In finance roles – you may want people who are diligent, process driven and have attention to detail.

And in development roles – you wish to find intelligent, highly technical individuals with imagination, common sense and who get a kick and take pride in producing great products.

In my view, in terms of a 'tech' business, if you want more creativity in your development team consider people who are good at art as well as maths. Uncover clues on their resume and dig deeper at the interview stage. People who are great at art as well as mathematics can often visualize solutions better. When you ask them,

"How did you come up with that idea?"

The response is usually, *"I dreamt it last night"*. Some of these individuals literally dream how it will look and work. They are frequently better at generating fresh solutions in a technical space. And they are worth their weight in gold.

If you want to increase creativity in your team, search for these people and it will lead to more ideas, more originality, and better products.

4.7 How can you galvanise your team into one unit moving in the same direction?

Communicate your vision and values to the team from the start and ensure that the people you hire are a cultural fit and share the same passion for the journey. Ensure you put in place a framework where healthy debate is encouraged and where people want to contribute. Somewhere people feel comfortable sharing their knowledge and views, challenge the status quo in a friendly, inclusive environment. And where people treat each other with respect.

Set clear objectives, treat people fairly, build trust, put in place a competitive and friendly working environment, and ensure that everyone is included and can have their say.

I remember one summer in my youth, during a student vacation, I had a job in a glass factory in Leeds. I was employed on a production line alongside many other people making windows and safety glass. It was a slog involving long hours, doing very repetitive, manual work. The management had allowed a culture of bullying to develop amongst the production workers, particularly of minority groups. Shortly after I had started working there, I decided to voice my opinion in support of one individual who was being bullied. This was ignored and the attention was then turned on making my time there uncomfortable.

I was only working there a matter of a few weeks though it made me appreciate what some people must put up with in their working lives, and what can result from a toxic environment with weak management and poor leadership.

As the leader you set the tone and people follow your framework.

Creating a high-performance environment also means looking after the team in tough times. Before and after running my own business, I have also been lucky to work for and with some great people, some leaders who would literally take a bullet for the team.

I remember one day, whilst working in a large company, one of the people in my team told me they had a serious illness and needed to go into hospital for an operation. They were worried about being off work for a prolonged period, whether they would continue to get paid, and how they would be able to cover their mortgage and bills.   Unfortunately, the employment contract we had in place contained a limited amount of sick pay entitlement. The person had no health insurance and statutory sick pay would certainly not cover basic living expenses, never mind their mortgage repayments.

I spoke to my boss at the time to find a way to help the person out. 'This guy has been a great employee and is a valuable member of the firm. Can we find a way to help him out please?', and the response was 'Ignore the bureaucrats, we need to look after the team. Yes, Mark, find a way to keep paying and overlook the contract on this occasion, you have my full support'. He stuck his neck out and that is what strong leaders do.

I have learnt a lot from other people. As well as being the right thing to do this creates trust and loyalty. You know your leader has your back.

Recognise the contribution of individuals to the team, promote excellence and champion continuous improvement in your products, and in everything you do across the company.

In the businesses that I have been involved in people have been encouraged to share their ideas and their knowledge with the rest of the team in regular off-site away days. At these events we would also update people on how the firm was performing, reiterate the shared vision, and what we all needed to focus on next. This was combined with team building events, dinner, and an overnight stay in a nice hotel - we made it fun. We were creating a group which was more productive than the sum of its parts.

One that could take on much bigger rivals, and win.

4.8 How do you motivate, maintain, and drive high performance?

Make sure that you set clear goals and objectives for each of your team. And where they are interdependent, that people are aware of where objectives fit together to encourage collaboration. Ensure that all objectives adhere to the SMART[4] criteria, as shown in table 6 below. They should be specific or targeted at a particular area, measurable and have a way to quantify success such as hitting a certain sales target or completing a project. The objectives should also be assignable so the responsibility for delivery is assigned to a particular area or individual, relevant, or realistic as to what can be achieved with the available resources. And time dependent, so the objective must be completed in a certain agreed time frame.

Table 6: SMART Objectives

SMART objectives	What are the key elements you should include when setting any objectives for your team
Specific	Targeted and tightly defined.
Measurable	Quantifiable in terms of what is delivered.
Assignable	Someone is responsible for making it happen.
Relevant	Realistic and achievable with given resources.
Time dependent	Time frame agreed with a set date for completion.

The targets assigned to individuals should all roll up to deliver the shared goals of the team. The performance of individuals in the organisation should be measured against their objectives and the rewards allocated in relation to these.

Many companies I have spoken to don't have any formal or informal feedback or any objectives set for their employees. If you don't give people something to aim at, then provide feedback and acknowledgement on a regular basis, how do they know they are doing great work. People carry on doing their job without understanding whether they are doing well or not. To get the most from your employees they need to feel appreciated, where they fit into the bigger picture and that what they do makes a difference. That they have a purpose.

Give constructive advice and feedback to your team regularly. Encouragement, perhaps a steer in another direction. Make sure you commend people when they achieve, win sales, hit milestones, and do great work. They want to turn up for work believing that they are adding value and what they are doing is contributing to the whole enterprise. This is what motivates, energises, and drives a high performance from your group.

Show a genuine interest in your colleagues and their development though be careful when providing any negative feedback and in criticizing individuals. People respond much better to praise and constructive feedback than to criticism.

As a blunt Yorkshireman, I have had to learn the hard way, through experience, how things should be handled. Nobody likes to be told they are wrong or have made a mistake and there is a right way and a wrong way to deliver the message. Also, in a technology environment you want people to try new things and, in some circumstances, particularly in product development, to take the odd risk. Above all avoid reprimanding people in public, subtly point out errors or issues, praise something you can find they have been doing well, then offer solutions and encouragement.

You should also avoid sending off-the-cuff emails lambasting people for mistakes or perhaps when responding to curt emails they may have sent you. It is far too easy to send an impulsive, scolding email when irritated with a colleague for making a complete hash of something. I know because I have done it, and it does NOT work. It doesn't resolve the issue and you don't get the best response from people. It doesn't energise or motivate; it has the reverse effect. It deflates, and it can escalate and create bad feeling. If you think of firing off an email to reprimand someone, don't do it. If you feel you must write it, don't send it, sleep on it, and leave it until the next morning. Then tone down your response and arrange to meet in person, find a resolution and move on.

Help colleagues find solutions, encourage and coach them to be the best they can be, to exceed their own expectations. Motivate and energise them to grow with the business. Lavish praise publicly when people hit or exceed targets and reward them well with bonuses and good pay rises. Set stretch goals and challenge your team to keep improving. Then watch them reach their potential and drive the business forward.

4.9 How can you retain the best people?

How do you retain the top performers? In the technology space where I have worked it has been a challenge to attract and lock in the best people. At ISL we had some great talent in the team, I was keen to offer several individuals share options to lock them in, though I was out voted on this point at a board meeting. So instead, we paid them significant cash bonuses linked to performance. This didn't retain them long term and eventually they were poached by larger companies offering remuneration packages we couldn't match.

When I started Business Insight, I decided that we were not going to make the same mistake. We took a different approach. This time around we ensured that everyone in the company had share options. Those on board near the start could put money in to acquire a sizeable chunk of shares and others joining later were given a small number of shares, even though they didn't invest any of their own money. I thought that having some ownership of the company, however small, would motivate everyone to a higher performance and lock them in long term.

It worked very well for some and not so well for others. For some people it was a motivating factor and did drive them to a higher performance, and they did consistently put in effort over and above what was asked. For other people, admittedly a small number, it was not a motivator and for me this was disappointing. A few people seemed to take what was given to them for granted. Holding the shares proved to be very lucrative. Business Insight was profitable within the first 18 months and the shares we issued to staff carried voting rights and entitled them to a dividend, when one was issued. In addition to the eye-watering sale price, we paid out significant dividends over the years as the company grew.

I think some people just don't have any respect for capital and they think 'well he has got plenty of money he can afford to give it away'. They may also have different drivers when it comes to work, remuneration and incentives. Based on what I have experienced I would advise to not be overly generous at the start. Keep share options up your sleeve to bring on board key people and to lock in star performers when they have demonstrated their worth. Also, a better way forward would be to issue B shares to star performers that don't carry any voting rights or dividends and only vest when the company is sold. Whichever way you do it finding a way to retain the best people is important and worth doing.

4.10 Lastly, how to deal with hires you get wrong.

Occasionally you will hire the wrong people. Over the last 25 years I have fortunately been right more than I have been wrong in hiring staff. Though I have made a few mistakes.

The worst kind of people are the energy sappers and the quite clever, able individuals that have a massive ego and who struggle to work well within a team or take any direction from management. They drain the energy from the team, and when you walk into a room, they often inhibit higher interaction between everyone, and create an unpleasant atmosphere. Of course, what happens then is that you, as a leader, end up spending a disproportionate amount of your time managing them or sorting out issues they have created.

In his book '*Winning*'[5], Jack Welch suggests grading the whole company into three groups. At the top you have the star performers, the major contributors to your business, then in the middle you have the engine room with the main bulk of people who perform competently and then at the bottom you have those not performing. He suggests managing the non-performers out of the company. This is fine but what about those that can do the job but are just difficult people to work with, temperamental or sullen people, who drain the energy from those around them?

My advice, based on experience, is find a way to manage them out as soon as you can. In a 'scale-up' business you can't afford the extra time spent on dealing with them and the problems they may create.

One way forward may be to put everyone joining the company on a probationary period of at least, say 3 months. At the end of which you should know if they are a good fit in the company or not. Liaise with your talent management or human resources consultant and move them on quickly before any negativity spreads to the rest of the team. When you do this always ensure that you treat people in a fair, kind, and compassionate way.

Of course, the best way would be to stop them coming in the front door and identify them at the interview stage. In 'Winning'[5] Jack Welch offers one killer question to ask at interview to try to weed out this type of person. He suggests asking them to discuss their current role and why they want to leave their current employer. Follow that up by asking for a reference and compare the two. That might offer some clues. You could also ask what their most challenging moment has been in life to date and how they coped, or perhaps how they have overcome any adversity or how they bounced back from failure.

In my view competitive team sports has a lot of parallels with business as people work side by side collaboratively towards a shared goal. Consequently, I would also ask someone at interview if they have played any competitive team sports. Get them to talk about their experiences where they were part of a winning team, what aspects they enjoyed and what aspects they found particularly challenging. People who have learnt to be part of a team from a young age don't struggle to fit in or integrate into a business environment in my experience.

Surround yourself with talented performers, people better than you, team players with a fantastic, can-do positive attitude, and create a winning team.

References /Further reading

1. https://www.cbinsights.com/research/startup-failure-reasons-top/
2. https://www.icaew.com/technical/financial-reporting/uk-gaap/frs-102-the-financial-reporting-standard
3. Merrill D. W., Reid R.H. (1999) 'Personal Styles & Effective Performance' CRC Press.
4. Doran, G. T. (1981). "There's a S.M.A.R.T. way to write management's goals and objectives". *Management Review*. **70** (11): 35–36.
5. Welch, J, S Welch, (2007) WINNING. Harper Business.
6. Collins, J (2001) GOOD TO GREAT. Random House Business

Key takeaways

• The first 10 to 15 people you hire are critical. Ensure you get this right, and they fit the culture.

• Hire people better than you.

• Ensure the people you hire fit the 'BATTLE' benchmark criteria.

• Seek out 'A' team people.

• Weave your team together carefully with complementary personalities and skillsets. Think about the optimal blend for you that works to maximise creativity and performance.

• Set the framework for the team to function.

• Ensure objectives are clear and everyone understands their role.

• Create an environment where people feel comfortable contributing their ideas and joining the debate, challenging the status quo, and moving the company forward towards a shared vision.

• Design a structure for growth covering all the functional areas for the business to operate effectively as it is scaled.

• Set stretch goals and link rewards to performance. Take care when being critical, praise openly and publicly. Ensure teams celebrate success.

• Lock in star performers and manage out energy sappers as soon as you can.

HOMEWORK

Now it is over to you. How is your business currently structured? Is it missing certain skillsets or professional expertise?

1. *Draw a diagram of the current structure of your business below. Does it currently allow you to easily expand? Is it threadbare in certain areas? If you are missing key skills draw the ideal structure below your current structure you think you require to support growth.*

SCALE for SALE

CHAPTER 5: HOW TO REFINE YOUR COMPETITIVE STRATEGY & EXECUTE WITH SPEED

'There are only two sources of competitive advantage: the ability to learn more about your customers faster than the competition and the ability to turn that learning into action faster than the competition'

— *Jack Welch*

Do you know what sets you apart from your competitors? How do you currently differentiate your product or offering from others in your market? Why should customers want to buy from you or work with you time and time again? How do you uncover or create a competitive strategy for growth? How much do you know about your market, different competitor products, and the quality of service provided to customers?

As a start-up having entered a new market, what is your 'secret sauce' to ensure you can compete against established companies? What is unique about what you do and how can you gain an advantage? In this chapter, I will outline some of the key ingredients to consider in refining your winning competitive strategy: a sustainable one, and a route to growth.

5.1 What is a competitive strategy?

A competitive strategy is your recipe for winning, a template to beating other companies to that customer order. Crucially, it needs to be one that remains relevant, and that you can repeat time after time.

To scale a fledgling company from nothing to millions of pounds of turnover, you need to have a robust competitive strategy that is sustainable over time. If you want to win more deals, perhaps from much larger players, scale your business and be a dominant player in your market, then you need to build a competitive advantage.

You need a deep understanding of the markets in which you operate and a clear game plan. A winning formula that differentiates you from competitors, that sets you apart and ensures that you win the lion's share of new opportunities.

5.2 What types of competitive strategy might you consider?

The common competitive strategies are focused on either lowering costs, product differentiation or going deep into a market niche to create an advantage.

5.2.1 Cost leadership

Gaining an advantage through providing products at a lower cost than your competitors is a common approach. This could be achieved through new technology to reduce overheads. It may also be through sourcing materials from suppliers at cheaper rates or stripping back the product offering to empower a lower cost strategy. Budget airlines would be an example of a low-cost competitive strategy. An example of a technology play would be in the insurance industry where developments such as artificial intelligence and RPA (robotic process automation) are being used to automate routine processes, replace humans in validating and managing claims, and consequently significantly reducing the cost base.

Many large companies, sometimes companies scaling up from a start-up position, pursue ways to lower their cost base through focusing on improving operational efficiencies. Strategies known as 'Lean' aim to remove waste and cut cost from processes without compromising on the quality of the product or service to the customer.

In technology businesses the largest cost is often the people or talent in the team. In the connected world that we live in your technical team could be located anywhere in the world taking advantage of the variation in the cost of talent. Some start-ups choose to locate their operations in cheaper territories to reduce the cost base. For example, in the last decade we have seen a lot of IT resources moved to India, cities in Eastern Europe such as Krakow and Poznan in Poland, and Bratislava in Slovakia. The cost of equivalent highly qualified data scientists or software engineers in these locations has been a fraction of the cost compared to London or New York. Of course, as more and more companies relocate or start operations in these locations the demand and cost of talent will increase, and the cost advantage will be eroded.

5.2.2 Product Differentiation

Another competitive strategy is product differentiation. How is your offering distinguished from your competitors? Do you provide something that has distinct features or functions compared to competitor products? Does it have more benefits for the customer? Does it have something that makes it stand out from the crowd and that can justify a price differential compared to other offerings? It may be a superior quality product, be made from different materials and packaged for the market in a different way to competitors.

In the markets where I have worked, we set apart our offering from other players through sourcing better data and by negotiating exclusive agreements with some suppliers. The combination of more granular data and top technical talent ensured our products were more accurate for underwriting and pricing property insurance, and it worked. This helped us to gain traction in the market and to safeguard our competitive advantage as much larger companies with more resources were not able to imitate our wares.

5.2.3 Market specialisation

Focusing on the customer needs of a specific market niche is another approach. Providing products and outstanding service that are extremely focused on the requirements and needs of a niche group can result in the company developing domain expertise, a strong reputation and brand loyalty for that area.

5.2.4 Create new market space

The strategies above are externally focused on what is happening in existing markets. One way to build a competitive advantage is to reimagine the future, innovate and create completely new products and services. This creates new market space and renders competitors in existing markets irrelevant. It is the focus of the book 'Blue Ocean Strategy'[13]. In essence, it is about creating new products in new markets. It is a high-risk strategy. Depending on the industry it can also take a long time before your solution gains traction.

Back in December 2009 I decided to take my young family on a trip to Lapland to visit Santa Claus. The weather took a turn for the worst and we ended up being stranded in Stockholm. Another family who we had met on the airplane helped us book into the hotel where they were staying and invited us to join them for dinner in the town. The husband was advising a local start-up company in Stockholm and one of the founders, Dan, also joined us for dinner. The start-up was called Spotify.

We had an extremely enjoyable evening, and it was kind of them to look after us. I had just recently started my second business, Business Insight, and it was interesting to hear about what they were trying to do. At the time buying music CD's was still popular and although it looked like streaming music on demand would happen, it seemed to me it could be a long way off. Creating new market space is a high-risk strategy though it can also be one that yields high rewards. Over 11 years on and most people now use a music streaming service. Dan is a billionaire and Spotify has become a global success.

5.2.5 Core competencies approach

Other approaches that might be taken are more internally focused, for example looking at the capabilities and core competencies within your operation. What is the core know-how and expertise that you have assembled and have at your disposal? Look at all the combined experience, knowledge, and skillsets of your team. These could be viewed as assets that could be combined uniquely to build a core competence in a differentiated customer offering.

5.3 What is the best competitive strategy for your market?

For any of these strategies to work you need to have a deep understanding of the market, the emerging trends, and customer needs. When you first enter a market, a prerequisite is to have done your homework, to have a clear view of different competitor offerings, understand the different distribution channels and routes to market, how all the various competitor offerings are positioned and what customers perceive of the value they provide. Once your initial venture is up and running, you need to carry on gathering information from clients and others in the market. It is essential to keep deepening your knowledge of market supply and demand.

How do you currently differentiate your product or offering from others in your market? Are you providing a superior product, an innovative new service that creates new market space or a better customer experience, and how does your price point compare to competitors? Do you know your total addressable market? Who are the incumbents selling similar products in your target area, and what are their strengths and weaknesses? Is your strategy appropriate for your market niche? How do customers buy via the different distribution channels? Is this changing and how will that impact costs?

A strategy based on a lower cost structure competing mainly on price may work in the Business to Consumer market, though this isn't appropriate as the main strategy selling highly technical products into a niche Business to Business market, where performance and quality drive the buying decision rather than purely cost.

The distribution channel will impact cost and vary depending on the type of product and whether it is B-to-C or B-to-B. Online sales to consumers have increased dramatically across most industries recently and the B-to-B market is moving in the same direction. Is there an opportunity in your market to gain a cost advantage with a new offering that accesses customers in a more efficient, more cost-effective way?

To win, you need to differentiate yourself from competitors and offer clear superior benefits to customers who make a move from existing suppliers. The best strategies are incremental, subtle, and hidden. In his book, 'Winning'[1], the former England World Cup-winning coach Sir Clive Woodward describes the plan that he devised and implemented to set England on the path to winning the 2003 Rugby World Cup. One of the cornerstones of his competitive strategy was something he referred to as 'Critical Non-Essentials' - minor improvements across many different areas from the hotel the team was staying in, to the way they analysed the matches and even to the type of shirt the players wore during a game. For example, Sir Clive had seen how video technology was being used in American Football to gain more significant insights in matches about different competing teams. It could also be used to assess individual player strengths and weaknesses.

He persuaded the English Rugby Football Union to invest significant funds in 1999 to have the technology installed at England's home ground at Twickenham, London. This enabled England to analyse all their home matches in depth, from many different parts of the ground, and so gain a much greater insight into game strategy, and competitor game plans.

Sir Clive also innovated and had the match shirts for the England rugby team redesigned. Instead of being loose fitting and easy to grab hold of, shirts were redesigned and made to be skin-tight, so players were more difficult to tackle during a game. No stone was left unturned and with each incremental improvement there was a cumulative effect, giving England a competitive advantage at the time. However, a lot of the innovations and ideas that Sir Clive deployed were quickly replicated and adopted by other countries, so the competitive advantage was short lived.

If you want to have a sustainable competitive advantage you need to somehow protect your idea, IP, formula, design. Or else keep on innovating and continuing to make incremental improvements to stay one step ahead of competitors. This needs to be baked into the DNA of the company. Otherwise, the daylight between you and your competition will narrow and then disappear. Protecting your innovation in some way, either contractually, legally or by restricting access to the trade secret is often not easy to do.

One of the most famous trade secrets is the formula for the syrup going into the Coca Cola[2] drink. This is kept in a vault in the Coca Cola company headquarters in Atlanta, in the United States of America. Only two employees are allowed access to the formula and the two are not allowed to travel together in case there is an accident.

The original drink was invented by John Pemberton, a biochemist, in 1886. The patent and formula for the drink was sold to an Atlanta pharmacist, Asa Candler for $1750 in 1891. Candler formed the Coca Cola Company and kept the formula for the Coca Cola drink a closely guarded secret. Maybe this is now part publicity, part marketing angle, though Candler's protection of the IP has proven to be sustainable and incredibly successful. In 2020 the Coca Cola Company had a market value of $200 billion.

5.4 How do you discover a competitive advantage in an established market?

Large analytical firms are sometimes burdened with bureaucracy, often lack focus and are slow to react to customer requirements. They are also sluggish to act and slow to change course when technology moves on or when market requirements change. As a start-up the big advantage you have is speed and focus. Seek out industry experts, bring on board a non-executive Director with a deep knowledge of your industry and a wide network of client contacts. Ask them to open a few doors for you, make some introductions and help you to deepen your understanding of what is happening in the industry. What are the key trends? What are the emerging customer needs? Do your customer research, find those voids in the market, and move swiftly to fill them!

Prior to re-entering the insurance risk modelling market, we started speaking to prospective clients, consultants, and people in the industry. What products were currently being offered by who, how strong were they and did they meet client expectations? Were clients generally happy with what was being provided and with the services? Did they live up to expectations?

There were already several companies established in our target market. These were large blue-chip organisations with thousands of employees, huge resources, and recognised brands. How do you work out a competitive strategy in this situation?

We delved further and found out as much as we could about the experience of the people building the products and the service provided to clients. What data sources were they using in their risk models, what was the resolution, how accurate were the products? What was the level of domain expertise, what technologies and techniques were suppliers using? And crucially where were the weaknesses?

Secondary research can help to uncover some of this information. To find out intricate detail about supplier offerings and where the weaknesses reside, there is only one way, and that is to get close to the customer base.

What we discovered shaped our competitive strategy and product development plans. We found out that customer support wasn't as strong as you might expect. One company had a visually well- designed product though the data behind it was weak. The incumbent suppliers were generalists and so lacked domain expertise to give the support and consulting back-up that the market desired. The granularity and accuracy of the products provided at the time could also be superseded. This information shaped the foundations of a competitive strategy. We put a plan together and believed we could provide a stronger product, with a better focused service and at an extremely competitive price.

We hired PhD level mathematicians with deep domain expertise to build our products, signed exclusive contracts with key data suppliers for newer, more accurate and more granular feeds of input data. We scoured academic research papers in the UK, the USA and other markets for new ideas and approaches. We discovered new insights in relevant areas that could be applied to enhance our products.

We also recruited a sales team with terrific industry experience - they understood the market, the customer issues and could engage with the client base in a knowledgeable way. They provided a deeper level of technical and consulting support. The specialist knowhow also enabled our team to test, tweak and tune the product set so that it fitted better in the customer workflow.

This combination resulted in a new suite of products that were technically a long way ahead of the competition at the time. It was a quantum leap. We had created a differentiated product of higher quality that was difficult to replicate and so had a sustainable advantage. This made the reason to switch supplier from a large blue-chip company to a small start-up operation suddenly quite compelling. It may sound surprising but some of those early contracts were worth hundreds of thousands of pounds (in the market it was typically a 3-to-5-year contract duration).

Focus on where larger competitors are weak and what the main factors are driving the buyers' decision-making. In the insurance market where we were working, accuracy of information and data was especially important, as was domain expertise in providing help and adding value. Not everyone will risk the comfort of switching from a large supplier to a start-up, at least not in the early days. Nevertheless, if you have a far superior product and a convincing business case to move, some will, and you will start to gain traction!

We launched products that proved to be more precise, built from richer, more accurate data sources and that assessed risk right down to property level. We also provided excellent client support and service to ensure our insurance company customers got full value from investing in a multi-year contract with us.

Convincing a large client that your customer service as a start-up will be better too is no easy feat. We assigned one of the senior team to each client account and made sure that any issues or problems were sorted out immediately. We were fortunate in having people in the team with a trusted reputation in the industry.

Clients also liked to have easy access to technical experts as well as senior decision makers in the company. We could move amazingly fast and could sort out problems at lightning speed, it did not have to go through several layers of bureaucracy.

Start-ups have agility and creativity in their favour, when working in unison this is a major advantage. Having domain experts and providing consulting or stronger technical back-up can distinguish your offering. It also gives you the inside track. Once you get close to clients you can start to build those long-term relationships, find out a lot more about how they operate, and understand their on-going and evolving requirements in much greater depth. Then keep moving rapidly to make incremental improvements to your offering to fill those needs and maintain a market advantage.

The products we sold at ISL and Business Insight were very technical. Geographic risk models, databases and price comparison software aimed at actuaries and underwriters to help them price risk. We were a small start-up venture, yet we were able to sell products to large blue-chip insurance companies for hundreds of thousands of pounds. Our competitors were huge organisations with significant resources and yet we continued to win deal after deal and gain significant market share in our niche area. We proved it can be done.

Do your homework and research, find the areas where customers are dissatisfied. Discover your competitive strategy, put together your plan and execute. Innovate, and move quickly to build a competitive advantage and then grow your market share.

5.5 How to review your competitive strategy and discover your 'Secret Sauce'?

OK, so how do you do uncover your effective competitive strategy for growth?

What process could you go through to give you an insight and a route to discover an effective strategy to help you scale your business?

Review the competitive dynamics of the industry.

The first step in reviewing your competitive strategy is to gain a thorough appreciation of the dynamics of how the market operates and the intensity of the competition within it. One of the most used management frameworks for this is Porter's five forces[3]. This defines the competitive structure of a market in terms of the bargaining power of buyers and suppliers, the extent to which substitute products or services compete, the potential and threat from new entrants coming into the market and the intensity of competition from existing competitors. I used this framework when planning the strategy for Business Insight to debate the competitive landscape and understand where the best opportunities were.

Table 7: Porter's 5 Forces of Competition within a market

Bargaining Power of Suppliers	Bargaining Power of Buyers
Intensity of competition (Competitors)	
Threat from Substitute Products	Threat from New Entrants

How is the market structured?

<u>In terms of who are the customers:</u>

How many are there? how much do they spend? How integral is your product to their operation, the more important it is the less price sensitive they will be? How differentiated are the different product offerings in the market? The closer the offerings are the easier it is for customers to compare and try to shop each part around the market to force prices down.

How easy is it for customers to switch suppliers and how expensive is it to do this? When we were supplying into large insurance companies operating across lots of different systems and offices the cost to switch to another competitor was often quite high. Consequently, to justify the cost of switching for customers we had to make sure that we had a differentiated, higher quality product, and that there was a compelling business case for them to make the switch.

There were also different segments of the market with different requirements and dissimilar price elasticity of demand (sensitivity to the pricing of our products).

We created a differentiated range of offerings with different price points focused on the needs of different companies across the market. New insurance companies entering the market had different requirements to larger established players. Even within the established group of companies there were insurers focused on specific market segments where the appetite for and relevance of our products varied. For example, insurance companies supplying specialist covers to high-net-worth individuals had a larger appetite to licence our risk model products and often amenable to paying more for them. The average premium for a high net worth individual, perhaps someone living in a property with £1 million reinstatement value, is much higher. And so are the losses from claims, so the requirement for the best quality risk models to assess the risk and price the premium accurately is essential.

In terms of suppliers:

How many of these are there and how interchangeable are the things they can supply to you? How essential are the component raw materials and what proportion are they of your costs? Do any suppliers work exclusively with your competitors and how does this impact your ability to compete? Are you able to find suppliers that have unique raw materials, and can you acquire exclusive rights to embed and sell into your market?

In the market where we worked there were a few suppliers providing raw materials to anyone who contacted them. However, we were able to identify suppliers with unique products and signed several exclusive agreements for our target market.

Look to identify potential suppliers, perhaps not currently providing anything into your market, where you can differentiate your offering and provide something better than your competitors. Then find a way to get an exclusive agreement in place to protect your position. You may have to pay higher prices for the services. You may also have to guarantee minimum levels of annual royalties or revenues to the supplier. Try to do this as you will make it easier to expand your own offering, make it difficult for competitors to copy your innovations and you will build more value into your company that an acquirer will pay a premium for.

In terms of existing competitors:

How many are there? How is the market concentrated? How diverse are the different players and how differentiated are the competing offerings? How loyal are customers to the different competing brands? How are they positioned in terms of quality and price?

In terms of new entrants:

What is the threat from new entrants coming into the market? How easy is it to enter the market? What are the capital investment requirements? Are there any legal requirements (e.g., licences)? Are there high costs involved to acquire specialist talent and resources to build products? Are there barriers to entry due to patents, know-how, experience, proprietary knowledge, or exclusive contracts relating to product inputs? Do existing providers in the market have economies of scale that inhibit new entrants?

In the Insurtech market there have been many new entrants in recent years with new innovative offerings using the latest technology, such as machine learning techniques. In head-to-head tests against these companies using actual insurer test data, we never lost a deal even though some of the competing products were impressive. I think it can be difficult to break into a market when there is a focused niche supplier with a team of experts that have been around for a long time, with deep domain expertise and that have strong relationships with clients. Even if you provide a much cheaper product, you must be better, more accurate, easier to use or deliver some tangible benefits and uplift over the existing incumbents.

In terms of substitutes:

What is the threat from substitute product offerings? What is the tendency of buyers to switch to substitutes? What is the price differential? What is the level of attraction to switch and how different is the offering (or perceived difference by customers)?

Please go through all the questions, collate the information, and put it together to view the competitive landscape within your industry.

Another factor to consider, though not part of the model, is the regulatory framework. Are there any government regulations within the industry you are operating in? There are regulations in the financial industry as well as in the supply and analysis of certain types of data. In future, there is likely to be regulations introduced governing applications of AI and data algorithms. This is important for technology companies and will probably increase in significance as an issue in the future. The permissions required to use certain data feeds or certifications required to provide specific technology services may increase costs and make it more difficult for start-ups to compete. Make sure you consider this aspect and have a thorough understanding as you plan your route.

Consider trends and external factors in your industry influencing competitive dynamics.

You now have a detailed analysis of the competitive dynamics in your market. What about external factors and trends taking place that may have an influence? It is important to understand any technology, customer buying trends or changes taking place or likely to take place in the near term that may impact your business plans. For example, technologies such as robotic process automation, machine learning & artificial intelligence and nanotechnology are likely to have an influence on many industries and future competing offerings from new entrants. Government and regulatory legislation change and shifting demand patterns of consumers could also alter market dynamics.

In the insurance industry, increased interest and involvement from government regulators, adoption of big data, machine learning solutions and a drive towards digitalisation have been recent themes. Some of these changes are likely to pick up pace after the Pandemic 'lockdown' and the rapid increase in home and remote working. What changes are taking place in your industry? How might your market look in 5 years' time? How will these changes impact your plans and strategy for growth?

How do you carry out a SWOT analysis on your current business?

The next step is to carry out an honest assessment of your business and where you currently stand in the market. What are the existing capabilities of the company and do these allow you to capitalise on any opportunities? What are you missing, is there a gap in the skills of the team? What could go wrong that might be outside your control?

A SWOT analysis or Strengths, Weaknesses, Opportunities and Threats is one of the most widely used strategic planning tools. What are the strengths of your product offering and business? Where are the weaknesses relative to the competition and your capability to execute any plans? Looking externally what are the opportunities that you could exploit using existing resources and assets? What are the threats to your business, perhaps from competitors, new entrants, technology, government legislation, or things that might have a negative impact on your business?

You should free up half a day with your management team, perhaps offsite so there are no distractions. Then go through each section, as shown in the example in Table 8 below, to pool your brainpower and capture all the points across these areas. Some people will have different points of view, so it will be a useful exercise to debate all the issues and discuss this as part of your business planning process.

Table 8: Hypothetical example of a SWOT analysis

Strengths	Weaknesses
- Deep domain expertise - Exclusive supplier contracts - Development capability - Established products	- Small, inexperienced management team - Resource constraints - Access to overseas markets
Opportunities	Threats
- Develop products X, Y, Z & cross sell - Expand into territory B - Expand consulting services	- New entrants with greater resources entering market - More government legislation - Losing supplier contracts

SWOT ANALYSIS (Example)

How do you select the best growth vector for your business?

The next step in revisiting your competitive strategy is to discover the best growth vector for your business to focus on. A starting point I have used in the past is referred to in management literature as a Growth Vector Matrix, based on work by mathematician Igor Ansoff[4]. The basic idea is replicated in Table 9 below. The four quadrants identify the potential ways to explore growing the company collapsed to the most basic categories. These are current products in current markets, new products in current markets, existing products in new markets and new products in new markets.

Are you going to focus on expanding the sale of your current products in the markets you presently operate in? Are you looking to develop some new products for your existing market, perhaps to meet the emerging needs of your customers? These are the lowest risk options and maybe the easiest and least cost options to implement.

Another possible route to growth is finding new markets for your existing products. Perhaps you can uncover new use cases for your established products in new markets to those where you presently operate. This is a higher risk strategy. I have spoken to companies in the past that have followed this strategy, developing one great product, then trying to sell into distinctly different markets after identifying other use cases. The result: slower growth, it doesn't work as well as focusing on a market where you have some domain expertise, contacts, and an existing reputation.

The most difficult strategy to implement is developing completely new products in new markets where you are not currently operating.

You need to decide what products and services you have or are thinking of developing that fit into each of the quadrants. You will need to have an in-depth knowledge of each of the market segments you are considering. The easiest place to start is your current market and existing customers. Speak with your customers, prospects and people in your network that understand these areas, find out what companies are interested in acquiring and what they are currently spending budgets on.

Consideration of other markets will require plenty of research. Especially if you have not had any experience or knowledge in those sectors and they are outside your domain. It is much higher risk to invest time and money in completely new markets but worth having a look at as the opportunity may be significant.

You could commission surveys, hire consultants with a deep knowledge of the target sectors you are considering, as well as searching online and public sources of information. If you join the Institute of Directors (UK), you can also get a certain amount of market research assistance as part of the annual subscription. I have used this service a few times in the past to save time.

You should explore partnering with other companies already established in other markets, where they have the client relationships but where you have value to offer. For example, where you have a product or data which may have a relevant use case.

The nature of your product and target market will also influence the channel to market. Digital sales and subscription-based software licensing via the cloud (software as a service) widens the reach and lowers the cost of entering new markets and expanding into new areas.

Table 9: Growth Vector Matrix as a framework to set out options for growth

GROWTH VECTOR MATRIX	Current Products	New Products
New Markets	MARKET EXPANSION (e.g. New use cases)	DIVERSIFICATION HIGHEST RISK
Current Market	EXISTING PRODUCT EXPANSION LOWEST RISK	NEW PRODUCT DEVELOPMENT

How do you discover the total addressable market value for each of your options to scale?

When assessing each opportunity for growth, it is important to have some indication of the present and future revenue potential. How much is the market spend on similar products? Which segments offer the biggest return on future investment? If this is a relatively new evolving market how much can you find out about current spend, and possible future spend from customers you are close to? How could you assess the potential across the whole market?

There are essentially a couple of ways to approach this, and a few sources of information required. Either a top down or bottom-up method depending on what figures you can get hold of. There is obviously the data you already have about spend in the market from your own customers. You could also gather research from press releases from competitors and customers about investments in comparable products. Some companies like to talk about investment in new technology, competitors want to increase awareness and their credibility when companies buy from them. So often you can find useful material on public websites. There are also on-line information sources, public accounts of large competitors, as well as published market research reports and articles in industry magazines. If you have a strong network of client contacts you could also phone up people directly and ask them, sometimes they will share information, sometimes they won't, but it is worth asking the question.

The first example below in Table 10 is a hypothetical example estimated from one data point. In theory you would ask as many companies as possible and calculate an estimate of the total addressable market based on a reasonable size sample. The approach below assumes that the level of investment in external products is linked to the size and income of the buyer. In the case of the insurance sector this may not necessarily be true, new entrants without any in-house experience data or resources may place a higher reliance initially on external products when they first enter the market (in this example risk models for insurance pricing).

TABLE 10: ASSESSING YOUR TOTAL ADDRESSABLE MARKET OPPORTUNITY

Hypothetical example of a top-down approach (P&C Insurance Market)

Company X spends £250K per annum with you on relevant analytical data products. You also find It currently spends £2M per annum on all analytical data products across all external suppliers, so your product represents 12.5% of the overall data enrichment/IT budget.

The annual premium income (gross written premium, GWP) of Company X is £60M.

So, Company X spends 0.42% of its GWP currently on relevant products.

And, for Company X the total annual spend on external analytical data services is 3.33% of its GWP.

Based on official sources the total market size (in terms of premium income) for UK property insurance is £7.5 Billion GWP per annum. Assuming a similar level of spend on data and relevant products by all other companies would indicate a total addressable market of around

Existing products - £31,250,000

All analytical products - £250M

One data point is not enough to rely on though if you repeated the exercise across several companies, you would be able to home in on a reasonable estimate of the market potential.

    Another approach shown in Table 11 below, taken from the bottom up may give a different view. This may be more accurate and appropriate if you already have a lot of customers, or wider range of different contacts willing to share information. The idea is to aggregate up the information on the total market spend using a much bigger sample, though there are numerous ways you could fill in the missing gaps. In this example, I have assessed the average spend by type of company and multiplied that up by the number of companies in each group to estimate the total market potential. For both examples, the estimated total addressable market was calculated at £31M. If these were based on real data, you would be comfortable with the estimate.

TABLE 11: ASSESSING YOUR TOTAL ADDRESSABLE MARKET OPPORTUNITY

Hypothetical example of a bottom-up approach (P&C Insurance Market)

Let's assume there is a total universe of 200 potential customers in your niche target market. We split these into groups by size of company (GWP) comprising of 20 large companies, 40 medium size companies, 120 small companies and 20 new entrants. In terms of annual spend on your products you find that the average annual spend by group is:

Customer Type	Number of companies	Average annual spend (£000) per company	Total Potential Market spend (£000)
Large	20	350	7000
Medium	40	250	10000
Small	120	100	12000
New entrants	20	120	2400
	200		31400

For this market segment around £31M is the estimate of the total addressable market based on this calculation.

How to build a Competitor Insight Matrix

We have looked in detail at how to assess the competitive structure of your market, how to segment different options available to you, how to estimate the potential size of each and how to relate this to the shape your business is currently in. The next step is to do a much deeper analysis of competitors to understand their strengths and more importantly their weaknesses. Collate competitor data similar to examples shown in Table 12 below. Use the information to build a competitor insight matrix to piece together a deeper understanding of what you are competing against.

Look at competitor company accounts, websites, brochures, industry periodicals and press releases for information. Speak to customers, suppliers, and industry consultants to piece together as much intelligence as possible. For each of your competitors, find out the market positioning, quality of the product, prices, reputation, and strength of their brands. This should help you uncover the most effective ways for you to compete in the market.

How do you bring it all together?

The last step involves amalgamating everything and putting together a plan of action. It requires first reviewing, then consolidating all the information, before assessing each of the strategic opportunities with your team. Then look at the most attractive openings, highlight any gaps in your capability you need to fill and select the best options for growth to pursue.

Table 12: Example data fields you could collate to gain insight on your competitors (not an exhaustive list):

- Turnover/profit
- Years in business
- Number of employees
- Price positioning (cheap/low quality, high/perceived premium quality)
- Notable customers
- Number of customers/estimated market penetration (I remember one competitor used to put the logo of every customer on its website)
- Main area of expertise
- Level of relevant industry domain expertise
- Experience of management team
- Depth of resource and size of development/technical team
- Product areas (of relevance)
- Product details (what do they use to build, is it legacy technology or the latest tech?)
- Customer journey/experience (How effective/efficient/good is this?)
- Brand loyalty (low, medium, high)
- Technology behind their products
- Data employed (materials used), this may not be relevant to you but basically collate any information that might be an area you can examine to find a weakness.
- Perception of customers/reputation (market view)
- Level/depth of service/support
- Quality of service (as reported from customers, poor, average, good, excellent, outstanding)
- Sales approach/level of discounting
- Size and quality of sales team
- Typical contract lengths offered
- Strengths (customer view)
- Weaknesses (customer view)

Look at the potential value of each and what would be required to win given your current position. It may be that you have identified some large opportunities in new markets where your products and expertise could be applied. It could also be where the competition appears to have some weaknesses.

Carry out a gap analysis looking at where you are now and what assets you need to take advantage of the different opportunities you have identified. How are you going to win, what will you do different, or better? Why will customers switch to you or buy from you if you are a new entrant?

Discuss the risks and likelihood of success versus reward and select your best opportunities for growth.

Once this is complete put your plan of action together. Work out all the associated costings, additional resources required and assign a budget. Develop your implementation plan, timescales and assign responsibilities. Put this into action and monitor progress against plan.

Go for growth!

References /Further reading

1. Woodward, C (2004) 'Winning!' Hodder & Stoughton
2. https://en.wikipedia.org/wiki/Coca-Cola
3. Porter, M, E (1980) Competitive Strategy, New York, Free Press
4. https://en.wikipedia.org/wiki/Ansoff_Matrix
5. Mauborgne R, Kim W.C. (2015) Blue Ocean Strategy, Harvard Business Review Press.

Key takeaways

• A competitive strategy is your way to win and the route to growth.

• Common approaches are lower cost, product differentiation, or to focus on a niche with specialized products.

• Higher risk strategies involve creating completely new market space, either inventing a new product or producing a completely new service, for example such as Spotify or Tesla.

• To uncover the best competitive strategy, you need to gain a deep understanding of the market, how it operates and its competitive dynamics.

• You also need a profound appreciation of what the customer wants to buy now and how that is evolving.

• The best strategies are subtle, hidden, and incremental. Unless you can protect the IP, competitors are likely to imitate and erode any short-term advantage. Gain a sustainable competitive advantage through putting continual improvement, innovation, and the pursuit of excellence at the heart of what you do.

• Assess the competitive landscape and how you fit in using Porters Five Forces Model.

• Consider the different strategic growth options. Work out the total addressable market opportunity for each.

• Do a deep dive on each of the competitors in your chosen market(s). Find out their strengths and weaknesses and uncover a way to win.

• Do a SWOT analysis on your current business. Assess the gaps and build a plan to support your option to scale balancing chance of success versus reward and potential growth.

HOMEWORK

Now it is over to you. Go through the suggested steps above and collate as much of the information as you can. Apply the framework to the market segments that you operate in. Apply a SWOT analysis to your business using the template below. Work out the potential market opportunities and use the business canvas model to document each option and to compare against your existing plan. Use these tools to uncover new strategic alternatives open to you. This should help to crystalise some ideas and inform debate within your company on the most productive strategy for you to scale.

Example SWOT Template to apply to your business.

STRENGTHS	OPPORTUNITIES
1-	1-
2-	2-
3-	3-
4-	4-
5-	5-
THREATS	WEAKNESSES
1-	1-
2-	2-
3-	3-
4-	4-
5-	5-

PART 2: ACHIEVING SUSTAINABLE GROWTH

SCALE for SALE

CHAPTER 6: HOW DO YOU TRANSFORM YOUR FIRM INTO A 'GOLDEN GOOSE'?

'Turnover is vanity, profit is sanity and cash the reality'
- Anon

When you start your company, you and the co-founders have to multi-task. Out of necessity, you must swap hats regularly and apply yourself to a range of jobs. Maybe, you created the initial product. Perhaps you also were the main person selling. Next, you hire the first few employees and make what seems like a small family. The focus is on getting the right product or service developed, and those first few customers on board. At times it can be chaotic, you must be a good generalist and do whatever it takes to get the business up and running.

In the next phase, you hire a bigger team with different complementary specialist skills, put in a structure, and appoint experienced leads into the main functional areas such as sales, product development, finance, and operations. The group morphs from a family size business into a tribe. The business starts to generate regular income, a stream of new customers, and cash flow improves with recurring revenues. The company is becoming established in the market.

Getting the foundations in place with a capable and robust core team is vital. A talented unit will make sure you are off to a good start and establish the firm in the market, but you are still likely to depend on key individuals in the business. Reliance on you and critical people will slow down growth. You will always be a slave to the company. The firm will not be attractive to acquirers if too many crucial elements are dependent on you or any of your colleagues. You need to remove the people dependency, put in reporting, systems, and procedures.

You also need to manage the business as efficiently as possible, including being in complete control of the finances. You need to have a good feel for exactly where the company is now regarding cashflow, and where it will be in three months. To build a business that someone would want to buy involves elevating it to the next level. You need to transform it into a cash machine or 'Golden Goose' as one of my colleagues, Peter Edwards referred to ISL. Something very profitable, generating strong cash flows, with high recurring revenues and growth rates over 15% per annum. And something that is not dependent on you or anyone else in the business.

When your business foundations are in place, and your products and customers are established, your start-up is progressing towards becoming a reputable firm.

What should you be doing next to transform your firm into a 'Golden Goose'?

6.1 What do you need in place to effectively manage the Profit & Loss (P&L) of the business?

You need to be able to do a few vital things to help you scale, and one of these is managing the P&L account or profit and loss of the business. If you can't understand your numbers back to front, balance the income and expenditure, and know exactly where the company is financially at any point in time, you will struggle. Cashflow is one thing that seems to cause problems for many companies, as highlighted in Table 13 below summarising a few key statistics from recent surveys of small business owners. It disappears all too quickly, and the business finds the runway has vanished before gaining a foothold in the market.

Table 13: Statistics highlighting the challenge of financial management for small businesses

- 29% of start-ups fail due to cashflow problems.
- Lack of capital/cashflow is cited as one of the top three challenges faced by small business owners.
- 22% of entrepreneurs struggle finding money to reinvest.
- 17% of entrepreneurs state not having enough cash on hand to pay bills is a major issue.
- 12% of small businesses struggle to keep costs down.

Sources: Guidantfinancial.com, Freshbooks.com, CBinsights.com

One thing that all start-ups are concerned about is running out of cash. It is the lifeblood of the company and something that requires careful management. Poor cost control can cause a business to fail, and incompetent financial management will almost guarantee that a firm goes bust quickly.

To keep control of your finances, you need timely and accurate reporting and a disciplined, prudent approach to spending. You need to know the company's cash position at any point in time, how much runway is available, and how much money is going out of the door every month. It is fundamentally important to keep control of costs when running a business, especially in the early days, to put in rules on expenses and ensure there is no waste.

Ensure your finance person produces detailed monthly management accounts and this includes key performance indicators (KPIs) across finance, sales, product development and customer support. Ensure you keep your finger on the business's pulse, know precisely where you are, and that any problems are flagged up in the monthly KPI metrics. Put a system in place to ensure you receive early warning when things start moving in the wrong direction. The KPIs will highlight when certain levers in the business need to be adjusted to bring your plan back on track.

Money going out of the door is certainly one area that is under your control. I have generally always viewed the company money as though it were my own, whether it was my own business, or whether I was working for someone else. I have always been a careful spender, grew up in Yorkshire, and I guess, being frugal is part of the culture. To control costs effectively, I would advise adopting a similar attitude, only spend what you can afford.

Colleagues in past employments have frequently asked me,

"Why are you staying in the $100 a night hotel when you can stay in the five* hotel on expenses for $350 a night?"

"Well, I don't like wasting money, and I am here to work, not on holiday", I would reply.

The typical attitude of many employees is that if the company is paying, I may as well spend up to the agreed limit. You need to make sure you put in rules and controls on expenses and spending across the business.

<u>Keep tight control of expenditure. When it is your company, it is your money that is being spent.</u>

I would advise you to:

- Keep your finger on the pulse with regards to finance; understand precisely where you are at any point in time. Get monthly reports produced and go through these in detail.

- Make sure you know where every penny or cent is going and that nothing is wasted or spent frivolously.

- Ensure proper controls are in place for personal expenses as well as guidelines for any capital expenditure. Make sure you have rules in place so that you must sign off all spending over a specific limit (e.g., $2000 or £1000).

- Issue guidelines so that everyone is aware of where they can and can't spend the company money.

- Get your finance person to prepare monthly management accounts with breakdowns on expenditure by category, what contracts you won, how much cash came in and what went out of the door. Compare this against budget and forecast, include KPIs such as:

- the total sales revenue for the month,
- the total sales revenue for the year to date,
- the EBITDA for the month,
- the EBITDA for the year to date,
- the average number of debtor days for the year to date,
- the change in the cash position for the month,
- the customer retention rate for the year to date,
- the total expenditure by category for the month,
- the total expenditure by category for the year to date,
- the cost per customer acquisition for the month,
- the cost per customer acquisition for the year to date,
- the committed monthly recurring revenue won for that month,
- the total committed monthly recurring revenue,
- the number of new contracts won,
- the number of new proposals issued,
- the number of new qualified leads for the month.
Etc.

Make sure your finance person can produce an accurate cash flow forecast for the year ahead, compare this against the budget plan, and update it monthly. Above all, as you establish the business, make sure you manage cashflow closely and know exactly how much runway you have available.

6.2 How can cost control be a source of competitive advantage?

In a technology company, often the largest cost element is the people or talent in the business. The people with the imagination, skills, and intellect to create value from ideas are often a technology business's critical assets. In the last company I worked in, out of around 9000 employees, 25%

had post-graduate degrees, the capability across the organisation to produce new technology solutions was phenomenal. If you can better control your cost base than your competitors, sourcing the same quality talent at a much lower cost can be a competitive advantage.

An experienced post-graduate analyst will cost you less than half in Krakow, Poland or in Bratislava, Slovakia compared to what you would pay someone in London; So, it is not surprising that many large companies have located operations there. Your people can now be based anywhere given the level of connectivity and acceptance of remote working. When you consider the fully loaded cost of a team of say 30 analysts over a five-year period the cost savings can be significant.

Technology companies frequently use global talent optimisation to scale-up capability, while keeping costs down as low as possible. Given the recent pandemic and the rise and acceptance of remote working do you need to be based in London or New York? Are there much cheaper cities where the costs are significantly lower and where you could scale-up your business?

Off-shoring and Near-shoring are strategies that many companies take up as skilled workers' cost can be substantially lower in some countries. When I worked in my last role, I received a phone call in early August from the company president. The group wanted to investigate setting up a nearshoring capability, and an initial desktop analysis had revealed eight different cities across Europe as potential candidates.

'You have six weeks to go and carry out due diligence on the cities, gather all the information and prepare a report with your recommendation', he said, then adding, 'Oh, you can hire someone and bring in resources to help you'.

After the phone call had ended, I remember thinking, doesn't he realise that half of Europe is on holiday during the first couple of weeks of August. This may be difficult, given the timescales.

However, I found out that many countries, such as Poland, Bratislava, and Ireland, have development agencies geared up to support and help companies locate offices there. It is possible to research and set-up a team in these locations a lot quicker than you may think. These countries also have generous tax breaks and grants available to encourage investment. The cost savings can be significant, and the process of setting up an operation in one of these countries is not as complicated as you might initially imagine.

It is worth exploring.

That said, for UK start-ups, BREXIT may make it more difficult and a different experience to the one that I had.

6.3 How do you remove key man dependency, reduce errors, and increase product consistency and quality as you scale?

To increase efficiency, maintain quality, and improve productivity as you grow, you need to put in systems and procedures as a framework. This will help you to scale and at the same time will remove key man dependency. First, you need to understand the business processes and capture all the knowledge stuck in people's heads about doing 'stuff'. Some you may be able to automate, other tasks you need to document to remove people dependency. Eliminate as much inefficiency, reliance on certain individuals and risk from the business as possible.

Effectively turn your business into a cash machine, something self-perpetuating, and that does not require you to focus your time on twenty-four hours a day, seven days a week. Transform the business into something that someone else, with a little training, could pick up and run.

In the 1990s, a senior colleague gave me a copy of the book 'E-Myth' by Michael Gerber[1]. The book was phenomenally successful and left a lasting impression on me. Gerber was first to coin the phrase' work ON your business, not IN your business'. One of the core messages in his book is if you want to remove any keyman dependency and scale a business, you must introduce systems.

Gerber made the point that to free up a business owner's time; you need to understand and standardise all the firm's processes and then systemise everything. Capture what you do, document all the steps and put in place procedures on 'how to' do things consistently, such that anyone could pick up the task and replicate it to the same standard. You need to remove all the specialist know-how and knowledge from inside people's heads, capture it, and then produce a procedure or set of instructions on how each process can be repeated to achieve the same consistent result.

By covering all the business processes, you transform the firm into a finely tuned engine that can operate without you. One of the primary examples given in Gerber's book was McDonald's, where every process is defined and optimised. It is easy to replicate the business anywhere, yet the quality of the end-product is maintained.

By systemising all the processes using this approach, a company is turned into a money machine.

We tried to bring this idea into the business where I was Development Director in the late 1990s. We hired consultants to define and document all the processes in our company. By a 'process' I mean what we do within the business in a particular functional area. When I refer to a 'procedure' I mean how we do something, and all the steps required to ensure that it can be replicated to the same standard time and time again.

The aim was to remove people dependency, reduce errors, improve product delivery and service consistency. We also introduced procedures to capture data to create an audit trail for reviewing performance. So, if there was a problem, you could track down the source of the error, and you could also use information you gather to measure performance and understand how to tweak ways of working to improve efficiency. We went through different departments in the business, captured the processes and defined the procedures required to get certain things done. The plan was to produce a manual of 'this is how we do it here', to create an initial baseline of how we accomplished different tasks that could then be tweaked and improved over time to increase efficiency. At least that was the grand plan.

We never completed the project to the depth or level we had initially hoped, though we did reap some benefits from the finished parts. I think many staff at the time thought we were over complicating things, and it was 'paralysis through analysis'.

Looking back, I would say it is worthwhile considering all processes across the business and focusing on a few crucial business-critical elements first. Document these processes across the different parts of the company and put in place procedures people must follow early. When the business has been running for a few years, it becomes more challenging to implement change.

I have heard numerous examples in large organisations where essential knowledge relating to parts of the business remains locked inside a few individuals' heads. It gives a lot of power to these people, and some are often reluctant to offload know-how and relinquish the control they believe they have in the business. Some people can also be resistant to change, and others may fear losing their jobs and being replaced by automation. People also get set in their ways with the attitude, 'this is the way we have always done it' and 'if it isn't broken don't try to fix it'.

When you own the company move early to stop this situation arising, don't allow the business to depend on you or any other person in your operation. You should bring in external help to ensure the project is undertaken rather than add this to the long list of your existing tasks. It will never become enough of a priority to focus on if you decide to do this independently.

All your team must buy into the ideas and reasons for undertaking the work. Present it to them from their perspective. For example, when a key person is sick and unable to work for a lengthy period, this may impact the business. However, if the key processes they are involved in are systemised, their absence will not affect the firm, and the workload they return to will not have accumulated.

With hindsight, we tried to do too much too soon when we first applied this approach. There wasn't enough buy-in across the teams in different locations, and we were not successful in capturing all the processes. However, we did manage to capture the critical processes in sales, finance, and development. We adopted the necessary procedures, and they proved to be important, mainly when people left the business, and new people joined. New people needed to take over immediately without any disruption to the service.

For example, one of the main areas we captured was updating all our risk models and databases that we sold into the insurance market to help set premium prices. Product updates were undertaken monthly for the software and every six months for our risk models across over twenty different variants. Each update was quite involved and required many person-days of effort. Every step was captured and documented, with a 'how-to' and where to source each input. We removed the dependency on the people that had created the products, who knew all the subtle nuances of the build process, and more importantly, how they should be updated.

The resulting procedure manual made future updates straight forward and easy to follow; if any worker undertaking the task was ill, someone else could pick it up and get the work done. You need to identify this type of business-critical process in your operation. Make sure you capture and document them. One day you will appreciate how valuable this work can be, as I found out.

In July 2001, I led the buy-out of assets from a company in the Marsh McLennan Group and started a new company, the analytical team consisted of just one person: me. We located the new business to our West Midlands office, the London analytics team that had built all the data products stayed with the group. They didn't want to relocate to Dudley. I needed to get all the products updated without any help from the people who had built them. Using the documented procedures, developed to systemise product updates, we managed to get everything done, handing off work to a new team as they were recruited over the following months. Before capturing the processes and documenting all the steps, the know-how would have been inside the heads of at least half a dozen senior employees. As they didn't join the new venture, it would have been impossible to do the updates quickly and without making errors.

Having systems and standard processes in place is undoubtedly vital in some areas, as was proven to be the case for me in this example. Suppose you want to scale, not be worried about losing certain people in the firm and be able to accelerate growth while maintaining the quality of your offering. In that case, you need robust and established procedures in place that anyone can pick-up and follow. When we first tried to systemise the ISL business, we were overly ambitious. It is better to focus initially on just the company's vital areas, protecting and minimising any disruption to clients.

In the book 'SYSTEMology'2, David Jenyns proposes a more simplified approach to systemise any business by first examining the journey that the customer takes with your company. The end goal is to create complete business reliability independent of the founder or any other key person. Jeynes suggests that you first need to understand the customer journey in-depth, the flow of processes, and the client interactions. You need to identify the vital steps in the customer journey and those required to maintain business continuity.

The methodology involves identifying the business's essential processes, across various areas such as sales, finance, operations, and product development. You need to understand the critical processes that impact the customer experience and that enable the business to function. What areas and functions within the company underpin the operation, and ensure things continue to run? The approach outlined in the book suggests bringing in outside support to get the processes captured and documented. You need to extract the know-how from people's heads and get this down on paper first.

Jeynes proposes seven stages to go through from initially defining and capturing all the critical processes through implementing the 'as is' systems in the business. Get these baseline processes in place first, not changing anything initially and then measure how things are performing. Over time you will be able to improve efficiency by capturing performance information and gaining insight into how things operate. You will be able to tweak things to make the business more effective, and this is the last phase in the methodology, referred to as the optimise stage.

In summary, to scale and then sell your business to someone else, it is crucial to remove the dependency on any one individual, including you. To turn a business into a cash machine or golden goose you must systemise it. To do that you need to define and capture all the critical processes underpinning the business, all the intellectual property in your people's heads, document and systemise it. Such that you could drop anyone into a role, and they would be able to read the procedure manual and get the job done to the same standard.

Focus on the leading twenty or so processes crucial to running the operation and get these done first. Once you have passed the initial start-up phase and are on the scale-up journey, I believe this should be a priority.

Once your business can operate independently of you, it will free up a lot of your time. You will find it easier to work on the company rather than being tied to it. You will also find it straightforward to bring new people on board and to integrate them quickly.

The business will also be more attractive to trade buyers and more saleable. There will be less concern about any founders leaving post-completion, and it will enable the acquiring firm to integrate your company more efficiently.

6.4 How do you maintain growth and keep your products fresh in a competitive landscape with rapidly advancing technology?

Following on from systemising critical parts of your business, I would advise looking at your product development process. To keep up with advances in technology, you need to be continually innovating, investing in research, and creating a steady stream of new products to take to market. In effect, you need to make a systematic way of creating a new product development conveyor belt and stay one step ahead of competitors. Where do I start, you might ask?

Get close to your client base and understand their requirements in depth. Listen to your customers, capture information, ideas, feedback on suggested product enhancements within a CRM system. Anticipate, and react quicker than your competitors to emerging market needs. Keep innovating and investing in research and development. We reinvested a significant chunk of revenue every year in research and new product developments. There are tax advantages in the UK to encourage technology companies to reinvest in research and development, as there are in other countries across Europe.

If you want a sustainable, growing business, you need to have a conveyor belt of new products that clients are interested in buying. When I researched competitors in our space, I noticed that many successful, growing companies, were reinvesting around 25% of revenues per annum. If you don't do the same, you will soon lose any advantage you may have, and others will overtake you. You can't afford to take your foot off the gas.

Once you have an established business with a sizeable customer base, you have an advantage over start-ups coming into the market of customer insight and knowledge. That information and the contacts you have are valuable but only if you make the most of your position. If you sit on your hands and don't keep moving forward, someone will steal your lunch. Consequently, always collect feedback and information from your customers systematically and review the data regularly.

Find out how your existing products need to be improved, what your clients want next, and how you can solve more of their 'pain' or business problems. Make sure you sustain your competitive advantage. Keep investing in the business and innovating. And continue moving forward, looking to improve.

6.5 What is one thing that some technical folks neglect, yet needs to be a central ingredient as you scale, to enhance your firm's profile in the market?

As you develop your business, scale, and put in place your product conveyor belt, you need to have one essential ingredient running through everything you do, and that is excellent design.

Product design could take up a whole chapter of its own and so is worth mentioning. Great design is essential and can significantly impact how the market perceives your business. You don't need to be a consumer products company such as Apple to embrace fantastic design. Yet it remains hugely important.

It is all about first impressions.

When people see an outstanding design pleasing to the eye, they immediately think it is quality, whether a reliable indicator or not of the underlying product. Think about the whole customer experience with your organisation and the journey that a client takes with you. Presenting your logo, your collateral, your website with a stunning high-quality design will immediately create impact and have a lasting impression.

When I think back over the years, particularly relating to technology start-ups, I have seen some innovative products that have not sold as well as expected due to poor design. If the interface, look and feel of the product is clumsy, and ugly, people perceive that the engine underneath, model, or service provided with it is also of the same quality. If it does not look visually appealing immediately to a potential buyer, they will switch off. They will not be drawn in to learn more about the product.

On the other hand, if the product is pleasing to the eye, with a slick, captivating design, they will want to find out more. I believe that you should invest in design. Apply this to your products, website, collateral, logo, and anything representing you, your company, and your brand. Don't put anything out in the market that does not look impressive. Invest in professional design from the start, do things properly. Act as a large company from day one.

By the way, that does not mean to go and hire a significant PR, design, or marketing agency as soon as you have some spare cash in your back pocket. Many top-quality designers work freelance from home, some such as the people we hired, Jo Euston-Moore and Lynne Aitken, worked on design and PR for us. They used to work for large London agencies, then started out on their own, balancing part-time freelance work with looking after their families. You can still get access to excellent quality talent, though you may have to work a bit harder to track it down.

What is certain though is that your website represents the business, what your logo says about the firm's quality and what ultimately your products look like to the client, is more significant to your success than you might appreciate.

In summary, please be advised:

Put great design at the heart of what you do.

References / Further reading

1. Gerber E Michael: 'The E-Myth' 1988 Harper Collins
2. Jenyns D: 'SYSTEMology: Create Time, Reduce Errors and Scale Your Profits with Proven Business Systems'

Key takeaways

• To facilitate growth and to turn your business into a golden goose or cash machine you need to put in systems, processes, and regular reporting. You need to monitor key areas, control costs, and have a framework to remove dependence on you and enable the business to scale.

• Manage the P&L of the business more effectively by collating financial information regularly and reviewing timely reporting on key performance metrics.

• Make sure your finance person produces detailed monthly management accounts. Include KPIs across finance, sales, product development, operations, customer support. Ensure you keep your finger on the pulse of the business and know exactly how things are progressing at any point in time.

• Another essential element is to control costs. Keep tight control of expenditure and put adequate checks in place so that you are aware of all major outgoing spend from the company.

• Consider offshoring or near shoring as an option to reduce the cost of talent. This can be a source of competitive advantage.

• To remove key man dependency, reduce errors and ensure the consistency of product quality, systemize the critical processes within the business.

(continued)

• Bring in external help to review your processes, capture what you do and how you do it, and document these. This is the first essential step in standardizing some of the processes within your business. Make sure you get started. If you add it to your own 'to-do list' the likelihood is that it will not get done.

• A further step in creating a sustainable cash machine is to continually reinvest in research and development. Set-up a system to produce a conveyor belt of new products to safeguard your position in the market. Don't think your existing product set will give you longevity in the market.

• Put great design at the heart of the business and everything you do from your logo, business card and website design through to the look and feel of your product interfaces.

HOMEWORK

1. *Draw a flow diagram of the customer journey from the first contact through to the delivery of the product, invoicing and follow-on serving.*

2. *Write down the main functional areas of the business and consider the different processes within each department. For example, Finance may include elements such as payroll, invoicing, cash collection, paying creditors, preparing monthly management accounts, cashflow forecasting, budget preparation.*

CHAPTER 7: HOW CAN YOU REFINE YOUR PRICING STRATEGY?

'You must never try to make all the money that's in a deal. Let the other fellow make some money too, because if you have a reputation for always making all the money, you won't have many deals.'

- *J. Paul Getty*

Pricing products is not uncomplicated. When first starting out, you need customers to test your product, provide feedback and help you discover the best path for your offering. You probably gave large discounts to those early adopters in exchange for assistance and input to refining your solution, that is more valuable than optimising the price point. Now, having established your start-up, with some paying customers on the books, it's time to revisit your charging strategy.

Before ramping things up you need to be certain you have a good appreciation where you should be pitching your fees. This is vital to put thought and research into. Too low and you will be leaving money on the table, it may even impact your ability to make a viable margin to support your scale up of the business. On the other hand, if you raise your prices too high you may not bring in any new customers at all.

7.1 What market and type of product are you supplying?

To some extent the type of product, the market you operate in, and how well you understand the customer base dictates the tactics or combination of approaches suitable for working out your pricing strategy. Table 14 below lists a few alternatives to pricing your product. Deciding on which to adopt depends to a certain amount on your product, the type of customer and the characteristics of the market you operate in. Is your solution inexpensive to produce with a vast number of potential buyers? Or are you targeting a niche market with relatively high upfront costs of supply? Are you selling to large companies directly or to consumers over the internet?

In the B-to-B market for example, you don't have the same transparency as you have in the B-to-C market. The approach to pricing would be different. For the B-to-B market the focus would be more about trying to first understand the value that is being delivered. If you have a tech product, for example, a unique app for the B-to-B market with some amazing machine learning algorithms behind it, you are not going to licence it for $999 if the value it delivers to the client is potentially in the millions of dollars or pounds.

On the other hand, if your product is some new gadget for the B-to-C market with lots of substitutes retailing at $99 or £99, with potentially millions of buyers, you would take a different approach. Perhaps focusing first on your costs, and then experimenting with different price points relative to the average market price, gauging demand, and homing in on the sweet spot. The price where demand for your product is maximised.

Table 14: Examples of different pricing strategies to consider

Pricing strategy	Description of strategy
Price skimming	Price as high as you think the market will stand for early adopters, then lower the price gradually over time as competition increases, to attract more customers.
Cost plus pricing	Know your cost of supply then add a profit margin.
Value pricing	Price relative to the value the customer derives from your offering. In the BtoB market what value does your product add to customer profitability?
Competitive pricing	Price relative to competitor pricing established for substitute products in the market.
Loss leaders	Price at a loss to grow market share, get established in a market or attract customers that you can then cross sell other products to.
Premium pricing	Price high to reflect premium quality of your product or the perceived quality or luxury status of your brand.
Price bundling	Price several complementary products together as a package at a lower aggregate price. The customer gets a lower price than if all the products were bought individually. You sacrifice a bit of margin but increase the volume of sales.

The psychology of pricing is also a factor to consider, people are often willing to pay higher prices for certain brands or from larger companies. There is a perception attached to premium pricing of quality, prestige, or security. For example, in technology buying, there used to be a saying 'you never get fired for buying IBM'. The reality often doesn't match up that a large established competitor will provide a better product or service, though as a new market entrant this can be to your advantage, it gives you a larger margin to work with.

As a small technology company, considering where to price in relation to larger players, you will have to work on your marketing, how you position your product against recognised brands, how you differentiate yourself and how you communicate added value. There will be a perceived risk in switching from larger companies to buy from you. This either needs to be reflected in your price or you need to convince buyers you are in the same quality bracket as established incumbents. Normally you will have to provide a better product at a cheaper price to entice someone to change, to take a risk, to go with a much smaller start-up firm.

7.2 What happens when you price technology solutions too low or too high?

My experience has mainly been focused on providing highly technical products and consulting services into large blue-chip companies. Inevitably what I say will be biased towards that market, though I think some of the principles behind how we approached pricing are common sense and could be applied more broadly.

In my opinion, you should pitch your pricing at the top end of what you believe the market will stand. It is easier to lower your prices than to increase them once they are established. The tactic of price skimming is the most adopted pricing strategy where prices are set initially high for new products and then gradually reduced over time to expand the customer base.

In the past I have had numerous debates with colleagues and tried to work out the optimum price for products. We had one software solution at ISL that achieved a high market share - at one stage over 90% of UK insurers licensed the product to understand market pricing trends. The price per module was quite low, though it was a subscription-based model with recurring revenues, and the attrition rate was virtually zero. At the time it was also a key input to actuarial software that insurance companies were buying at massively higher prices.

We probably could have trebled the price and increased our revenues significantly, even allowing for a drop in market share. We took the decision to leave the pricing as it was. Having virtually the whole market to cross sell other products to justified keeping things as they were.

There is a downside though.

Pricing your product too cheaply will put doubt in the mind of the customer about quality –

'It surely can't be that great if they are selling at that price'.

Raising your prices significantly, on the other hand, once products are established is difficult and could irritate customers, tarnish existing relationships, and deter some from even looking in detail at your other offerings.

Another example, in complete contrast, was what happens when you price too high and there is resistance from companies to buy, even if the value delivered can be justified. We used to sell software that helped insurers understand the risk of subsidence, enabling home insurance to be priced more accurately. When it was first launched in the 1990's there were no similar offerings in the market, so the price was set extremely high. The initial licence fee was in the hundreds of thousands of pounds. This was at a time when there was a high market demand, industry losses per year were in the hundreds of millions of pounds, yet less than a dozen companies licenced the product at that price point.

The strategy was to link pricing to the value delivered, though at the time data and risk models weren't viewed as business-critical purchases, even though they added value. Insurers were making sizeable returns from their investments on the stock markets, there wasn't enough pressure to make an underwriting profit, and so there was a ceiling to what they would spend on data to support underwriting solutions.

Not only did it mean a much lower proportion of the market was captured, but it also encouraged competitors to enter with cheaper substitutes. There was money to be made and a lot of headroom for new entrants to undercut us, even if their offerings were not as strong.

That is why it is so important to get your pricing in the right ballpark early in the scale up of the business. You need to have a thorough understanding of the market and what customers will be prepared to pay. It requires some work as finding that optimum price point can be elusive.

7.3 How could a niche technology start-up approach pricing in the business-to-business market?

Understand your cost of supply.

To begin with, of course, you can look at product pricing from a cost of supply point of view. You could set your price based on the cost-plus profit margin approach. What does it cost to buy the components or raw materials, and then produce, sell, deliver, and support your product? You need to know your breakeven point. Consider the costs of production, supply, and support over the term of the contract. It is research you must do at the very beginning of your journey, not all opportunities are worth pursuing.

A client from a large direct insurer phoned up once asking me if we were able to provide a monthly telephone market research service for a niche area. This would have involved making thousands of telephone-calls a month to collect market pricing information and was before the internet had taken off. He told me the maximum they were willing to pay for the service, so after researching the opportunity I responded, we were not able to supply at that price. His price expectations were miles away from the actual cost of providing a quality product.

At the time we had a 90% market share in our niche sector, so it was straight forward to make a few phone calls to existing customers and find out the market appetite and potential for the service. Even if we had been able to sell to most of the market at the price people were willing to pay, it was high risk, the likely profit was never going to be attractive enough, if indeed we ever made a profit.

In effect, we would have been busy fools.

When you are in the process of discovering your optimum product, you need to find out if there is a market worth going for. What is your total addressable market size by value compared to the cost of supply? And what is your likely market penetration? Will your target customers pay enough to make the project worth following?

Understand the value you are delivering to your customers.

Putting effort into understanding what value your product or service delivers for your target market is the next step. Another approach to setting price in this context would be value-based pricing. You should question early adopters about the benefits and the usefulness of your solution.

Try to equate this in monetary terms.

What savings were made?

How much did it increase efficiency?

What has been the growth in business achieved since the customer adopted your product?

In the businesses I have been involved with we have had solutions that made a tangible difference to the accuracy of insurance pricing models. The amount of money paid out in claims per year by company ranged from tens of millions to hundreds of millions of pounds. Just an incremental improvement in the accuracy of risk pricing translated into significant value for insurers. It was possible to precisely quantify the added value of our offering. The types of product we were providing became business critical to profitability, companies that did not invest in similar solutions to improve their pricing accuracy were at a disadvantage.

For your business, take a step back and consider the benefits of your product or service. Then think of ways to put a monetary value on it for the client and think about what it is worth to potential customers.

Research the price range of competitor products and to what extent they are substitutes for your offering.

You need to do some research and discover at what level your competitors are pricing their products.

If they are selling their products cheaper, find out why?

Perhaps they are cheaper for a reason, maybe the products they offer are not as accurate, not as rich in content or functionality. Maybe the competition lacks the domain expertise to provide adequate support, back-up, or the customisation you can offer. You will need to have something that differentiates you to justify a higher price.

When the price is dramatically different you need to have a good reason for a customer to choose you over a rival.

We frequently had clients say to us, 'I can buy a risk model from company X at half the price you are charging, and they have thousands of employees in the company'. Often clients are not comparing apples with apples in such a scenario, so you need to have your arguments ready.

We used to respond with facts explaining why there may be a differential on price, with the main one being that our product was more accurate, delivering better results. This can be further explained by mentioning some of the differences in inputs, design and capabilities of a specialist team that may account for the variation in fees. For example, at the time we had exclusive data inputs, PhD level data scientists building our products, and decades of experience involved in development and support, ensuring that the client was able to gain maximum benefit from our solutions.

We also used to allow clients to test the products for a limited period, to verify the accuracy of what we were saying. The proof of the pudding so to speak was in the 'test'.

An analogy we also used was pointing out that Michelin Star restaurants in London are all providing food, but you don't get anyone complaining that prices are too high because you can buy a beefburger at McDonalds for £4. The product quality and customer experience are not comparable, the price differential is there due to the cost of the inputs, the people preparing it and the people delivering and supporting the customer experience.

How essential is your product in the customer workflow?

To some extent the value you deliver, how essential the product you supply is in the client workflow, and the price elasticity of demand for your product will determine how high you can increase your prices.

If you can build a strong competitive advantage over substitute products and can clearly prove the extra value you add, putting some daylight between you and competitors, then candidly, pricing relative to the competition becomes largely irrelevant.

In my view you need to price for profit and you also need to have an in-depth knowledge of what you are delivering is worth to customers. Don't sell yourself short.

Price needs to be fair relative to the value you deliver.

This is one of the things I learnt from an experience in my first business. At the time we provided bespoke software to a FTSE 100 company to facilitate the pricing of property insurance in the UK. When the deal was originally agreed the contract had a fixed annual price, under a hundred thousand pounds. The client did not have any insurance business, the price was fair. Several years later, the software underpinned several hundred million pounds of premium income and the contract was still on the same fixed price.

We had massively under-priced the contract by not linking it to the growth in the client business. We hadn't considered the true value to the client of what was being provided. Prior to the seventh anniversary of the agreement renewal date the client sent an email but unintentionally left a senior management discussion attached. They had forgotten to delete notes from their internal discussions on the email trail before contacting us. In their deliberations they stated how much it would cost them to bring the software in house – an eye watering amount of money! And how much their business was dependent on the service we provided. It was remarkably interesting reading.

To replace our software was going to cost them significant amounts of investment, and probably take 12 months of development and testing before being able to go live.

We believed the current deal was too one-sided, and we now knew clearly from their discussions we had the upper hand.

Should we triple the price on renewal?

Should we insist on a minimum renewal term of several years?

What would you do in this situation?

We had good relationships across the business. I knew the chief actuary very well and had been talking to him about buying all the other products we had available. After some discussion internally we sent them an email back, leaving the original email trail in place.

We decided to propose a modest increase in the price of the software covering support costs and suggested they look at licencing our other products, obviously subject to our other solutions working for them. Within six months they had licensed everything we had, the annual revenue was much greater, and they had signed a 5-year agreement. They became our largest customer, a reference site, and an advocate for us in the market.

There are a few lessons we learned from this. The first is to make sure you think carefully about other things in addition to price. Also think about the future relationship, build scenarios into your contractual agreement to ensure you get a fair deal, that you are not out of pocket. If the client business grows massively and your product is a vital piece of the workflow, you want to make sure that you have a fair slice of the upside.

Another key point is that if you do find you have made a mistake then approach the client honestly and fairly. Treat people well and always act with integrity. It will not always mean things go your way, in the long run though you will maintain trust, be someone that people want to work with, and you will have longevity in the market. We could have trebled our price and insisted the client sign up to a multi-year deal. We would have made a short-term gain, though it would have forced their hand to bring the software in house as quickly as possible, and they may not have looked as favourably at buying other products from us or providing references. Our response generated a lot of goodwill and a lot more revenue over the longer term.

<u>Carry out market testing to understand how responsive demand is to price.</u>

Depending on the size and extent of your target market you could experiment testing out different price points with different customer groups. If you are offering a premium product compared to the rest of the market you may wish to pitch your prices considerably higher. But how much higher? This may depend on the value you can prove your products provide.

When you know your breakeven position, understand the value customers derive from your product, and have information on what your competitors are charging, you will then be in a strong position to find the right price point for your product.

I would advise going through all the above steps to gain insight into the optimum price range for your products. Then put together your price book or spreadsheet with all your pricing information, put in automatic annual increases for inflation and review your pricing regularly.

If there are not clear differentiators between you and your competitors, you may wish to look at being more creative with your pricing and offering bundled deals. Perhaps offer some individual products at a discount to competitor pricing though you could look at combining several products, offering higher discounts for bundles, or including some consulting time to provide a more customised solution.

When thinking about your price point you could also present a price that appears to have been scientifically calculated. For example, if you decide you are pitching your list price around £35,000, why not have £34,575 or £35,380. It will appear that it has been meticulously calculated or that you have applied a cost-plus margin approach, whether you have or not.

However you set your prices, please ensure you allocate time to it and think about the different approaches.

It will be worth the investment!

References / Further reading

1. Simon, Hermann *'Confessions of the Pricing Man: How Price Affects Everything'* Springer
2. Cracking the code in Startup Product Pricing Strategies, Startups.com, September 21st 2017

Key takeaways

• It is essential to price accurately at the start of your journey. Set your prices too low and you will be leaving money on the table. Set them too high and you may not sell anything.

• Once established it is more difficult to increase price in the market than it is to lower it.

• Pricing too cheaply may put doubt into the mind of the customer regarding the quality of your product.

• Make sure you understand your cost of supply.

• Find out the value you deliver to customers. How vital is your product in the customer workflow?

• Research competitor product pricing and understand how they compare in value they deliver to clients in the market. Where does your product fit into the competitive landscape?

• Always deal fairly, openly, and communicate honestly with your clients if you believe you have priced something incorrectly and intend hiking up the price on renewal. You need to make a margin but also think about long term relationships and being a trusted supplier.

• Carry out market testing to understand the optimum price point.

• Think creatively about pricing if you have a lot of competition. Discounting, bundling, and providing consultancy to customize solutions can differentiate you in the technology solutions space.

• Consider the psychology of pricing. The perception of pricing low relative to the average market price may be lower quality. Increasing your price significantly may result in more sales, particularly if your solution delivers high value.

HOMEWORK

1. *What is the fully loaded cost of supplying your product? Write down all the elements below and estimate the associated costs of each.*

2. *Where are competitors pitching their prices? How does the quality compare to your current offering?*

Competitor	Competitor Product	Price per annum	Estimated number of customers	Quality relative to your product

SCALE for SALE

CHAPTER 8: SEVERAL WAYS TO SUPERCHARGE SALES

'If people like you, they'll listen to you, but if they trust you, they'll do business with you'

– *Zig Ziglar*

Sales is one of the areas of the business that entrepreneurs worry about most. According to a survey of small businesses in the UK by Factworks[1], 79% of owners questioned felt the biggest challenge they faced was attracting new customers.

For many business owners, sales are an uphill struggle, a task they least like doing - it fills them with dread. They labour to get traction with customers, need to work extremely hard to cultivate deals, and have difficulty closing business. To them, the sales profession appears like a dark art, shrouded in mystery.

For some entrepreneurs though, selling seems natural and is the best part of the job, they love to get out of the office, are interested in meeting people and finding out how other companies operate. For these businesspeople, it seems straightforward, like riding a bicycle.

Whether you are a natural salesperson or not, what is certain is that until you make a sale you don't have a business.

Having a great product that solves a problem is a key requirement, but if you want to scale your business, you need to consider how to be more efficient and effective at selling. You need to create a slick sales capability, something giving you more certainty in being able to grow your revenues quickly.

You want to make sure that the whole approach to selling and the experience for customers is consistent right through your whole organisation.

8.1 What is the easiest type of sale and why? How can you ensure you get more via this route?

It may seem obvious but it's much easier getting more business from existing customers than searching for new ones. Consequently, when looking to win more deals to grow your business start with your existing client base first. If you have built strong relationships these are the low hanging fruit to revenue growth.

When you focus on delivering a fantastic service and delighting them, they then turn into advocates and evangelists for your business. Word of mouth is a powerful marketing medium.

When clients talk about your products and services, they will recommend you to friends and colleagues. Then when they move jobs, they will buy from you again. Some become consultants and recommend you on every project. It can have a snowball effect.

The record number of sales from the same person, a client called Phil Webb, generated revenue for us from six different large blue-chip Insurance companies over several years. Phil changed employer a couple of times before becoming a consultant. He then recommended our company several times as a trusted supplier, and this produced a large chunk of recurring revenue over many years. Advocates can be better than your own salespeople, they are independent, and the sale has almost been closed for you by the time the prospect phones you. You just need to cut them a fair price and terms, and it is easy business.

The first way to supercharge your sales is to focus on cross-selling to your existing customer base, provide a great service and turn clients into advocates and evangelists for your firm.

You have probably already listened to podcasts about selling and perhaps read numerous books and articles about sales. When you have a foothold in the market, and loyal customers satisfied with your product, what is the one thing they all tend to agree on as the most efficient way to get more customers?

Focus on referrals.

It is the most cost effective and easiest way to grow your business beyond your existing client base.

Why?

It all boils down to trust.

Referrals are a lot easier to convert into sales. People that have been referred to you from a trusted source are warm leads. The prospect has already 'ticked the box' of you being a reputable company that can deliver a useful product. The trustworthy source is likely to be a friend or contact whose opinion the prospect respects. Customer leads originating from this route will be more open to communicating, to sharing their problems and requirements. And to listening to what you have to offer them.

At the time of writing this during the 2020 pandemic, with face-to-face meetings suspended, a referral from a trusted source was the most common route to new business.

So how do you generate a lot more referrals?

You need to put in place methodical ways to generate recommendations. Put together a system that produces endorsements, that fashions introductions to more prospects, and that gets you reference sites whose opinions potential customers will trust.

To achieve this be proactive in asking clients for referrals, ask them to be reference sites, and for introductions to their key contacts that could be interested in your services. This may seem a bit awkward and unnatural at first, though it is something you should get used to. Once you get to know people well and they trust you, then often they will be happy to help you and it will reap rewards. This approach works and will generate business.

When at contract negotiation stage with existing clients and they pushed hard for discount, we would always in return ask for them to be a reference site, for a press release, or to be the subject of a case study. This can be an easy way to close negotiations as a win-win for both parties, you get valuable marketing, PR, and access to more prospects without it costing the client any money.

Receiving glowing praise from a leading blue-chip company to put on your website is useful marketing. Having reference sites and getting warm introductions to other clients also makes the whole sales process a lot easier. Of course, they are unlikely to agree to recommend you to others if you don't provide a great service or they don't trust you.

The essential thread you require through all these points, for sales growth and longevity in the market is **TRUST**.

If people trust you, your company, and believe you have their best interests in mind they'll do business with you, and they will continue wanting to work with you in the future. They will also be advocates for you in the market telling other contacts about what a marvellous product or service you provide. And they will be willing to refer people they know to you that may be interested in your product or service.

OK, so how do you win the trust of clients in the market if you are a relatively new business you might ask. Well, it will not happen overnight, in my view you develop this over time by consistently delivering a terrific product or service and putting the client first. From trust in your brand, the reputation of your company slowly builds over time, through all the customer interactions with your company at every level. Make sure this is consistent and that the quality of the service or product remains high, and just as important that the attitude and interaction with customers stays constant.

Whoever a customer meets within your company they should receive the same warm and friendly, attentive, and responsive service.

You may not get everything 100% perfect for your customers all the time, there may be the odd issue, for example, software bugs, system outages, the odd error in data models, as was the case in the products we supplied. However, if you commit to doing the best you can possibly do, put the customer first, go the extra mile to solve problems and put things right when there are issues, then you will build trust.

To really ramp up your sales, build out from your existing customer base, through referrals and introductions to people from sources they trust. In building trust and putting the customer first it all starts with your attitude, behaviours, and is something that needs to flow through the whole firm.

A lot of companies aspire to the 'Trusted Advisor' status with clients, though in my experience, many companies talk about it, but few deliver on the promise. Putting the customer first, looking to continually improve and achieve excellence in what you provide must be engrained in the core of your business from the top down and be part of every employee's key objectives.

'Everyone is on the sales team'.

As one of my old colleagues used to say frequently. As mentioned earlier in this book, you need to be customer centric, to put the client first and always go down the path you believe to be the best for the customer, not necessarily the one generating you the most short-term revenue. Above all, you should always be focused on providing solutions that are in the best interests of the client. Treat everyone fairly, always behave honestly, openly and with integrity. You should be looking to build long term lasting relationships that over time generate trust.

Make sure that everyone in your organisation is focused on putting the customer first and providing the best possible product or service you can provide. Over time as you build trust, you will turn existing customers into advocates that promote you in the market.

Presentation and proposal materials should be standardized, depicting the same quality, presenting the same values, and communicating a consistent story to the market. You should make sure that everyone in the company represents the business in a similar manner when interfacing with clients and that the sales team all go through the same approach in their meetings, for example, questioning, listening, understanding client requirements, then communicating your story, what you do and how you can help solve their problem.

You should also track customer satisfaction, get your account managers to call every client at least once a quarter and ask them a few questions, find out if they are satisfied, where you are doing well, and more importantly where you need to improve. Stay ahead of the pack.

If you think of sales in this way, you will be on the right track to fast growth.

Consequently, the second way to supercharge your sales is to BUILD TRUST and put in place systematic ways to generate referrals.

8.2 How do you increase client engagement and interest in your products?

The best way to increase client engagement is to focus on being a solutions provider. Focus on solving problems, under promise, over deliver and act in the best interests of the client.

To get to that position and to be effective in sales your sales guys need a vital skill.

The sales team must be good listeners.

They need to be attentive to what the customer is telling them. I am amazed by how many sales executives I have met that never let anyone get a word in and talk constantly. I was once told that you have two ears and one mouth, and you need to use them in that proportion in sales. How do you know what the client is interested in buying if you just talk about yourself, your products, and your company? Yes, they may have an idea about what you can provide, but unless you know where the current needs are focused you will struggle to find a solution, or to get them excited and eager to buy your product.

One of the most successful salesmen I have worked with, a chap called Martyn Hayward, was Sales Director at ISL. As a seasoned professional he knew how to run a sales process, how to build relationships, negotiate, close deals, and look after customers. He never failed to exceed his sales target during the eight years that I worked with him. Customers loved him and I had the pleasure of accompanying him on numerous sales pitches and seeing him in action.

Martyn was a great listener, a fantastic storyteller, and a master at building rapport with clients. I remember accompanying him to have lunch with one of the senior executives of a large insurance company in London. After we had covered some of the business items Martyn chatted to the client and quizzed him about bird watching, whether he had spotted certain varieties and where he thought the best places were in the UK to spot certain rare species. The client was animated during the discussions over lunch and the meeting went very well. On the walk back to the station after the appointment I said,

"I didn't realise you were interested in birdwatching Martyn?",

"I'm not", he replied. *"But I know that it is Ray's hobby, so I did a little preparation and background reading last night"*.

Martyn kept mental notes on all his customers. He knew when their birthdays were, what football team they supported, what hobbies they pursued, what they were keen on, and even the names of their wives and children. He went along to meetings and listened, focused on solutions, then picked up more business.

To succeed in sales, you need to be effective in helping people solve their problems and become a trusted supplier, that is all about building long term relationships, not about short-term sales targets.

There is no magic wand, key question, or hard sale in the sort of selling that produces long term client relationships.

You should ignore the old sales clichés like

'*Sales is like ABC – Always Be Closing*'.

This conjures up the image of the double-glazing salesguy or pushy car salesman who looks to sell his product at all cost, regardless of whether this is in the best interests of the client or not.

In my mind, the ABC of sales should mean:

'*Assist, Benefit and Comprehend your customers*',

or maybe a better saying would be:

'*Sales is like ABS – Always Be Serving*'.

This should form part of the values within your business and be something that all your employees sign up to.

When you actively listen and show a sincere interest in clients and what they are doing, it achieves two things. To begin with, the person will appreciate the attention, the focus on them as an individual and someone making them feel important. Secondly, by you actively listening, they are more likely to give you more details about their business problem or requirement. You will understand their firm in a lot greater depth and in turn find it easier to identify solutions for them using your products. It will also enable you to figure their emerging needs to inform your future product development.

Meet regularly with clients, find out what their interests are, ask questions, get them talking about the problems and challenges they are facing. Build rapport, keep notes on what your clients are interested in, show an interest in them and their business. What sports are they interested in? What teams do they support? Do you they have any kids? Actively listen in meetings, always thank them for their business with a personal note and stay close to them.

Be a great listener. People like people who listen and who show a genuine interest in them.

Use this information as the bridge to build a relationship and be a solution provider rather than just pushing your products. Provide great service, be honest with people about what you can and can't do and show a genuine interest in helping them achieve their objectives.

Don't go along with a mindset to sell them anything, take a sincere interest in the person first, the business and look to help solve problems.

So, the third way to ramp up your sales effort is to put the client first, be great at listening and focus on unravelling client problems and being a solutions provider.

8.3 How should you structure your sales team for growth?

When you are scaling up there will be a temptation to go out and hire an expensive, experienced sales leader. Many companies do this, they bring on board a well-qualified sales director, at a premium, rather than getting by with more junior salespeople until the business can afford the extra overhead. This type of investment is a big gamble when you are in the early stages of scaling up your company and money is tight. In the insurance technology space, an experienced senior sales professional can cost upwards of £150,000 to

£200,000 per annum when all the components of the compensation package are included.

It is a strategy that I have tried out on more than one occasion and let me tell you, it usually fails and is an expensive mistake. We hired lots of expensive salespeople when we were scaling up a business under the umbrella of a large corporation. Generally, this didn't work, the overhead from hiring senior sales leaders increased massively and it took a long time before we saw an impact on revenue growth.

I would take a step back and think about exactly what you need and what you are missing.

Are you finding it tough to win new business?

Is your sales pipeline thin or your sales process falling over at a certain point?

Do you need to upskill the existing sales team?

Are you missing a sales leader within the founding group or senior management team?

Do you require a more experienced manager to oversee the sales function?

Do you have any 'hunter' salespeople in the team who focus on winning new business?

Bringing in one expensive individual, expecting that person to wave a magic wand, then for lots of new sales to suddenly be generated is a big ask. If the person is from outside of your industry, doesn't have existing domain knowledge or already have a network of senior client contacts, producing new revenue quickly is probably impossible.

The technology sales I have been involved in have tended to be high value low frequency deals with a relatively long process. It takes time for new people to get traction in the market. It has taken senior salespeople we have hired eighteen months to two years to have much of an impact on our numbers. It obviously does depend on what you are selling and the length of the sales cycle but if you are looking for an instant impact, consider other solutions.

What is the blend of individuals in your sales team? Ideally you need to have 'hunters' in the team who are out and out salespeople, high energy, gregarious, charming, experienced in running a sales process, and in bringing in new business. These are normally expensive people, though you could go for less experienced individuals, offering them a package with a low base salary but with a generous commission structure. If they are capable, they get well paid, if they don't work out your downside is limited.

You also need 'farmers' or account managers who can look after your client base, coordinating and managing the requirements of existing customers, ensuring you retain business and can cross-sell your other products. Farmers should be client facing people, easy to get along with, proactive, who like spending time with people and getting out and about visiting customers. They don't need to be at the same extrovert level as the 'hunters', and are usually less expensive people to bring in. But they do need to have plenty of energy, be willing to put in effort and to be out in the market, meeting and speaking to clients.

This is crucial, particularly if you want to be a trusted supplier – you need to have strong relationships and rapport with clients to help generate repeat revenues. Otherwise, the relationship becomes purely transactional, then the likelihood of retaining business, cross-selling or upselling is diminished. I have experienced different ends of the spectrum over the years from account managers and salespeople reluctant to leave the office and not even taking clients out for coffee, to a colleague at my last company, who would meet different clients for breakfast, lunch, and dinner most days of the week.

You also need a sales manager who can manage the team, collate data on the pipeline, monitor activity, and help to coordinate and report progress. You don't need to bring in an expensive sales professional to do this role. In my view, the guy who is a great sales 'hunter' often is not the guy that makes a great sales manager. The skillsets are completely different. In fact, I have noticed that the best new business salespeople usually don't make great sales managers. They don't like managing people, usually want to be out seeing clients, and want to bring in the business themselves.

At ISL we had a sales leader and a very competent sales 'hunter' within the team. This person was part of the founding team, had extensive market contacts, and a deep understanding of our products and their applications. This worked very well. We were able to control costs as the person was a shareholder and agreed to be paid below the market rate until we could afford to pay his full rate.

When starting Business Insight, we lacked selling experience and the initial sales team consisted of outgoing technical people. In the early days we couldn't afford to hire an expensive sales leader, so instead we decided to upskill the existing team. I brought in a sales trainer, Bruce King[3], to improve our skills, to freshen up our approach to selling and to show us a few different techniques to close more deals. The tactic worked well and had an impact on our numbers. A few years later, when we could afford it, I hired an expensive sales leader – he lasted less than 6 months.

Therefore, the fourth way to supercharge your sales, in my opinion, would be to first look at the team to ensure you have a good blend of the right types of people. Make sure you have a blend of the right personalities.

Then invest in training your team to sharpen up their sales skills.

8.4 How do you find out where things are going wrong if sales begin to dry up?

You need to put in place structure, systems, and a clear process you can measure at each stage to monitor the performance of your sales function. Then you can start to collate sales metrics, review these monthly in your management meeting, and identify at what stage things are going wrong. The typical sales metrics (or KPI's) to collect and review are detailed in the appendix at the end of this chapter.

To begin with you first need to define your sales process into a series of steps you typically undertake, from the first interaction with the potential client through to the delivery of the sale. Document this and all the steps that your sales team must follow for each prospective customer. Then collate information at each phase, measure, monitor and report on the numbers regularly. Licence a CRM software tool so you can easily capture and manage the information for each stage and each interaction with a client.

You will easily be able to track clients through the pipeline and over time, with more data, accurately forecast the value of your pipeline at any time. You will also spot when things aren't going as they should if too many customers drop off at a particular juncture in the process. Once you have robust estimates for all your sales metrics, forecasting sales accurately becomes a lot easier and more feasible.

Base your numbers on fact not fantasy, on reality not guesswork and you will find it much more possible to hit your numbers. For example, in one of my previous businesses I knew from the data we had collated that a qualified lead had a 25% chance of progressing through to a closed sale. If we got a client to the contract stage, then the chance of signing a deal was 90%. Once you have been collating the data for a while and have robust metrics to hand, you can estimate the value of the pipeline, identify when things are going off-track and what is required to get things back in line if the numbers start to fall behind.

An example sales process for a software\data analytics company might go something like this:

Step 1: [Week 1] Identify or connect with suspects in the market, either through cold calling, conferences, personal networks, client referrals or companies phoning you up directly.

Do you have a product or service of relevance to their needs? Are they interested in meeting to discuss further or see a demo/overview presentation about what you do?

Step 2: [Week 4] Meet the suspect, present a top-level overview of what you do. Understand their problems, needs, and qualify them as a prospect (use the STAR approach to qualifying leads, see next section). If they fit the criteria, then the goal is to move them to the next stage for a deeper dive of what is available.

Step 3: [Week 8] If not agreed during the meeting, follow-up and determine with the prospect if interested to move to deeper discussions. More detailed information from either side will then be shared to understand the potential fit. A confidentiality agreement is usually issued and signed by both parties prior to the next stage.

Step 3: [Week 14] Bring in technical leads from both parties, present a deeper dive of the products available, question the prospect in more depth to get a full understanding of their requirements. This meeting is likely to be followed up by further technical questions, the handling of objections, more discussion around their requirements and initial ballpark indications of cost.

Step 4: [Week 20] Arrange a test of the data model or software for an agreed period and for a limited sample size. A contract is usually issued to ensure that the IP of the products are protected, and the use is restricted to evaluation only. Written indications of licensing costs are issued prior to engaging in a test to ensure the client is aware and this is within budget expectations.

Step 5: [Week 30] Meeting to discuss the results of the test and to close the deal. Either it works wonderfully well, and they want to buy, or it doesn't, in which case you need to try to understand why. Sometimes it is somewhere in the middle and that is where the salesperson earns his money by revisiting the results with the technical guys to dig deeper, to understand the results, and to make a solid case to licence the products.

Bizarrely, sometimes the results can show potentially huge added value, yet the prospect still doesn't buy. This will be due to poor qualification, for example, the person you are liaising with perhaps does not have the authority to make a decision to buy.

Step 5: [Week 32] Proposal is issued, and an agreement negotiated with the client. Sometimes this is a bundled deal on a multi-year contract for hundreds of thousands of pounds.

Step 6: [Week 34] Contract issued reflecting the final terms of the deal that has been agreed.

Step 7: [Week 40] Contract signed, final specification for product delivery and date of installation agreed.

Step 8: [Week 42] Delivery of product to agreed specification.

The above process is just one example of selling into a large blue-chip company, there are more hoops to jump through in this scenario compared to selling a lower value items to small firms. The basic idea remains the same, to define each step of the process and each interaction with the prospect. Capture the data at each step and understand what the likelihood of success is at each stage. You can then work out the value of your whole pipeline by multiplying the potential value of prospects at each juncture by the likelihood of them progressing through each step to a sale.

The fifth way to supercharge your sales is to:

- define your sales process into a series of steps.

- then collect information on each step, monitor and report on the success of progress of prospects through your pipeline.

- build up an understanding of what typically happens at each stage.

- identify when things are going wrong at what stage and learn to forecast the value of your pipeline accurately.

8.5 What will improve the quality of your sales pipeline that a lot of companies struggle to do well?

You can save yourself a lot of time and effort by ensuring you focus on the best prospects. This is especially important for high value technology products where the sales cycle can be long, and the work involved extensive. You need to ask questions early on, for example in step 1 and step 2 above, to find out if the prospect is a good fit.

Look to pick out the stars to put in your sales funnel or pipeline.

> **The 'STAR' Method (Spend, Timing, Authority, Requirement) for prioritising prospects:**
>
> **Spend**: - Does the prospect have the available budget to buy your product?
>
> **Timing**: - Is the timing right for the prospect to buy your product?
>
> **Authority**: - Does the prospect have the authority to make the buying decision?
>
> **Requirement**: - Does your solution fill a need of value to the prospect?

If you qualify your leads according to the above criteria, the quality of prospects progressing through your pipeline will improve, and the overall success rate will increase.

The sixth way to supercharge sales is to improve the quality of prospects you put in the sales funnel by qualifying each one with a consistent rigorous approach.

8.6 Why do you need to embrace digital marketing?

You need to embrace digital marketing if you want to generate faster growth in future. It is strange to think that until just before the recent pandemic hit, 25% of small businesses in the UK did not even have a website[4]. I think this will not only be a thing of the past, but if you don't have a strong digital marketing plan, a social media platform to build a profile with customers and an online presence in future, you will be dead in the water. It is especially the case if selling to large companies for big ticket contracts. You need a quality website reflecting your company brand, telling your story, something compelling that resonates with your customers and that connects you emotionally with them.

The ease of access and availability of information means potential clients often do substantial research about you before they will even speak to a salesperson or agree to a meeting. According to survey data[4] 60% of potential buyers look at websites, read online reports, download brochures, and form an opinion about a business before they contact anyone in the company. Your on-line image, brand, and website is your shop window. And is now more important than ever.

It is business critical now to have a quality website, digital plan and approach that makes use of this channel. Social media, podcasting, blogging, vlogging (or video blogging) and having an on-line dialogue with your client base has become an essential part of a marketing strategy these days.

You should also look at search engine optimisation and the use of different social media in connecting with your client base and getting your message out. Consider webinars, online discussion forums, blogs covering topical things of interest in your market and e-newsletters, informing your client base about your product releases, and keeping them updated.

Even as the world goes back to normal, post-pandemic there is sure to be an increased emphasis on digital and everything surrounding it.

If you don't embrace it, you will be at a disadvantage.

So, the seventh way to ramp up your sales is to ensure you focus on your digital marketing plan.

Lastly, you could also look elsewhere, perhaps to other related markets, to see where your products may be relevant. For example, some of the solutions I have been involved in building have been applicable not only to insurance but also to home buying and the property research market. One of the property databases we built in the past, RESIDATA, we even sold to the UK Government to help in housing research projects being undertaken at the time. This was introduced by a partner company not competing against us in our market.

Search for potential partners with complementary products and those that are not competing with you directly in your own market. Also look for those in other markets where your product could be used for another purpose or in another context. Then try to cut a deal where the partner sells your product as part of their service or as an additional add-on solution, and make sure you incentivise them to generate more business for you. If structured in the right way, and assuming you trust and can work with the partner, this can be another lucrative revenue stream that doesn't involved a lot of resource from you.

In conclusion, the eighth way to supercharge sales is to find partners offering complementary products or services, join with them to access a wider network of clients. And access another sales resource to sell more of your product.

References / Further Reading

1. www.entrepreneur.com/article/242432
2. The Digital Evolution in B2B Marketing, CEB Marketing Leadership Council in partnership with Google (www.CEBGlobal.com)
3. King Bruce: '*How to Double your Sales*', FT Prentice Hall
4. www.merchantsavvy.co.uk/uk-sme-data-stats-charts/
5. Mourad, Maroun 'The Insurance Management Playbook: A Leader's Guide'
6. Schiffman S '*The 250 Sales Questions to Close the Deal*' Adams Media.

Key takeaways

• Sales is the one thing entrepreneurs worry about the most. 79% of owners feel the biggest challenge they face is attracting customers. Without sales you do not have a business.

• Focus on delighting your customers, deliver a great product or service. Then turn them into advocates and evangelists.

• Cross-selling to your existing clients should be your first focus and easiest route to more business.

• Build trust, ask for referrals and put in place a systemised way to generate more leads from existing customers.

• Put the client first, be great at listening, focus on unravelling client problems and become a solutions provider.

• Avoid bringing in expensive sales leaders, this is unlikely to be a silver bullet solution and is unlikely to fix sales in the short term, if you are having trouble with the numbers. If you want instant impact bring in a specialist trainer and upskill your team.

• Define your sales process, collate data at each step. Measure and monitor your pipeline, and proactively manage your sales through each stage from suspect through to signing a contract. Use this system to identify problems and where things are going wrong. Then fix them.

• Sharpen up the quality of leads you put in your sales funnel by qualifying them using the same consistent approach. Only put client STAR's (SPEND, TIMING, AUTHORITY, REQUIREMENT) in the funnel that have been properly qualified.

(Continued)

• Embrace digital marketing and make sure you have a robust plan in place.

• Search for partners in your market and other markets where either your product could complement another solution or where it could add value elsewhere. Then structure a deal and let other people sell for you, reaching a wider network of clients and generating other additional revenue streams.

HOMEWORK

1. *How much of your business originated through a referral from an existing client or contact, and how much business has been cross-sold or upsold to existing customers per annum?*

2. *Define the steps in your sales process and the customer journey through from the first interaction with your salespeople.*

APPENDIX: Sales metrics to collect and review monthly

Sales metrics to collect and review monthly

Number of inbound prospect enquiries by email and telephone per month Number of outbound prospect (cold calls) calls and emails per month Number of outbound prospect calls (from referrals) per month Number of prospect calls per Sales FTE per month Number of prospect visits per month [or video calls] Number of prospect visits per month [or video calls] per Sales FTE	LEAD GENERATION
Number of new qualified leads generated in the month % Qualified leads as a proportion of all initial prospect meetings Number of qualified leads progressing through to the testing phase per month % of those wishing to test the products as a proportion of all qualified leads Number of clients progressing through to the contract stage per month % Clients negotiating a contract as a proportion of all testing the products % Clients negotiating a contract as a proportion of all qualified leads Average value of contract closed per month (per quarter) Average length of contract closed per month (per quarter) Number of signed contracts (new business) in month Value of signed contracts (new business) in month	NEW BUSINESS GENERATION
Number of new signed contracts (renewals) in month Value of new signed contracts (renewals) in month Average value of signed contracts (renewals) in month Number of new signed contracts (cross-selling and upselling) in month Value of new signed contracts (cross-selling and upselling) in month Average value of new signed contracts (cross-selling and upselling) in month Retention rate (contracts renewing in quarter) Client visits in month Client visits per sales FTE	CONTRACT RENEWALS CROSS SELLING UPSELLING

SCALE for SALE

CHAPTER 9: MANAGING DURING A CRISIS AND HOW TO TURN IT TO YOUR ADVANTAGE

'When written in Chinese, the word 'crisis' is composed of two characters. One represents danger and the other represents opportunity'

- John F. Kennedy

Once you have been running your own business for a while, you will soon find out there are plenty of ups and downs, moments of elation, and disappointing times when things don't go your way. Running a company is a bit like being on a rollercoaster ride. The highs are enjoyable and exhilarating, whereas some of the dips can be challenging, and disheartening.

Occasionally you may get something significant happening, a crisis, something that knocks the wind right out of your sails, and the company. Stopping you in your tracks.

Something major that threatens the business, and initially at least, that causes you mild panic, alarm, and worry. Something that gives you a sinking feeling in the pit of your stomach.

How do you handle this type of crisis when you haven't been through anything like it before? What sort of approach has worked well in the past for others in a similar position?

How do you avoid waking up every morning at 4am in a cold sweat, stressed out about whether you will have a business or not?

9.1 What should you do first in a crisis?

How you first respond in a crisis is crucial and can be the difference between being able to continue scaling up, or failure. It may be tempting to react when panic sets in, without thinking things through clearly. Unless it is life threatening, please resist your initial gut reaction to do something immediately. You may make the wrong move. You might even make things worse than they are already. Do not do anything in haste, and so initially, in my view, DO NOTHING.

Take a step back, make sure you have all the facts about what has happened, and find out what the impact may be on the business. Try to assemble a full understanding of the different options open to you.

Speak to your colleagues internally, seek out guidance from your mentors outside the business, find people who have been through similar crises before and listen to their advice - what worked for them, what approach might work in your business, what are the courses of action open to you, and what might these mean for your company. Only then, when you have the full picture, should you plan your response and act.

Back in the Summer of 2010, I was settling down to watch the evening news on television, when it was announced that the Office of Fair Trading (OFT), a government regulatory body, had launched an investigation into the pricing of car (auto) insurance. There was a suspected breach of competition law. And the product mentioned on the BBC News was one I had been involved in supplying. Any wrongdoing, if proven, could lead to a significant fine, and in a worst-case scenario, a custodial sentence or prison for the company directors found to be at fault.

To say that concern, and mild panic set-in would be a slight understatement. The only thing I can compare the feeling to was one time when I lost my daughter whilst out shopping when she was aged five. She had wandered off while we were in a crowded store as my back was turned and seemed to disappear into thin air. She was probably only missing for about 10 or 15 minutes, but it was a terrifying experience. It is difficult to think clearly to begin with in such situations, anxiety and fear can take over your feelings.

At the start of the investigation by the OFT we also received legal letters from insurance companies. Internally, some of my colleagues were urging me to act straight away, to contact senior people in government, and to send a letter out to all our insurer client base. First and foremost, as the leader, you need to present a calm exterior to your team and reassure them that all is under control, that you are putting together all the facts and that the best way forward will soon be found. It is your job to take some of the pressure away from the team in this situation, allowing them to concentrate on continuing to develop the business.

Fortunately, I resisted the temptation to do anything impulsive or to act rashly. I waited until I had all the facts and understood the ramifications of each possible course of action open to us. I spoke with our legal advisors, requested the opinion of a Senior Barrister (Queen's Counsel), and sought the guidance of external mentors.

It was our belief that the products we offered facilitated price transparency and increased competition; they were in the consumer interest, not against it! It seemed perplexing at the time.

We put a strong team together of legal specialists and product experts, brainstormed how we would get our point across, then we put together our evidence and prepared a robust response. We met with senior people at the OFT and send out a letter to all our clients with a summary of our understanding of the advice received.

9.2 How do you prevent waking up at 4am, worrying about the situation the company is in?

What you should do is formulate your Plan A, based on what you believe to be the most likely outcome. Then work on your Plan B and consider how you approach this, and what you need to do if the outcome is different. Once that has been completed, formulate your Plan C and work on that. When you have concrete plans for different scenarios you will find you can consciously push worry and fear out of your mind. You can only do this when you have put a plan in place and have a couple of contingency plans in your back pocket should the best outcome not come to fruition.

Then trust in your plan A and put concerns to the back of your mind.

9.3 How can you turn a crisis to your advantage?

A crisis can be a tough time for a founder and for the business. However, these are often the circumstances that can define you as an entrepreneur. Challenging situations can present opportunities for the business if reframed in the right way. These can be occasions to innovate, to adapt, to find new solutions and to leapfrog competitors and get ahead of the market.

As Churchill once said,

'Never waste a good crisis'.

In our case, during the issue we had with the competition authorities, we submitted a detailed report to the government regulator (OFT) and then arranged to meet one of the directors in person to understand their concerns. Although we didn't think an investigation was warranted, we found the inside track and understood their worries. We found out what the OFT considered to be acceptable and so we quickly modified our product. In the meantime, all our competitors suspended supplying their products into the market.

When we contacted the client base, we were completely upfront, telling them what we had discovered about the investigation, showed them our modifications, and offered them the opportunity to switch to the new product or exit the contract we had with them. Interestingly, the response was more positive than I could have anticipated. Customer loyalty increased. Some customers even wrote to the OFT stating how vital the products were in enabling competition against much larger rivals. Consequently, we had a clear run, and proceeded to mop up a lot of business. Instead of closing one half of the company, as we might have feared when first hearing of the investigation, we ended up exceeding our growth targets for the year.

9.4 Where might opportunities emerge following the Global Pandemic of 2020?

In the 2020 pandemic we experienced lockdowns, countries were shut down and almost the whole western world moved to online working on mass. Most traditional businesses struggled to adapt, and the hospitality, airline, and traditional retailing industries have been hit particularly hard. Clearly, the pandemic has advanced remote working and the take-up of digital services by several years. Many people who were previously used to travelling into their city office five days a week, and averse to using video conferencing software, are now comfortable working remotely and are now experts at using tools such as Zoom. Prior to the pandemic only 4% of Americans worked remotely from home (source: Economist).

What the pandemic has done is accelerate the shift to digital and to remote working for many companies. The tech giants, online retailers, and those offering remote conferencing services such as Zoom, have seen a huge surge in growth. Those with a strong on-line offering have also coped well.

In every crisis there are always opportunities for entrepreneurs. To get the world back on its feet we need more entrepreneurs taking risks, turning their ideas into a reality, creating more start-ups, and generating new jobs. I think there are going to be lots of new technology firms emerging in online education, digital healthcare, analytics, and automation in financial services. For example, in the insurance market I think there will be a surge in new applications to automate claims validation, improving the customer experience and speeding up the settlement and processing of claims.

We have also seen many small companies pivoting their businesses and developing extremely innovative, new services. One example near where I live is a new start-up that had planned to open as a wine bar and shop just as the pandemic struck. Instead, they repositioned themselves to sell on-line and held regular wine tasting evenings via Zoom for their customers, with expert talks, quizzes, and advice on what to buy.

Prior to the pandemic we had run my previous company with a small office and most of the team working remotely. The reasons behind that were to recruit the best talent, without being restricted to certain geographic locations, and to keep costs under control. If you allow people to work wherever they want, you can attract a wider pool of people, they value the flexibility of working from home. They can also save the time and cost of commuting, which can be significant and so they will often work for a lower salary.

In the new normal, now that most firms are set-up for remote working, and the workforce having experienced the flexibility of being based at home, I can't see things going back to how they were before the pandemic. For entrepreneurs it will lead to the increased mobility of start-ups. More people will realise you don't need a large, expensive city centre office location, particularly if you are an expanding tech company.

Why scale-up your business within an expensive city office and be limited by the cost or availability of the local talent pool? In future, more companies will cut down on expensive city centre locations and instead focus on getting the right talent on board for their business, regardless of where they currently live. An office will still be necessary in some form though it will be cutback. People will still need some face-to-face time, some social interaction for their mental well-being, and to spark ideas and do creative work together.

Undoubtedly there will be opportunities. You can turn a crisis into an opening, if you take a step back, think outside of the box and consider all the different options open to you.

9.5 How can you plan for unknown events with an unknown impact on your business?

The simple answer is you can't plan for every eventuality or know exactly what the future will hold. Nevertheless, you can develop contingency plans and have processes in place that mitigate any problems emanating from a particular part of the business. You can also regularly test your business interruption preparedness, that lines of communication work, that plans are robust and clear, and that people know what is expected of them should such a situation arise.

You can start by gathering key people from across your business and brainstorming all the risks that could have a detrimental impact on your company.

What are you aware of that might go wrong?

What are the possible things that could impact the firm?

What is the scale of the impact of each of these threats?

How can you plan for these and what processes, planning or checks and balances can you put in place to help prevent or mitigate any potential loss to the company?

What is under your control that can influence or minimise any risk?

Could you buy insurance cover and how much cover might you need?

Once you have a thorough understanding of the risks, appreciate their impact, and have them ordered by threat level to the business, you can plan. Put together plans, consider processes and checks, essentially things that you can control that could mitigate any of the known risks that could impact the business. Then assign roles and responsibilities in the company for each of the actions and procedures to implement during a crisis to ensure continuity of the business.

A thorough business continuity plan is more than just disaster recovery, it covers all aspects of the business with workarounds, processes, where back-up assets are located, how to do certain key tasks, supplier details, and contact numbers. It covers everything that needs to be put in place to ensure the operation can get back to 'normal' as soon as possible and continue to run when there is disruption.

Once this has been completed you need to make sure people know what it contains and that they are trained properly. The plan needs to be regularly tested to ensure people know what they are doing. It is important the key people in the chain of command understand how to respond when there is an incident, what they need to do to ensure the assets are protected, how to recover off-site back-ups and how to get the company back-up to speed as quickly as possible.

Beyond that it is extremely difficult to foresee and plan where an unknown event might flow from. Though you could plan for what action you might take given a particular impact to part of the business. For example, you could consider what to do following an event that wipes out one half of your firm, perhaps due to supply chain problems, new government regulations or some new technology. Whatever it is you could consider how you might respond and what actions you might need to take. Consider how you would repurpose resources in such a situation, how you might expand other areas of the business to compensate and what changes would be required.

You can also make sure that you have more detailed technical continuity plans in place in case of specific threats. For example, cyber-attacks are becoming more common these days, so every business should have a process in place to back-up and protect all the assets of the company. There should also be a technical disaster recovery plan in place that has been tested in case the worst happens and you are the target of a cyber-attack.

When you have considered all the risks that might disrupt your business, put thought and planning into effective responses; at least you will have helped to make your company a little more resilient. This will help to mitigate any known threats. Your team will have more awareness of what to do in such a situation, whether it is a known threat or something unexpected, and you will have a structure in place to call upon with assigned responsibilities. It will also be useful for you and your team to have gone through the thought processes and planning, and to have some protections in place, should a crisis hit the business that you had not previously considered.

Even if what you have in place is not sufficient, you should be able to act quicker and adapt plans already well-thought-out to assist you in resolving the issue.

It will certainly be better than having done nothing, and having no contingency planning, no business continuity solutions, or any disaster mitigation strategies in place. Whatever happens, any work or effort put into this area is not wasted. Having some protections in place for the business will help you to sleep more easily at night.

When you eventually progress to selling the company having plans in place will show potential purchasers you have a well-run outfit, that risks to the firm have been considered, and contingencies have been well thought through. It will make the business look more resilient to outsiders. They will appreciate that, if there was a crisis to hit the business it can, through the plans in place, be controlled and minimised.

References / Further Reading

1. A Guide to the preparation of a Business Continuity Plan (aig.co.uk)
2. How to Build an Effective and Organized Business Continuity Plan (forbes.com)
3. Alan Berman (March 9, 2015). "Constructing a Successful Business Continuity Plan". *Business Insurance Magazine.*
4. Surviving a Disaster: A Lawyer's Guide to Disaster Planning (americanbar.org)

Key takeaways

• When a crisis hits the business, resist any impulse to do anything too quickly before you know all the facts and are aware of what impact on the business your actions might take. You don't want to make matters worse.

• Take a step back, try to gather all the information, make sure you have the full picture and understand the consequences of different options open to you.

• Seek advice and guidance from mentors with relevant experience you can tap into.

• Assemble a team of advisors, ensure you have great legal support and counsel.

• Present a calm exterior to your team. They may be worried, and this can impact their daily contribution to the business and have an impact. Reassure them and make sure you take the pressure off them and act as a buffer so that they can continue to keep the business going as normal.

• Get your Plan A, Plan B, Plan C etc. in place for different potential outcomes ensuing from the crisis. Once you have these in place, consciously push fear and any anxiety about the crisis to the back of your mind.

• Look at the crisis from a different perspective. Try to reframe the situation. Does it present any opportunities for a young agile firm like your company to tweak your offering? Could you introduce new products or new innovations that could help you to leapfrog your competitors?

• Consider putting time and effort into a risk audit to understand the existing range of risks facing your business. Then work out what you need in your business continuity plan, disaster recovery plan and what things you can put in place to help safeguard the business.

SCALE for SALE

(Continued)

• Any planning and effort you do will not be wasted. It will help as a safety net to protect against known risks and give you a head start, plus a structure to work with if any currently unknown risks hit the business.

222

HOMEWORK

Answering the questions below will help you to start the thought process to put together a business continuity plan, helping to make your company more resilient to the impact of risks and crisis events. Please refer to the references and further reading for more in-depth support in putting your plan together.

1. *What are the main threats to your business that you are aware of that could impact your revenues, growth, reputation, supply chain, operations? What would the potential impact be to the business revenues of each to help you put these in order of importance?*

2. *For each of the above threats list factors under your control or any processes you could put in place to help prevent, mitigate, or warn against such risks impacting the business.*

PART 3: WORKING TOWARDS A SUCCESSFUL EXIT

SCALE for SALE

CHAPTER 10: PREPARING FOR YOUR EXIT

'By failing to prepare, you are preparing to fail'

-Benjamin Franklin

Selling your company is, for most people, the most important and largest transaction of your life. If you have a technology company, especially one with a strong track record, the proceeds from a sale can be eye-watering and life-changing sums of money.

You may have had some success in scaling up your initial start-up, are profitable and can show several years of sustainable growth. Now you have decided you want to release some capital in the company, to 'de-risk' your investment, enhance your life while you are still young enough to enjoy it.

Well, here is the reality- deciding to sell your business is like entering to do a marathon rather than a jog around the park in a local fun run. Unless you prepare meticulously, hire the right professional advisors, and put a huge amount of planning and effort into the process of selling, the business will fail to sell. Consider trying to sell a house without easy access to data to understand market value or without the same advertising reach via agency websites, estate agency shops, or in newspapers. Then multiply the effort involved by ten.

If you want to have a successful exit and sell for life changing amounts of cash, then planning, hard work and preparation of your company is essential before going to market.

When thinking of your exit, you need to start preparations early. Preferably when you start the business, though certainly a long time before you go to market.

You need to have a robust, resilient business, to have crossed the t's and dotted the i's as you scale. If you don't you will have a mountain rather than a hill to climb in making your firm market ready when approaching your exit.

Think of an Olympic athlete who trains every day, puts in an enormous amount of planning and attention to detail, preparing to be in the finest possible condition, for that pivotal moment in their life when they are on the track, to achieve the best result imaginable. Compare that with the business owner looking to sell his company who has never been through the process before, has not considered what is required and has no idea what his company is worth. How likely is that person to get the result they long for, or even to reach the finishing line?

10.1 How easy is it to sell a company?

Selling a business is certainly not easy.

Many deals fail to close or fall over at different stages during the sale process. According to industry statistics in the USA, 90% of Private companies taken to market fail to sell[1]. In the UK, three out of four private companies brought to market fail to close a deal.

Scaling and then selling a company is challenging. In a recent survey of a thousand venture-funded start-ups by TechCrunch.com[2], trade buyers acquired just 16% of companies across eight different funding rounds. Many went bankrupt. Only a tiny percentage progressed to an Initial Public Offering (IPO). This is when a company sells part or all its equity to the public and lists the business on a stock exchange.

Many entrepreneurs don't think about selling their company, or how they will exit, until the business is mature, they are approaching retirement, or have fallen out of love with what they are doing and want to sell. Commonly, there isn't much thought given to an exit until late in the day. And then the amount of preparation, and tidying up, to get the business into a fit state for someone to buy ends up being a massive amount of work.

To give yourself a great chance of a successful exit and to avoid a lot of work later, it will help if you think about your exit, not towards the end of your journey, but at the start. This realization didn't hit me until after I had already been through the loop once.

When I look back at the successful exits that I have had, I have thought about things that went well, where we made mistakes and where I would do things differently next time around.

At the time of selling my first business, I knew something about the process of buying a company, having been on the buyer side from my time in the corporate world. Yet, there were still large gaps in my knowledge. You don't know what you don't know. I probably had more experience of mergers and acquisitions than many entrepreneurs, even so, I still managed to screw a few things up. Fortunately, we got the deal over the line, though with hindsight, we left plenty of money on the table.

The second time around, having learnt a little more, we put time into the exit planning and preparations. We also thought about what type of an exit we had in mind; for example, we decided the ideal buyer should be a company focused on our niche area, where a buyer could maximise the synergies. A strategic buyer, we thought, would pay a higher price for the business. Yet looking back, although happy with the outcome again, we still made a bunch of mistakes.

I think selling your business is a lot trickier and more complicated than most entrepreneurs realise. It was certainly a lot tougher both times for me than I had thought possible, before entering each process, and I had successful outcomes.

If you haven't been through the process of selling a company before, how can you know what is expected and what the potential pitfalls are? Most business owners know little about what to expect, or how much time and effort are involved. What things might have an adverse impact and how can you mitigate these? I hope, by sharing some of the tips and the traps to avoid in this section, through my experiences of the buyer and seller side, you will be a little more aware, and this will be of help to you.

10.2 What are the things to consider when timing your exit?

There are a few vital things to consider before you embark on the sale process. The first question to ask is:

Why do you want to sell now?

Is it the right time for you, the business, and are market conditions promising? Timing a sale is difficult, a desire to sell could also be driven by a whole host of reasons. Such as wanting to retire, a yearning to enjoy the fruits of your hard work or perhaps due to ill health, or maybe the business has progressed as far as you are able to guide it.

Whatever you do, don't sell due to an external event, for example, a pandemic, or maybe because you think the sales will fall off the edge of a cliff soon. This is called a 'fire sale' and is not likely to get you the price you want. Ideally, there needs to be some upside for the buyer, something to generate interest, to get them excited about wanting to acquire the business. A way for them to make some money and receive a return on their investment.

What are your reasons for selling?

What are your reasons for selling and do these make sense to a buyer? A logical reason will make the process run more smoothly. For example, you may feel that your business needs to be part of a larger company to get it to the next level, to help realise the full market potential. Further expansion may also require you to invest significant additional capital, and you may not wish to carry that risk.

A larger company with deep pockets, wider distribution capability, greater marketing resources, customer contacts, overseas offices, and a bigger brand, for example, may be better placed to take your firm onto the next phase of growth.

How is the business performing?

If you try to sell when your sales are falling or about to drop off a cliff you are unlikely to get a good price. Equally, if you sell with plenty of upside left, are you going to miss some lucrative growth?

There needs to be some upside for the buyer, to whet their appetite, though will this result in you selling far too early and you leaving money on the table? It can be a difficult one to call.

Is the market favourable for sellers?

Are economic and market conditions good now, and what is the outlook for the next couple of years?

Find out the current state of the market for selling firms in your sector. Has there been a lot of activity? What has been the appetite for similar businesses and what multiples have been achieved in recent years? There is a saying that the best time to sell is when the sun is shining.

Having said that you also need to be aware of the supply to the market. Are there any other similar firms in your sector looking to sell? If there are several then it may not be the best time, and you may need to rethink or delay your go to market timing.

How much do you need to achieve in a sale to make it worthwhile?

One of your first steps is to be clear about what you need from a deal. What amount would you accept and be happy with?

What to you would be a fair deal, and a successful outcome?

Are your fellow shareholders aligned?

A major point for consideration and sometimes a source of disagreement between board members is how much you each would need to achieve from a sale.

What price would the company need to achieve on completion for a sale to be worth pursuing?

What is the board's vision for the potential shareholder value of the company? And where are we today?

Is there a lot of growth remaining in the business?

Is there a consensus in your team on what price, if realised now, would make the sale of the company a success?

Often start-ups that have gone through that initial scale-up phase successfully, get approached by large corporates, and sell-up too early.

In recent business literature it has been reported that European entrepreneurs tend to sell-up much earlier than comparable entrepreneurs in the USA. It can be very tempting to take the money when larger 'fish' knock on the door interested in acquiring your company.

To prevent falling into this 'trap', you need to do two things.

Firstly, take a step back and assess the current state in the development of the business, and take a realistic view on how much larger the business could grow.

Ask yourself, how well is my company performing?

Do you already have a few years of solid growth under your belt? How confident are you about the next few years?

Would your company flourish more easily under the umbrella of a large corporate with significant resources to help you? Or are you likely to hit your numbers anyway?

Identify the main barriers to further growth, and work out what would be required to unlock or remove them? How easily and quickly can this be done? Undertake a gap analysis and quantify what is required, what it will cost and what the impact would be on revenues should you invest further.

Secondly, have a frank discussion with your board about whether there should be further investment now or whether you should take the business to market. Discuss the risks involved, and the likelihood of successfully scaling further. Compare this against selling the business now or putting things off for a potentially larger pot of cash later down the line. The responses you receive may be different from everyone on your board depending on how close they are to retirement and their appetite for risk. In the case of my last business, we had several shareholders wishing to retire and keen to take their money off the table.

There was no appetite to invest more money, so the sale to a large corporate made sense.

<u>What are your intentions after selling the company?</u>

You also need to decide what you intend doing after the sale. Are you staying with the business, as part of a larger group, or are you leaving to go to do something else?

What do you want to do? Do you have the risk appetite to stay vested in the company? What realistically is the potential of the firm?

Could you scale it much more and do you have the skills and confidence to take the firm to the next level? Does the business require a larger, better resourced company to take it further?

Overall, you need to weigh up your own personal circumstances, the current position of the company, market conditions, and the price a sale might achieve in the niche area in which you operate. You will also need to discuss these points with your board before ultimately deciding whether to proceed further.

10.3 What options could you consider when selling the business and what are the differences?

Your exit strategy, personal plan and the answers to the previous section will in some ways dictate which buyer options you consider.

Are you considering a sale to your staff, management team or staff plus some new investors (Management Buy Out or Management Buy In)?

An IPO (Initial Public Offering) selling shares to the public on a recognized stock exchange?

A Private Equity firm, where they invest heavily, though are likely to be nervous about key founders leaving the business?

Or are you going down the route of a trade sale?

If you, as founder, want to de-risk, move onto something else and take a safe route to get your money out, then an MBO/MBI or trade sale may be the best options. On the other hand, if you and the founding team are still keen to stay involved, taking the firm on the next stage of growth, while retaining the bulk of your investment, and keeping the business as a standalone entity, then Private Equity (PE) or an IPO may be routes to investigate.

Management Buy Out (MBO)

I have been through one Management Buy Out, on the buy side, and two exits as a seller via trade sales. An MBO may not yield the highest return, as there is no competitive process if selling to the staff. Though it enables the company to continue as a standalone business, is probably the quickest path, lowest risk, and gives the best certainty of getting your money out – assuming the current management and staff have access to funding. The existing team may decide to bring in additional, experienced management with the funding, to fill the void you leave.

An MBO can be easier as the staff and management will be aware of all past and current issues, how the business is run and any potential problems. So, the due diligence process should be a lot quicker and the warranties a lot lighter. You could also stay involved as a Non- Executive Director, perhaps a couple of days a month, to assist with any problems that might crop up. You may also decide to stay partially invested to share in some of the future growth of the company. The main questions are whether there is enough talent and capability in the existing team to take over running the company. And where they would get enough funding or backing (perhaps from Private Equity) to make this a reality.

When approaching my MBO back in 1999, I had access to funding after my involvement in ValueInsurance.com. Consequently, I phoned up the Chief Financial Officer in the group head office, in New York, to ask about buying Intermediary Systems and Geological Information Systems, subsidiary companies in the group. There had been a recent divestment in a risk modelling firm I'd been involved in, called EQECAT.

The timing was perfect. The strategy of our USA owners, a reinsurance broker, at the time was to focus more on consulting with access to all vendor risk models, rather than owning a share of one of the main suppliers and being tied to one view of the world. So, I knew if I pitched the proposal right, there was a chance he would be receptive. His first question back, after hearing me out and then pausing for about ten seconds, though it seemed much longer, was:

"Have you got the finance?"

"Yes", I replied,

"Oh, well OK, let's have a more detailed chat the next time I come over to London",

Eighteen months later we signed on the dotted line. Extracting a subsidiary from a large multi-national S&P 500 company takes a lot of time. There are many hoops to jump through in large organisations, and it is probably fair to say that it will be a lot slower than executing an MBO from a private company.

Trade sale to a large corporate

A trade sale, to a large corporate company buyer, where there are clear synergies and growth initiatives to take advantage of, is the most common route to exit. It is also likely to yield a larger return on your investment than selling to staff or management. And is more likely to enable you to have a clean exit from the business, if that is what you want. A trade buyer usually acquires the equity for the whole company. There may be an earn-out element though it is generally small relative to the size of deal.

In a buyers-market you may have deals proposed that are heavily structured towards an earn-out and where you are locked into working for the new company for a long period. This is something I wouldn't necessarily recommend. Don't cede control unless you have taken the bulk of your money out and have the option to head for the door should things not work out.

In most trade deals, beyond a warranty period of maybe a couple of years, the proceeds from a sale are yours.

Private Equity (PE)

With other options you remain invested. For example, selling a majority stake to a PE firm may enable you to take some money out of the business, though you would be expected to keep a significant share invested. You would also be committing to another 5 years or so of involvement in the firm.

IPO

An IPO is when a company lists on a stock exchange and sells its shares to the public. The returns can be considerably larger than the other options, sometimes huge, as we have seen for a few of those that make it to an IPO.

One of the biggest differences between this and selling to a PE firm is the cost of the preparation, time commitment with bankers, lawyers and accountants, and the regulatory filings necessary. You first select an investment bank and then go through the due diligence, regulatory filings, setting the price range and then taking to market[4]. The whole process is longer and more time consuming than other routes open to you. There is also risk associated with this, along with the significant cost to implement, of changes in the economic climate impacting share prices and investor appetite.

In addition, there are normally restrictions on when insiders can sell their shares, for example, a 'lock-up' period of at least 6 months after listing on a stock market is typical before you can sell any of your stock. Of course, the price by then may have dropped considerably.

Some of the IPO's in 2019-2020 have listed and seen remarkably high valuations. For example, Zynga, a social games maker, saw the share price go so high on its debut to the stock market, that it made the founder Mark Pincus an instant billionaire. You need to consider the current economic climate, the likelihood of success, and how well shares in your type of business have fared in the market. This is more risk to consider, though balanced against this are the rewards, for the minority successfully making it down this route they can be enormous.

Which route is the one for you?

An entrepreneur with big, ambitious plans for their company, would perhaps consider taking their business to an IPO.

In my view the firm would need to be highly scalable, the products relevant in international markets and the opportunity to reach unicorn status possible. The returns going down this route can be immense, though you are taking bigger risks, and even fewer companies succeed down this path. Not only is this a risk appetite versus reward issue, but also a question of skills, abilities, and competence, as well as motivation and passion.

One thing to consider, as was my dilemma: Where do your skills, capability, strengths, and passion reside? The skillset required to start a company from a blank sheet of paper, then get it up and running are different to establishing the firm as a cash machine. Taking the business to the next level, scaling it further into a larger corporation, and running larger pools of people across multiple site locations is more about management, strategy combined with politics and administration – a different skillset yet again.

Most entrepreneurs are great at starting and building businesses, are superbly creative, yet are not comfortable in corporate life, managing huge groups of people, and coping with ever larger amounts of bureaucracy as the company grows. This is probably the main reason that 50% of founders get kicked out of the companies they founded or removed as the CEO within 18 months after a major funding event.

Where is your competence? How adaptable are you? What energises you?

You need to be clear what you want before you progress down one of the paths available for the company.

A question of control

One of the main variances between the options available to you is the amount of control and influence you want to retain in the business. A trade buyer would acquire the whole company equity and the founder or founders would become employees with the strategy dictated from above by the group company. You switch from being a decision maker to a decision taker. The first six months to a year post deal execution will be focused on integration into the group structure and adoption or transition to the culture of the acquiring group.

In other options you will have more influence post deal, there will be a greater potential upside, though there is always the possibility you may be replaced in your current role by someone else. A PE firm, though taking a controlling share and vote, would still be largely reliant and keen to retain the management team. They would look to the management to have more of a say in leading the strategy and future direction of the business. The first year is more likely to be spent looking at how costs can be more efficiently controlled, at leveraging expertise from the PE's network or other businesses, and what additional talent or investment is required to ramp up growth.

That said, the PE firm will be looking at your business and asking; 'Is this founder up to the task of leading the next phase of growth?' You have ceded control so if there is a downturn in the business and the numbers start looking poor you might find yourself out of a job.

10.4 What should you do first once you have decided to sell?

The first thing to do having decided you want to sell your company is to hire professional advisors with experience in your niche market. Given the importance of the transaction, make sure you have the best possible advice to give yourself the greatest chance of a positive result.

Investment Banks

There is a whole raft of advisors that can provide support with different parts of the process. Investment Banks are hired to help take a company through to an IPO. They do get involved in trade sales and marketing businesses to PE firms, though they are an expensive option, so it will normally be medium and larger companies who hire their services when going down this route.

Specialist Merger & Acquisition Advisors

M&A advisors help prepare businesses for sale, run the process on behalf of the seller and can lead negotiations with potential buyers.

In the successful transactions that I have been involved in we have always hired professional M&A advisory firms. Though this will cost you a few percentage points on the deal it is money well spent. Hiring professional advisors that have a lot of experience in selling companies is extremely important in my view. At the start they can help you prepare the business for sale, by initially carrying out a gap analysis comparing where you are now to where you need to be. Being able to highlight what needs to be tidied up is hard to appreciate, especially if you haven't been through the process before.

Advisors can then guide you, step by step, through the whole process. From getting the company into a 'go to market' ready for sale state, to approaching potential purchasers, negotiating on your behalf, evaluating offers, and then assisting in taking a deal through to completion.

Professional advisors will also have a network of buyer contacts across different markets that they can tap into. They will help to prepare a Confidential Information Memorandum, slide deck and high-quality supporting sales materials. You will need these as sales tools to support the process, and you want them to have been professionally produced, with great design, reflecting the quality of the business. It will be noticeable if they are PowerPoint slides you 'cobbled' together yourself the night before a presentation with potential acquirers.

Advisors will also help in thinking about synergies, and in tweaking and tailoring each presentation, to make sure that you customize each pitch appropriately. More significantly, they can act as a buffer between you and the buyer, resolving issues and running negotiations on your behalf without any emotional involvement. Having gone through the process with similar companies in your sector, they will have the experience of how to handle different issues, how to approach blockages cropping up from time to time, and what has worked to resolve them in the past.

When selecting advisors to work with you should do some due diligence of your own. You want to make sure you pick a firm that has sold similar companies in your sector before, that has contacts with acquiring organisations most relevant to you and a deep understanding of your business area.

Speak to a few different outfits with experience in your field and select a team you feel you can work with, you can trust, and ideally with a network spanning different industry sectors including the niche you work in.

The larger corporate trade buyers, especially in the technology space, will tend to have their own in-house merger & acquisition specialists. Candidly, the professional advisory firms will often have strong relationships with these people, and notably also, associations with senior leaders higher up the food chain. Being able to tap into those contacts, get the inside view on previous deals, and get a steer on how to ensure a productive process is what you are paying for.

I would also suggest considering advisors with an international reach as well as the domestic market buyer networks to tap into. In the technology space, international buyers are sometimes eager to break into a new territory or new sector. The appetite to enter a new market may drive a higher valuation, as international companies will frequently be willing to pay a premium to gain entry to new foreign territories. They look to acquire a foothold through a local team, and then use this as a base to expand out from.

Some advisory companies specialise in certain sectors and have much better networks in their main area of focus. One thing I would recommend is to do your homework, ask around the market, look on-line and in your trade press. What recent deals have completed and who were the advisors?

Find a firm with experience, knowledge and contacts in your niche area and a track record of successful deals.

I worked with Deloitte to sell my last company, following a personal recommendation from a friend, after the sale of his business, a large transaction successfully completed in the UK technology space. We were very satisfied with the work they did in helping to sell Business Insight and with the commitment the guys that worked with us showed.

In the sale of ISL we were guided by another large firm. It was certainly worth having advisors help us through the process, though in that case, I did not feel they were quite as effective. In hindsight, they lacked sector specific knowledge, buyer contacts, and experience in our niche area. So, choose carefully. There are plenty of good M&A advisory firms out there. Ideally you need to start looking for a firm to help you at least two years out from your ideal time of sale completion, to ensure the business is in a sale ready 'go-to-market' state 12 months out.

What you should NOT do is try to run the process by yourself after getting an approach from an interested buyer. You are unlikely to get a full price, or a well-structured deal, and the odds are it is likely to fail - as I found out on the one occasion that I was involved in selling a business without a specialist firm running the process.

<u>Lawyers</u>

You will need the support of a quality legal firm with involvement from the moment you start engaging with potential buyers. From the confidentiality agreement, negotiation of the letter of intent, through the due diligence phase and running a data room, to the final negotiating of the sale and purchase agreement, warranties, and disclosure letter. It is another important element where you need experienced support, a prominent firm and not a small outfit from your local town.

A word of advice:

When selecting a legal firm to help, one thing I would recommend is to check that none of the legal advisors, or people involved in the negotiations have any previous personal connections or worked with the people on the other side of the table. I had one aborted transaction and during this we had trouble communicating with the buyer's lawyer who worked for a local firm in London. The guy never turned up to a meeting, instead insisting on joining by phone or communicating by email. We struggled to make any progress on anything. I later found out that he had previously worked with our lawyer earlier in his career. Whatever the history there, it hindered our deal.

On this occasion, the lack of cooperation made us feel that we weren't going to get a fair agreement. We walked away from the table after a lengthy process, and after incurring significant cost. We had not appointed professional M&A advisors focused on our market sector. In hindsight, this was a mistake, and an experienced firm may have been able to step in and resolve the matter.

Accountants

Specialist accountants, particularly in relation to deal structure and the tax implications, are also worth tapping into to ensure that the agreement is structured as well as it can be for you, that your forecasts and accounts are robust, and that they are presented to showcase the business in the best possible way.

Tech due diligence firms

Tech due diligence firms are positioned to provide an independent view on the expertise within the target firm. For example, many firms state that they are technology specialists in artificial intelligence (AI), machine learning or data science, yet when you dig beneath the surface you often find the level of expertise is thin. It is a marketing gimmick rather than a core competence. Frequently PE firms don't have the depth of technical knowledge in house to assess whether a firm has core expertise or not, buyers are therefore suspicious, and so an independent view can help move due diligence along quicker.

How much might these advisors cost?

It depends on the scope and amount of work required. The lawyers in the process and accountants offering tax advice will usually bill you by the hour, and the number and seniority of people involved. Having been through the process numerous times, they should give you an indicative estimate of the likely cost before you engage them. For a deal between £10M and £50M, the price should be less than 1% and negligible in the grand scheme of things.

The cost of strategic M&A sell-side advisors will depend on whether you hire a firm to do an exit only transaction, carry out partial marketing targeted at several potential buyers or hire them to do a whole strategic and marketing exercise. You might also bring in a specialist firm two years out from a sales process to help with preparatory work, to increase credibility amongst potential buyers, and to assist with developing future strategic growth initiatives. They will help construct a convincing, attractive narrative to create a 'buzz' and heightened interest around the business, though it will also involve more time and cost more money. Consequently, there can be a large spread in the costs of M&A advisors related to different deals.

Generally, though, there will usually be a fee to cover the initial time cost of advisors working on the deal, plus in addition, a much larger success fee linked to the final enterprise value achieved. The size of the deal, the length of time and amount of work involved, and the complexity of the business will all be factors influencing cost. It is also worth considering that a deal value of £6M often involves as much work for advisors to complete as a deal of £12M. There are published reports via the internet on the typical costs of advisors from past transactions[5].

By and large, hiring a reputable firm to do a full marketing exercise, with some preparatory work, including lawyers' fees to do all the legal work, may cost you between 3%-5% of a deal with an enterprise value between £10M and £50M. A range of 3%-5% is in line with my own experience. An exit-only transaction, perhaps where the buyer has already shown interest or made an approach, would involve a lot less work and so the cost of M&A advisors would be significantly less.

10.5 What are the risks to be aware of when taking your business to market?

Taking your business to market is not without risk or cost for that matter. You need to protect your potential downside when selling your business and think about the consequences of a failed process.

Professional advisors can be expensive, and if the process fails or is aborted part of the way through, bills will still have to be paid. When hiring advisors incentivise them with a fee structure linked to the success of the deal, negotiate terms that protect your downside, and agree a much lower fee to cover costs should the process fail or be abandoned part of the way through.

The amount of management time required to sell a company is substantial. There is a potential cost to your business from you and your management team being taken away from the day to day running of the firm. Before you enter a process think about who will run the day-to-day operations, how the business is going to operate and who can keep things moving forward if you and other leaders are focused on the sale. Ensure you have adequate cover and that things will not slip.

You also need to consider risk to the confidentiality of your intellectual property (IP) by taking your company to market. The wider the number of potential buyers receiving materials about your business, the greater the risk. Make sure you safeguard your IP throughout the process as much as you can. You will have to balance lengthening the sales activity and the risk of IP leakage in a wider search, against a realization that you may not manage to engineer a competitive auction for the firm, and consequently, may not achieve a full price.

In past transactions we decided on the tactic of only approaching a small number of potential buyers we thought would be the best fit to take the company to the next level. I have always had some concerns about giving away ideas, IP leakage and drawing attention to exactly how well we are doing in our market niche.

When you take your company to market, you will need to share some of the success stories and your growth ideas. A buyer will also want to see documentation and proof of what you are saying during the due diligence process. You need to balance protecting your IP against maintaining trust and not appearing to the buyer to be hiding anything.

There is always a danger that you will help competitors.

The process might also ignite interest in your market from companies currently focused elsewhere. If the process is not successful, you might feel like you are in a worse position than if you hadn't taken the business to market. Competitors may now be armed with information and a deeper understanding of your products that could be used against you in future business pitches.

Once competitors know your products, who your customers are and the details of your contracts, you can't take that information back. Confidentiality agreements are also difficult to enforce, and not everyone will behave honourably.

When considering what information to provide think about whether you may have a problem if the deal fails to close.

Will you be at a major disadvantage in the market if a specific piece of information was in the public domain?

Does your competitor now know your secret sauce?

Some items, such as product specifications, software code, customer names (excluding those in the public domain) shouldn't need to be revealed at all until after the deal completes. There will also be protections in the Sale and Purchase Agreement (SPA) for the buyer to enforce if you have misrepresented anything. There is no need for the other party to have access to your detailed IP.

Hold back as much commercially sensitive information as you think you can, after discussions with your advisors, to as late in the process as possible.

10.6 What are large corporate companies and PE firms looking for when acquiring smaller tech businesses?

Larger acquiring companies are usually looking to widen their capability, acquire new expertise and deepen their knowledge base. They also search for businesses to help them gain access to new markets and new territories.

Frequently they will examine the fit of target companies across a few parameters or key distinctives. Such as the level of domain expertise in the target company, whether the company has any unique data assets, new technologies or relevant intellectual property.

Acquirers will also give a lot of thought to potential synergies with their own company. Where are opportunities for costs to be saved? Where could new revenue streams be generated? Do the returns from combining resources from both companies exceed the sum of the parts? For example, where the target company has a software platform with potential for expansion, perhaps a product with potential use cases in other markets, or products that could be launched into new territories.

Some larger companies absorb smaller competitors to increase their market share before they grow to be more of a threat, as we have seen in the technology space on numerous occasions in recent years.

PE firms look to make money and get a return for investors in their fund. They want aggressive growth and typically want a 35% return over 3 to 5 years. They will push hard to get growth quickly either by leveraging assets from other firms they own, finding ways to reduce costs or helping firms to scale further through access to their networks and through supporting expertise to management.

What is certainly common to all buyers is their quest for fast growing, well run firms. They will all be seduced by the future growth opportunities of the business. In the time leading up to writing this book there has been more of a fixation with revenue growth at the expense of underlying profit margins, certainly in the technology market. My own view is that you ideally should also have a focus on profitable growth, it is the best way to ensure you don't fail before you are able to scale or before you run out of runway. Consequently, give some thought to how you position your business for sale, the potential synergies with potential buyers, and the growth initiatives that would be compelling for larger companies operating in your sector.

Do you have a 5-year strategic plan identifying how the company is going to continue increasing its revenues?

Do you have some striking growth initiatives with a compelling narrative that a buyer would find attractive?

10.7 What is a typical sales process?

The process to sell a business is more involved and takes a lot more time and effort than many founders anticipate.

In the exhibit on the following page, there is an example of a typical sale process and the chronological steps involved in completing a deal with a trade buyer. You should be bringing in professional advisors experienced in your sector ideally at least two years out from when you would like a deal to complete. This example is a timeline outlining the main activities and milestones that an advisor might put in front of you. It is in line with my own experience, when it worked, and will give a reasonable chance of success. It spans a two-year timeframe.

This includes all the time you should contemplate earmarking to do preparatory work required to get your business into shape. For example, where are you with compliance? What contracts do you have in place? Are there change of control clauses in your contracts with clients or suppliers that you need to get altered before you go to market?

In the Tech industry, making sure the contracts are in place and the IP is secure are vitally important. All the contracts need to be airtight and up to date, reflecting current legislation across all the different areas of your business. From employees and the lease for the office, through to raw material suppliers and your customers. Do you have robust, signed contractual agreements in place or has business been undertaken on a handshake or an exchange of emails?

Steps 1 & 2 – Research & approach advisors.

The example schedule below, is a typical timeline that I have witnessed across several different tech transactions on the buyer and seller side. It starts with the time you need to factor in to research company valuations, and to speak to several professional advisors, about what they can each offer, and to gain a consensus opinion across several perspectives on the range of values you might achieve. This needs to be discussed with your board, to decide if the value range meets your expectations, to discover the advisors providing the best fit to assist in the process, and more importantly, whether you wish to progress further.

Steps 3 & 4 – Appoint advisors, then risk audit/gap analysis & plan.

You then need to choose and appoint your professional advisors. They will work with you to initially review the business and carry out a risk audit and gap analysis.

Where are you now and where does the business need to be to take it to market, to have a reasonable chance of a successful exit.

Your advisors will help with an initial audit of key areas of the business, making sure that a process wouldn't be tripped up by something unacceptable to a buyer, such as a lack of airtight contractual agreements being in place.

Step 5 – Validate growth initiatives & work on financial plans.

You need to showcase the business in the best possible light and have compelling growth initiatives that will attract buyer interest. You have to work with your advisors putting together a strong narrative, a vision for the future and reflect this in a plan.

You should articulate your base, best and worst-case scenarios in your projections with assumptions and numbers attached to each.

Your advisor will also examine your financial statements and help to ensure that they are presented in the most attractive way. For example, if you, as owner, are in the numbers, your costs should be taken out and highlighted as a separate line. Equally, if you have any one-off outlays or Non-Executive Directors, these costs should be taken out and that should drop through to the profit line.

You need to scrutinize your business model, plans, and revisit your forecasts and financial statements. This all needs to be professionally presented and 'polished' to take to buyers.

Steps 6 & 7 – Research lists of companies to approach & send out a 'Teaser' to gauge market interest. Initial 'warm-up' conversations.

When the business is nearing 'go-to-market' readiness, your advisors will research the lists of potential companies that may be interested. They will test out the market appetite, gauging buyer response by sending them all a one-page flyer, giving an anonymized overview of the business. They refer to this as a 'Teaser' which advisors use to 'warm-up' potential purchasers, assess interest, and initiate some early discussions without having to worry about confidentiality agreements.

Steps 8 to 11 – Advisors discuss interest with board, prepare Confidential Information Memorandum (CIM), research potential synergies with companies showing interest and create focused CIM's and slide decks for meetings.

Following feedback from the Teaser and initial conversations that the advisor has had in the market the board will agree on the next steps. Will you approach a limited number of buyers or open the process to a wider group of companies? You will need to research and work out how to articulate and highlight any synergies with potential parties showing an interest in deeper discussions.

In parallel with this you will be working with your advisors and management board on preparing all the marketing materials, such as a Confidential Information Memorandum, and management pitch deck. [Please note an example list of what is usually included in a confidential sales memorandum is in the appendix at the end of this section. A pitch deck is also usually produced as a summary from this for management to present the business to buyers].

Steps 12 & 13 – Agree NDA's with interested parties and then issue marketing presentation materials (management slide deck)

The next step is to send out a confidentiality agreement to each company showing an interest, get that agreed and then send them the focused management slide deck. Don't send out the more detailed CIM until you are sure of the level of interest and that they aren't just fishing for information. A number will then hopefully respond, want to arrange a meeting with the management team, and to go through the slide deck in detail.

Example Sales Process

Typical steps involved in selling your business in a trade sale to a large corporate buyer

Legend: ■ Elapsed time

PERIODS (MONTHS): -1 1 2 3 4 5 6 7 8 9 10 11 12 13 14 15 16 17 18 19 20 21 22 23 24

STEP IN PROCESS	START	DURATION
Research, discuss and agree exit options with board. Set expectations.	1	2
Approach advisors/Understand realistic value range	2	2
Select Advisors/Agree workplan milestones/Negotiate contract terms	3	1
Prepare for sale / Risk Audit / Ensure contracts are airtight/ Resolve any issues	2	12
Validate growth initiatives / Develop financial Plans & forecasts with advisors	4	2
Advisor does research and sends 'Teaser' to long list of potential buyers	6	2
Initial warm-up conversations (Advisor led)	6	2
Advisor discusses market interest with board, agrees next steps and buyer list	8	1
Prepare confidential sales memorandum & slide decks for presentation	9	1
Research synergies & create focused slide decks for list of target buyers	10	1
Agree NDAs with interested parties	11	1
Issue marketing presentation materials (slide decks/sales memo)	12	1
Agree/deliver initial presentations/meetings with interested buyers	12	2
Further meetings with buyer subset/requests for further info	14	2
Non-binding proposals/Letters of Intent received	15	2
Competitive auction, advisor negotiates, front runners emerge	17	1
Evaluate offers & deal structure, select preferred buyer	17	1
Negotiate, agree & execute Letter of Intent	18	2
Buyer Due Diligence of business	20	4
Negotiate Sale & Purchase Agreement\Warranties\Disclosure letter	22	3
Agree completion accounts\Close contract negotiations	24	1
Execute contracts	24	

Steps 14 & 15 – Management team present to interested parties, then there are requests for further information and potentially further meetings.

There will then be several focused presentations from management to potential buyers of the business. There may be further follow-on meetings and discussions, lots of questions to answer, requests for further information and hopefully plenty of interest. You will issue the CIM and more financial data to those requesting more detail prior to putting in a non-binding proposal.

Steps 16 & 17 – Letters of Intent received, competitive auction. Front runner emerges.

You then need to wait for proposals from interested parties, or what is called a 'Letter of Intent', outlining an offer for the business.

This can take some time, particularly for large corporate buyers. They will need to produce their own in-house business case, look at the growth opportunities, compare the seller case versus their own models, and put these in-front of their investment committee. The value range will be calculated and an initial offer prepared, before being agreed and formally signed off by the main board.

Having been on the buyer side I know this process can take some time. Large corporate acquirers going through the process regularly will have guidelines and a standard procedure that they always follow. The advantage is they usually have dedicated resource and once committed to a process it should have a strong chance of running its course. Unless obviously, there is a major underlying problem with the target company.

Once the offers come back in, the advisors will look at each in detail, the structure, the terms, and the fine detail, before discussing the next steps with the board. When there are several front runners, the advisor will agree with the board who to go back to, and then try to negotiate better terms. There may or may not be several rounds of bidding before a preferred buyer is selected.

Step 18 – Negotiate Letter of Intent (LOI) with frontrunner, agree and execute.

There will be some fine details to agree, for example how long will you be staying with the business and on what terms. If you are not quite happy with the structure of the deal, you need to find out if this can be tweaked slightly. You also need to determine the terms of the earn-out and any targets to be achieved. Once this has been ironed out and agreed the LOI can be agreed and executed.

Step 19 – Buyer due diligence of business

The buyer will then start the due diligence of your business, looking at every aspect in detail. There will be list upon list of questions to answer across all different areas of the business. Your lawyer will also set-up a virtual data room where all the documents relating to the firm can be inspected such as contracts, financial statements, plans, board minutes etc. There will be numerous conference calls with technical staff to verify the competence of the technical team and the finances will be put under a microscope.

The due diligence phase can be extremely time consuming and drag on for months. It is a major distraction for the management team and can have a knock-on effect on the day-to-day operations of the business.

Step 20 – Negotiate the sales & purchase agreement (SPA) (warranties/disclosure letter)

Once the due diligence phase has been running for a while, often a month or two, the buyer will issue a sales & purchase agreement (SPA) to acquire the business. There will then be a period of negotiation where the document is fired back and forth until each point has been agreed. This will be running in parallel to the due diligence phase.

It can take some time to get the agreement to a position that is acceptable to both sides. It has always been months of elapsed time in the deals I have been involved in. It can be quicker though regularly the negotiations take a lot longer than you expect.

Step 21 – Agree completion accounts/close contract negotiations.

Invariably you need to get together in person with the buyer side to agree the final few outstanding points. You will also need to agree the position of the accounts when the business is transferred over.

There are a couple of options. The first being to agree the cash, debt and working capital position of the accounts in advance at an agreed date prior to completion, something called a 'Locked Box'[3]. This will give some certainty to the final price and be written into the SPA prior to the completion of the deal.

The alternative is to produce a set of completion accounts based on the position of the business on the day the deal is completed, and the agreement executed. The completion accounts need to be prepared and agreed by both sides, and any adjustment made to the final price in the SPA prior to signing. This can lead to disagreements between accountants on both sides at the eleventh hour, so the Locked Box is more popular.

Step 22 – Execute contracts, then go out and celebrate!

Whew! You have finally made it to signing the paperwork.

As you can see there is plenty of work and numerous different steps to go through.

Frankly, there is a lot to do before you even go to market – certainly if you want to give yourself the best chance of a successful outcome.

Of course, you can skip a few steps in preparing the business, in searching for the best advisors that fit with your company, and in doing thorough research. That will most likely result in failure, the deal being derailed after putting in substantial time, considerable effort, and incurring significant cost.

Two of the most common reasons that deals fall over are due to either the business not being prepared internally, or the market not being prepared externally.

For a tech business, if you don't have airtight contracts and clear ownership of the intellectual property rights the deal will immediately de-rail as soon as you enter the buyer due diligence phase. Trade buyers are also not immediately going to spend millions of pounds or dollars on a firm that they aren't aware of or where they don't know the management team. Frequently advisors will suggest promoting the company to potential interested parties a couple of years before taking it to market. Buyers then have time to get to know the management team, and to understand the organisation in a little more detail.

Adequate preparation and socializing of the business are essential if you want to increase your chances of a successful outcome.

Things are made a lot easier if you think about your exit when you start your company. Look to set everything up properly from day one, mindful that eventually it will be sold. That way the whole process from start to completion can be considerably shorter, though it will still usually be around 12 months, from the initial go to market 'ready' state to completion of the deal.

Whichever route you take, the time required is considerable, and the demands on management time substantial.

Before starting a process, you need to have some idea of what your company is worth. In the next chapter we briefly cover some of the common ways used to estimate value and what a business might sell for in the market.

References / Further reading

1.https://www.forbes.com/sites/richardparker/2016/10/24/the-business-for-sale-marketplace-why-90-of-listings-never-sell/

2. https://techcrunch.com/2017/05/17/heres-how-likely-your-startup-is-to-get-acquired-at-any-stage/

3. Locking_in_Value_Sept_2018.pdf (deloitte.com)

4.www.corporatefinanceinstitute.com/resources/knowledge/finance/ipo-process/

5. www.statista.com/statistics/952326/worldwide-advisory-fees-for--successful-mergers-and-acquisitions.

Key takeaways

• Selling a company is not easy. Understand your own motives and reasons to sell now. Is the business in good shape and are market conditions attractive?

• Is this the right point in the company's development to sell? You should discuss, consider alternatives, and reach a consensus with your board on the best way forward.

• What do you intend doing after the sale? Are you staying with the business or leaving to pursue other things?

• Hire professional M&A advisors experienced in your market niche to help sell your business.

• Thorough preparation is vital before you go to market. Carry out a gap analysis with your advisors to understand what is required to get the business into a 'go-to' market ready state.

• Protect your downside when hiring advisors and ensure your business is not neglected during the process.

• The sales process is often long and involved. Be aware that it takes a lot of management time and can be a major distraction from your day-to-day responsibilities.

• Safeguard your IP and the company assets throughout the process. A lot of deals fail to close, make sure you are not at a disadvantage in the market should this happen.

• Large companies looking to acquire small businesses are searching for unique assets, new technologies, and synergies with their own operation. They are also in the hunt for fast growing, profitable, well run firms.

• Give some thought to how you position your business for sale, the potential synergies, and the growth initiatives that would be compelling for larger companies operating in your sector.

HOMEWORK

Now over to you. Before you enter a sales process, you need to know exactly where your business is in its development, what the end goal is, and be aligned with your board. Answer the questions below and the list will help to guide you before you start the process.

1. *Write down your reasons for selling now. What is your aspirational price for selling the business? Is this aligned with your board?*

2. *Write down a short list of M&A advisors with experience in your sector. Have they successfully sold similar businesses? Do they have relationships with senior leaders in potential acquiring companies? What are the initial valuation ranges for your business they believe could be achieved when going to market?*

3. *Make a list of large companies you know of in your sector that may be interested in acquiring your company. What potential synergies with your business immediately spring to mind if you were acquired by each of these firms?*

4. *What growth initiatives do you have that a buyer would find compelling? What impact will they have on revenues and when can they be delivered?*

CHAPTER 11: WHAT IS MY COMPANY WORTH AND HOW MIGHT I GET A FULL PRICE?

'Valuing a business is part art and part science'

- Warren Buffett

Before you embark on taking your business to market, through a long and potentially expensive sale process, the obvious first question to ask is:

'*What is it worth?*'

And the simple answer to that is: Only what someone is willing to pay for it at the time.

People will have different perspectives on value, depending on what is driving their interest in your business, the availability of similar companies, market conditions, and how they view the potential synergies with their own firm.

Private companies are illiquid assets. And what you consider your business might be worth, after years of hard graft, toil, and personal investment, may bear little comparison to what someone is prepared to pay. You may think your operation is worth millions, and that may be true. You may have some exciting new technology platform, slick software, an enviable client base, a recognized brand, and high recurring revenues. But until you take your company to the open market, you will not know for sure what price it will attain.

How do you get an idea of the valuation range before you decide to embark on a process to sell?

The future cash flows that you believe will be generated by the business primarily underpin the value, and any calculation of what the company is worth.

So, firstly, you need to understand what is driving the cashflows? How fast can the business grow its revenues, and what sort of return on capital does it earn? Then you need to think about the market in which your firm operates:

How big can this business get?

What is the state of the market in which the company operates?

Is it expanding? Or is the firm going to be reliant on taking market share from competitors once past a specific size?

A combination of the cash flow potential and the return on capital drives the intrinsic value of a business.

One question you should be asking is what type of organisations are likely to be interested in acquiring my firm? Are they likely to be technical companies, data or information businesses or analytics focused? Are they going to be domestic or multi-national firms? What values are these companies currently trading at on public stock markets? The typical share price multiples of large corporate buyers will have an influence on what they are prepared to pay for your firm.

If acquiring companies in your sector are trading on public stock markets at over 20x multiples of the ratio of enterprise value to EBIT, then acquiring your company at a multiple of 10x-12x the same ratio would be attractive to them. The scalability of some technology businesses has led to sky high multiples in the USA on the NASDAQ in recent times. In turn this has led to continued high prices paid for private tech businesses in trade deals.

Speak to a few professional advisors experienced in buying and selling companies in your niche market, as a sensible first step. You can tap into their knowledge base, understand the current market activity, and access their archives of recent historical sales information. It will help to estimate a valuation range.

Repeat this exercise with two or three advisory firms and use this as part of a beauty parade to select the partner you can work with. The information you receive will inform your board discussions on how you move forward from there.

11.1 What are the common methods used to value a business?

Comparable Company Analysis (using EBITDA Multiple)

One of the most common ways to value a private company is through comparison to similar businesses in the same industry, both public and private.

Professional Advisors will select relevant, publicly traded companies and work out the current valuations of those businesses. Valuation in this context usually involves first calculating the enterprise value (EV), a measure of a company's total worth. It is the market capitalization of a firm's equity plus the cash and after subtracting any debt.

They will also collate data from recent private company transactions in your market and compare this against the profile of your company. They will search for firms of similar size, with comparable growth rates, levels of debt and returns on capital, and find examples of sales of matching firms. The calculation of a value range to associate with your business will then have more meaning. The enterprise value for this group being the total price, including cash and debt, that the company was able to achieve when taken to market.

Specific metrics of the businesses within each group are related to the enterprise value (EV) to measure performance and for relative comparison with other companies. The ratio of EV and each metric provide some easily comparable figures. Within each group these are then adjusted to be relevant to your company. The public company data must be adjusted for marketability, size of business and any other risk factor relevant to your firm.

Your advisor will calculate the valuation measures for each peer group of public and private company data, estimating a tentative range of metrics to compare back to your business. The range of performance ratios will help to understand the potential value of your company, and an advisor will use this as a basis to give a tentative estimate of what your firm might sell for when taken to market.

Valuation expressed using this comparative method is usually as a ratio of EV divided by recurring revenues, normalised sales turnover, or more generally accepted, a metric such as 'EBITDA', which stands for 'Earnings Before Interest Taxation, Depreciation[1] and Amortisation[2]'.

EBITDA is a measure of operating profitability and cash flow generated by a business and is an easily comparable, standard measure of how a company is performing. It is a standard metric, and probably the most used in estimating private company valuations, with a few advantages, such as allowing easy comparison between territories, and ignoring disparities in local taxation and interest rates. It is also useful for comparing companies with different capital structures, as often there are significant variations in the capital requirements between different sectors, and in the rates in which capital assets depreciate.

EBITDA as a metric does have some drawbacks though, as it ignores the financing costs of the business, takes no account of size, or the capital required to run a company. It can also mask or exaggerate the performance of firms that are highly capital intensive or heavily indebted.

Table 15 below shows the average EV/EBITDA multiples for all publicly traded companies in selected technology sectors across the main markets around the World. It is based on data published by Professor Aswath Damodaran[3], a leading authority on asset and company valuations, regarding all publicly traded companies.

Globally, across all markets and industry sectors, the average EV/EBITDA multiple in January 2020 was 14.1 (reducing to 11.2 when excluding Financial Services). The 'Technology Firm' definition used below was based on my grouping of the Industry sector data. It has a higher valuation on average compared to other industry sectors, and on a global scale, the average multiple across all Technology firms was 19.4x in January 2020.

TABLE 15 SHOWING PERFORMANCE MULTIPLES (IN TERMS OF EV/EBITDA) FOR ALL PUBLICLY TRADED COMPANIES ACROSS SELECTED TECHNOLOGY SECTORS JANUARY 2020

PERFORMANCE MULTIPLES BY TERRITORY (Jan 2020)	USA		WESTERN EUROPE		JAPAN		EMERGING MARKETS (including CHINA)		GLOBAL	
Industry Sector	Number of Firms	EV/EBITDA	Number of Firms	EV/EBITDA	Number of Firms	EV/EBITDA	Number of Firms	EV/EBITDA	Number of Firms	EV/EBITDA
Biotechnology (Drugs)	503	13.3	202	22.7	24	69.1	206	32.8	1024	16.0
Pharmaceuticals (Drugs)	267	14.6	116	13.9	40	14.0	638	17.4	1263	14.5
Green & Renewable Energy	22	17.2	48	12.8	8	12.1	108	10.7	213	11.6
Healthcare (Products, Information & Information Services	371	23.0	276	31.0	70	25.6	312	32.1	1128	22.5
Information Services	69	26.4	30	21.1	17	17.3	75	17.2	215	25.3
Software (Entertainment & Internet)	116	20.5	76	18.5	80	10.5	80	24.1	411	20.7
Software (System & Application)	363	24.0	283	21.9	136	16.2	372	32.4	1375	24.3
Aerospace/Defense	77	14.9	49	13.6	2	8.4	89	17.2	238	14.7
Technology Firms	1788	18.8	1080	22.5	377	19.8	1880	24.4	5867	19.4
Total Market (All Industry Sectors)	7053	17.5	6702	12.7	3854	9.5	22402	12.7	44394	14.1
Total Market (without Financial Services	5878	13.8	5897	10.6	3665	8.9	20162	9.8	39677	11.2

SOURCE: Professor Aswarth Damodaran, Stern School of Business, New York University, January 2020

OK, so how is this useful?

An advisor assessing the value of a software or analytics company trading in the UK or USA would look at the table, noticing for software and information services businesses the average EV/EBITDA multiple for publicly traded companies was 21.1 in the UK and 23.6 in the USA. They would then look at a selection of individual companies and estimate a range of values most relevant to the business they are valuing. To relate these data points to the private market, you need to take account of the lack of marketability and adjust for the size of the firm.

There is no easily accessible market for buyers and sellers of private businesses. So, when comparing valuations of listed companies, professional advisors will apply a discount factor to the EV/EBITDA multiple to arrive at an estimate for a private firm. Referred to as a discount for lack of marketability, valuation professionals will often have assessed pre- and post-IPO pricing of similar companies to estimate the appropriate adjustment factor.

Based on several published studies the discount factor is estimated to be in the range of 30%-50%[4]. So, if we applied this to the broad range of values in our definition above this would reduce the average multiple in the private sector for a software or information technology business to between (10.6 to 14.7) in the UK, and a range of (11.8 to 16.52) in the USA.

If the private company is also relatively small and heavily reliant on a few people, then a further adjustment will be applicable for smaller businesses to reflect this risk. For example, the average multiple may be discounted by a further 30% to take this risk into account, resulting in a range of (7.42 to 10.29) in the UK and (8.26 to 11.56) in the USA.

Discounted cashflow method

The discounted cash flow (DCF) method is another common way to value a company. It involves looking in detail at the financial plans of the firm, working out the likely stream of future cash earnings of the business, and then discounting these back to the present value using an estimate of risk. The discount rate or WACC (weighted average cost of capital) accounts for the time value of money and includes an element to compensate for the opportunity cost of the equity. It also includes an element to pay for the opportunity cost of the capital invested in the company, and any riskiness to the cash flows based on the company, e.g., if it is a small business.

You need a detailed financial plan and forecast, a deep understanding of applicable markets, and have a sense of what growth rates are realistically possible over the long term. Then the DCF method can generate a reasonable estimate of value.

To get started you first need to consider what today's products and services are worth, in terms of future earnings and cash flows. Then you need to give some thought to the opportunities, growth prospects and market potential that could sustain the future cash flows and expansion of the business.

The formula for the discounted cash flow method is $$\sum_{t=1}^{t=n} \frac{CE_{yeart}}{(1+r)^t}$$

This mathematical notation represents the value of the business as a sum of all the future free cash earnings at today's value, where CE represents the free cash, after tax and additional capital requirements. The additional capital requirements being in terms of operating expenditure (OPEX) and any additional capital expenditure (CAPEX), in year t. The on-going capital requirements, OPEX and CAPEX are both cash consuming, although hitting different parts of the balance sheet, and so need to be considered within the valuation.

The resulting calculation represents the future cash earnings in each year from year 1 to year n, these are discounted to the present-day value by the discount rate r, and then summed.

Or in a longer form notation:

Value (sum of DCF) $= \frac{Cash\ Earnings\ year_1}{(1+r)} + \frac{Cash\ Earnings\ year_2}{(1+r)2} +$
$\frac{Cash\ Earnings\ year_3}{(1+r)3} + ...$

$$... + \frac{Cash\ Earnings\ year_n}{(1+r)n}$$

Where 'r' is the discount rate or WACC reflecting the opportunity cost of the capital investment, the equity risk premium, and the risk to the cashflow. This discounts each future free cash amount after tax in each year to estimate the value of the cash today. These are all summed across the time horizon 'n' of your plan to a terminal value. In practical terms the projections forward will only be as valid as far as your assumptions of the business and market could be deemed reasonable.

It is exceedingly difficult to forecast beyond the usual planning horizon, typically five years. However, to calculate a current value for the business you must also consider what the operation is worth beyond that point. There are different ways to arrive at the perpetual value of the firm and a common way is to assume a multiple of the Year 5 cashflow number as the terminal value.

Another way is simply to assume that the business as it stands now would plateau beyond your forecast horizon, and then keep growing in perpetuity at a nominal rate, perhaps the rate of inflation plus x%, whatever you believe to be justifiable.

The formula to calculate the terminal value (Tv) using this method is:

$$Tv = \frac{CE_n(1+g)}{r-g}$$

Where:

CE is the free cashflow value in the last period of your forecast horizon,

g is the perpetual growth rate and

r is the discount rate and is usually referred to as the weighted average cost of capital (WACC).

The WACC is the blended average of the return required for debt and equity financing, and will depend on the mix of each, as well as the risk associated with the business being able to execute the plan. For example, a start-up with low or no revenues would have an extremely high WACC, perhaps more than 25%, reflecting the risk to future cashflows and the return required to compensate equity financing. For more established businesses, with more certainty around the future cashflow, the WACC would be lower.

The DCF method is highly dependent on the quality of the financial forecasts and the discount factor chosen.

When a seller presents a financial plan and forecast during a sale process the first thing a buyer will do is try to scrutinize the accuracy of the projections and plan. They will try to assess how credible your estimates are of future earnings.

What frequently frustrates buyers, as I have heard from colleagues and seen myself, are sellers putting in financial plans with 'hockey stick' type growth curves, with unsubstantiated, weak assumptions underpinning the forecasts. A lot of the time such plans are based on fantasy and guesswork and have little chance of being successful.

Putting in an aspirational but realistic plan is essential to maintain credibility in a process. It also enables a fair assessment of the value of your business. The buyer will have their own ideas on potential synergies and so will enhance the plan that you submit to justify any deal internally. If it starts from a credible base you will stand a better chance of gaining traction and of it moving along quicker in the process.

You should focus on producing a believable 5-year plan with ambitious but achievable stretch targets for future growth. Think carefully about your assumptions, the requirements for future capital, the trends in the market, and prepare evidence to justify the numbers in your plan. A time horizon longer than 5 years is exceedingly difficult for someone to estimate whether the assumptions and growth rates remain valid. Stick to the art of the possible. A buyer analyst will typically assess your assumptions, and model, before enhancing this and extrapolating the cashflows further.

Table 16 below shows an example of a fictitious software company in the B-to-B Widget market with strong recurring revenues and a growth rate of 15%. The business is still relatively small, has established a base in the market of £3M, has strong recurring revenues, is debt free, equity financed and the WACC is estimated at 15%. The perpetual growth rate is assumed to be 5% beyond the initial planning horizon. Using the DCF method to discount the forecast future cashflows and the continuing value (or terminal value) of the business to the net present value, the enterprise value in this example is £14M.

If we apply the EBITDA multiples method from the previous section for a software business, we find that the numbers are in a similar range. For example, a typical multiple for an established niche business in software or tech might attract a multiple in the range of 10x-12x EBITDA. Applying this to the Year 1 figure would indicate a similar valuation range of £13M-£15M.

TABLE 16 SIMPLE EXAMPLE OF A COMPANY VALUATION USING THE DISCOUNTED CASHFLOW METHOD

Hypothetical example for a software\analytics company (WIDGETS Market)

	Base	Year 1	Year 2	Year 3	Year 4	Year 5	Terminal Growth
Revenues	£3,000,000	£3,450,000	£3,967,500	£4,562,625	£5,247,019	£6,034,072	
Revenue Growth Rate		15%	15%	15%	15%	15%	5%
Operating Margin	35.00%	36.00%	37.00%	38.00%	39.00%	40.00%	
EBIT	£1,050,000	£1,242,000	£1,467,975	£1,733,798	£2,046,337	£2,413,629	
Taxes	£199,500	£235,980	£278,915	£329,422	£388,804	£458,589	
EBIT(1-t)	£850,500	£1,006,020	£1,189,060	£1,404,376	£1,657,533	£1,955,039	
+ Depreciation	£10,000	£70,000	£90,000	£110,000	£80,000	£110,000	
- Capital Expenditures	£150,000	£60,000	£60,000	£60,000	£150,000	£50,000	
- Change in Working Capital	£100,000	£100,000	£120,000	£120,000	£150,000	£150,000	
Free Cashflow to Equity (FCFF)	£610,500	£916,020	£1,099,060	£1,334,376	£1,437,533	£1,865,039	£1,958,291
EBITDA	£1,060,000	£1,312,000	£1,557,975	£1,843,798	£2,126,337	£2,523,629	

	Year 1	Year 2	Year 3	Year 4	Year 5	Terminal Value	SUM
Terminal Value						£19,582,911	
Discount factor (WACC)	87%	76%	66%	57%	50%	50%	
Present value (PV) of FCFF	£796,539	£831,047	£877,374	£821,914	£927,254	£9,791,456	£14,045,584

Sum of present value of free cash flows	£4,254,128	
PV of Terminal Value	£9,791,456	
Enterprise Value	£14,045,584	

EBITDA multiples method	10x	12x
Year 1 EBITDA	£13,120,000	£15,744,000

The WACC (Weighted Average Cost of Capital) used to discount the future cash flows to the present value is set at 15% in this example. It is the blended cost of capital and includes debt and equity financing.

For more details and a deeper dive into this area please refer to the references at the end of the chapter. For an owner/founder it is worth having a basic understanding however I would also recommend hiring some professional help in estimating a value for your business. Also recalculate the numbers using several methods and different scenarios, worst case, best case and baseline.

Trying a few alternative methods to value your business will help to home in on a sensible valuation range, and what you might expect when you go to market. It is worth having an appreciation of what is involved, though, I would always suggest that you enlist professional help to undertake these tasks in detail.

Replacement cost method

Another way to value a business is to consider what the asset value of the business is and what it would cost to replicate its current position.

In terms of physical assets such as factories, offices, computers, cars, if they are owned, they will be on the balance sheet at the current value. Any orders in the pipeline to be delivered, booked contractual work and cash in the bank, will also be straight forward to assess. Looking at just what the firm is worth in terms of the assets or asset replacement costs will result in an incredibly low estimate of the value of the business.

It becomes difficult when you consider intangible items such as programming code, trademarks, patents, intellectual property, and domain knowledge within the team. These are exceedingly hard to estimate what they are worth to any degree of accuracy. The peculiarity with technology companies as well is that this is where most of the value resides.

Finding new ways to assess and value intangibles will become a necessity in the future as technology businesses get bigger and bigger. In terms of replacement cost you could estimate the cost of the programming effort required to produce a product. What about the value of the design, look and feel? This is the valuable part, the unique design that generates sales. Also, if the brand and the team are highly respected, trusted advisors within their niche area, how do you put a replacement value on that? What is a specialist team with deep domain expertise worth? Assembling one from scratch would certainly not be cheap and would take time.

This method, however, can sometimes be useful to value early-stage companies with no revenues but expected or anticipated potential. It is also an exercise that some large companies undertake when sellers have vastly unrealistic expectations on price. The buyer will ask their team what it would cost for them to just replicate the business and do it themselves. To estimate a replacement cost valuation, you still need to find someone who has been through building a similar business before and understands the area. Someone with a deep domain knowledge of the industry and the niche market in which the business now operates. That person may be able to produce a reasonable estimate of costs to arrive at the same position from scratch. Have access to the right network and be able to hire a specialist team, understand the requirements to produce an initial prototype, and then have the client contacts and relationships to trial and refine the solution, before launching in the market.

A buyer may go through this exercise to have this as another datapoint and option when assessing the reasoning behind the acquisition case. They will balance this cost against the time saving through acquiring the target company. Another reason perhaps why it is important for sellers to set realistic price expectations. Ideally, there always needs to be something left on the table, some upside for the acquirer, to whet their appetite.

The best deals are a 'win-win' with both sides feeling they got a fair deal. That is easier said than done, and why putting some effort into preparing the business, having an irresistible narrative and plan for your growth initiatives, as well as enlisting the help of professional advisors, is vital. Ensure you get several valuations using different methods and accessing information on as many relevant transactions in the market as possible. This will help to make sure you have a clear indication of what your business may be worth and don't leave too much money on the table.

When we sold ISL back in 2004, the company had a high market penetration, a recognized brand, and a full order book with lots of long- term contracts. It had strong recurring revenues, was very cash generative and extremely profitable.

We also had a strong management team with very capable Sales and IT leaders, Martyn Hayward, and John Bunch, who were both passionate about the products and impressive in-front of clients, as well as being technically astute. We had approaches from two large technology companies to buy our business so called a board meeting to discuss the options. One of our main investors, Peter Edwards, a successful entrepreneur, questioned the reason to sell.

"Are you sure we should be selling the Golden Goose?" he asked.

The company had a couple of million pounds in the bank, a blue-chip client base, an enviable cash flow and plenty of opportunities to grow. We used advisors though the method of valuation was along the lines of 'What is the going rate for a software company in the market now in terms of a multiple of EBITDA, and how much would each of the shareholders accept?' The CFO of the acquiring company later told me that it was one of the best deals they had ever done, they recouped the purchase price within a noticeably short period. A detailed DCF analysis may have highlighted that more negotiating was required.

A technology company, growing at 15% or more, will effectively double its revenues every five years. With high recurring revenues and low capital requirements the value can increase rapidly. I am not advocating a hockey stick growth curve based on guess work to put into your financial forecasts. What I am saying is that when you become part of a much larger group, particularly if in the same sector, you will have access to greater marketing and distribution

Mark Harrison

resources. An aspirational, stretch plan becomes much more doable and higher growth sustainable. Think about this when you are negotiating a fair deal.

The two main drivers of value in a business are the growth rate and the return on the capital invested. Companies that have low returns on capital require a lot of investment to generate significant growth.

Technology companies, as mentioned before, tending to be capital-light and lean, are businesses that have a high return on investment. A small increase in growth can lead to a massive increase in value.

There are several options open to you when assessing various ways of creating more value in the business. For example, you could compete harder in your existing, established niche to increase your market share or you could search for opportunities in other industries and look to expand there. You could also acquire another firm that complements your own offering to create growth. According to results from past studies, highlighted in the publication' Valuation: Measuring and Managing the Value of Companies'[5] by McKinsey's Koller, Goedhart and Wessels, the best way, in terms of the greatest returns, to increase value, is to introduce new products. The reasoning being that organic new product development usually doesn't require much new capital investment relative to the returns generated.

In my view, you should always be looking to advance the capabilities of the team. Invest in skills and knowledge, and in research and development, to increase the IP and intangible value of the company. Breakthrough technologies, product designs, proven expertise, and critical competencies of the company, when greatly improved, will all feed through into future growth and can create significant value. Investing in these areas can also help to increase the attractiveness of the firm and put it on the radar of buyers.

277

The synergies become bigger, easier to spot, and the possible opportunities for buyers are much more evident and more apparent. The business becomes a more attractive asset and one for which major consolidators search. They look for companies that can enhance what they have. Creating a multiplier effect when combined with a larger pool of existing in-house capabilities and domain expertise. Like adding a missing piece to a jigsaw puzzle, it completes the picture and results in output that is greater than the sum of the parts.

11.2 What do you have to do to achieve a full price?

Some of the standard methods of valuing a business, as outlined above, such as the discounted cash flow method, can involve a lot of work and go into a great deal of detail. Having a reasonable idea of the intrinsic value of your business is incredibly useful, particularly in helping you to substantiate your expectations of price.

It is certainly worth having a detailed financial forecast for your company and then using this to undertake a DCF valuation of your plan. Work with your advisors to understand the sensitivities to your assumptions.

How much capital are you likely to require in future periods? Consider the useful lifetime of your products. When will you need to invest in rebuilding your existing products from scratch? How much are you going to invest in research and the development of new products? In the technology space, for example, software may have a useful market life of 10-15 years, depending on the niche, whereas data models used in predictive analytics will have a much shorter period of practical value.

A buyer will take your financial plan and then build their own in-house model. It will include the synergies that they are expecting to gain from the acquisition and the bigger they are, the greater the multiplier effect on generating stronger, and more massive cashflows. Whatever number you have from your model, assuming it is based on fact, not fantasy, the buyer number is likely to be larger. Often buyers pay larger multiples for companies for strategic reasons, and the synergies, and so expectations of achieving more significant growth.

Having worked in several large companies and then going through two exits, I would say find a trade buyer whose core business is in your sector. As mentioned earlier you will need to be mindful about protecting your IP. However, this aside, they will have a deeper understanding of your market, and what you do. Any synergies are amplified, and any earn-out more achievable as you can latch onto their distribution capabilities and access a wider client base.

An overseas buyer looking to break into your market is also worth consideration. They are likely to pay a premium price to acquire a business giving them a local team, a base to build on, and the ability to fast track their international expansion plans.

However, when you get into a sales process, there is <u>only one thing that will guarantee you a full price, and that is an auction process with competitive tension.</u>

Without it, a buyer will put in a bid at the bottom end of their price range, and it will be tough to get them to move. If you don't have a few offers, you won't have the leverage you need to negotiate the price up.

On the other hand, if your advisors can engineer an auction, and some tension between several interested bidders, then you may see 'deal fever'. And what sometimes happens is that one party becomes so determined to secure the deal, perhaps it is a vital piece of their strategic plan or the jigsaw they have in mind, that they increase their bid substantially. All the valuation methods and detail then go out of the window, and the result is that you get a price at the top end of your expectations.

It happened to a friend whose company was the focus of an auction with many bidders, one viewed the asset as strategic to their UK plans. The winning bid was a multiple exceeding 40x EBITDA, over 60% more than any other offer.

For a full price, think about the appetite in the market, how to create eager demand amongst potential suitors, and work with your advisors to find a way to orchestrate a competitive process.

11.3 What consideration should be given to different deal structures?

Another thing you will need to give some thought to is the structure of the deal. Having received an initial offer and negotiated for a higher price, a buyer might table a higher bid closer to your expectations, with the uplift based on hitting earn-out targets. How much value should you attach to the earn-out?

Which of these two deals would you prefer:

£10 million cash on completion, including £0.5 million held in escrow for 12 months to cover any potential warranty claims. With no further payments. In other words: **£10M Total with £9.5M Guaranteed.**

Or

£5 million cash on completion, including £0.5 million held in escrow for 12 months to cover any potential warranty claims. Then an earn-out of up to £10 million paid after three years, dependent on hitting specific performance targets. **£15M Total with £4.5M Guaranteed.**

In a seller's market you may see more deals like the first option, though if a recession bites and we move into a buyer's market, you may find more offers comparable to the second option. In some ways, you could say this may depend on your risk appetite, and as the founder, your confidence in the numbers you have presented, and how well you believe your company might develop under the new owners.

This is the sort of scenario to consider and agree with your board.

What is your risk appetite?

In my opinion, always view an earn-out as the cherry on the cake, not a significant part of the cake itself.

Once you have signed away your company, you will be an employee, not an owner, so control over the earn-out will be limited. The cash on the table is a certainty, an earn-out isn't, and you may not get what you expect, particularly if the growth targets are aggressive. For example, there could be a downturn in your market for whatever reason, you may not get the sales support you were expecting, or a new competitor armed with a better product might emerge. Things might not work out as well with the buyer, you may not realize the expected synergies and any earn-out targets may then seem out of reach.

One thing that is also important is to understand what the CAPEX requirements are, how many FTEs (full time employees) are needed, and how much expenditure is required for marketing, to continue growing. This is imperative if an earn-out is part of the deal. This needs to be part of a plan, requiring early agreement with the acquiring firm, otherwise there maybe be tension and disharmony after completing the deal. I think the key message from this is to find a buyer that you feel you can work with. Most trade buyers will want to keep the management team and will be delighted if you can bring in high rates of growth. Ask early for what you need, make this part of the earn out and growth plan.

There may be more deals structured towards earn-outs or staged payments contingent on hitting specific performance criteria as we emerge into the post-pandemic era. If there is a deep recession, we may enter more of a buyer's market.

Give some thought to the structure of any deal put in front of you with a large earn out element. Apply a discount factor based on your chances of achieving it given all the potential pitfalls, be realistic about what you might receive.

Discuss the options and any deal structures offered with your advisors. I had an earn-out on the sale of my first business, though both exits were structured with most of the cash up front. In this case, the earn-out for me was the right way for the buyer to keep me aligned with their aspirational growth targets. It worked; we hit our numbers.

On my second exit, I didn't have an earn-out, this wasn't part of the deal, though the people in the group company were friendly and easy to work alongside. And that is an essential factor to consider when thinking about the earn-out element. Can you work with these people? Will they ringfence your operation to some degree and cut you the slack required to allow you to focus on the earn-out targets?

Are you happy to stay on board for another three years or more? Do you get on well with the buyer management team?

Do you think you can fit in well with their way of working, culture, and organizational structure?

It would be best if you gave some thought to all these questions when considering whether the deal structure and earn-out element work for you.

References / Further Reading

1. https://www.investopedia.com/terms/d/depreciation.asp
Depreciation is an accounting method of allocating the
cost of a tangible or physical asset over its useful life.
Depreciation represents how much of an asset's value has
been used up. Depreciating assets helps companies earn
revenue from an asset while expensing a portion of its cost
each year the asset is in use. So, for example, if you
purchased computing equipment and the useful life was 5
years, you would spread the cost equally over the period
its use or 20% of the cost hitting the accounts each year
(assuming straight line depreciation of useful value).

2. https://www.investopedia.com/terms/a/amortization.asp
Amortisation is a routine decrease in value of an
intangible asset and in this context is like depreciation but
applied to intangible assets such as software, or goodwill.
For example, you have invested significantly in the
development of computing software which can be licensed
to clients on multi-year contracts. The useful market life
of the software could be 15 years, and in such a case you
would spread the development cost over the 15 years
matching the income from licence fees.

3. www.damoradan.com

4. www.investopedia.com/terms/d/dlan.asp

5. T Koller, M Goedhart, D Wessels: 'Valuation: Measuring
and Managing the Value of Companies' McKinsey &
Company, Wiley.

Key takeaways

• Valuing a private business is difficult; it is an illiquid asset and until you take your company to market you won't know for sure what price you will realise.

• Market conditions, the availability of similar firms and the potential synergies with buyers will all impact appetite for your business. Value is fundamentally underpinned by the future cashflows that your firm can generate and sustain over time.

• The two main levers of value are the rate of growth that the business can reach and the rate of return on capital it can produce. The major considerations then are: How big could the company get and is there capacity or will there be growth in the target markets to support this?

• Make sure you enlist professional advisors to help in undertaking a thorough valuation of your firm across all relevant methods.

• One of the common methods of valuing private businesses is a comparative company analysis, either by assessing the current values of similar publicly traded companies, or by looking at the sale values achieved through recent transactions of similar private firms. For comparative public company statistics, multiples are usually calculated from a ratio of the enterprise value to EBITDA. For comparative private company data, transaction values achieved are divided by the EBITDA. Value estimates are then usually expressed as a multiple of EBITDA.

• Another common technique is the discounted cashflow method where all future free cash flows generated by the business are discounted to today's value and then summed.

(Continued)

• The replacement cost method involves looking at the business and working out what it would cost to replicate the organisation as it stands. This tends to produce valuations at the low end of the scale.

• The most effective way to create more value for shareholders is organic product development, investment in IP and in the skills of the team. The larger the capabilities of the team, the easier it is for an acquiring company to spot synergy with their own operation.

• The best way to ensure you get a full price is to ensure you have a competitive auction.

HOMEWORK

Now over to you.

1. *Start by making a list of similar companies to your business that you are aware of that are publicly listed. Also consider similar private companies in your market, and in other related sectors. This will be a useful starting point for discussion with a professional M&A advisor.*

2. *What relevant transactions are you aware of in your sector, do you have any information about these, was the information made public?*

SCALE for SALE

CHAPTER 12: HOW CAN YOU IMPROVE YOUR CHANCES OF A SUCCESSFUL SALE?

'Accept the challenges so you can feel the exhilaration of victory' – General George S Patten

12.1 What should you do before you start a sales process?

Many sellers read about the large multiples in newspapers, often some obscure event, such as Facebook paying $1 billion for Snapchat when it was still a start-up with only 15 employees.

They then have unrealistic expectations about the value of their own company compared to what buyers are willing to pay.

Repeatedly a reason some deals don't progress is the large gap in expectations between what a business is worth and the price a founder wants to achieve.

Please do your homework, speak to a few Merger & Acquisition (M&A) specialists in your field, search out transactions that have successfully closed in your market over the last few years. Try to get a feel for the sort of price range you might be able to achieve on the sale of your company.

Get several professional advisory firms to put in a proposal with their estimate of what they think your business is worth. Look across these estimates and take a realistic view on the value of your company, given what you have found out and the current market climate. How does this compare to your expectations and what you would find acceptable? Is it still worth pursuing a sales process now, or should you carry on building your business?

So, the first thing to do to improve your chances of a successful sale is to:

Do a reality check of your expectations.

Know that selling a company is a very time consuming and a lengthy process that takes up an enormous amount of management effort. Many deals fail to close, though advisors used during the process, including external lawyers, accountants, and tax advisors, will still have to be paid. And, at the same time, you still need to carry on running your company and sustaining the enticing growth targets that you have in your forecast. It is a marathon rather than a sprint, so you need to prepare yourself mentally before you initiate the process. You need to ensure that you don't get 'deal fatigue' and want to throw in the towel later down the line.

I liken the sales process to an experience I had taking part in a charity event called the 'Bogle Stroll' back in 1987. The Bogle is a 55-mile race on foot during the night around Greater Manchester, in the North of England, in aid of local charities. It starts at midnight from the centre of Manchester, with thousands of enthusiastic participants ready for the challenge, walking or jogging through the night, usually in cold, inclement weather. I was on a team of 15 people. We had a couple of nurses in a car following us, to patch up blisters, and hand us food at various checkpoints.

In the 1987 event, the weather was terrible. We had snow, blizzards, and extremely low temperatures. It was tough going; we were cold, our fingers were like icicles, we were soaked to the skin, and had blisters on blisters by the time we had completed three-quarters of the route. It was torturous and just seemed to go on and on. When we stopped, to tend to any blisters, and have a brief rest, it didn't appear easy to get started again. Crossing the finishing line around lunchtime the following day was a massive relief.

There are many parallels to running a sales process to sell your business. It takes a lot of your time; it takes much effort, and it can be physically and mentally draining. And very frustrating.

Being prepared mentally is vital.

Professional advisors will help and provide support, but you should realise that it will be very demanding. You will need to contribute a significant amount of your time.

Ideally, you need to have a solid management structure and succession plan in place before you take the business to market. The company can then operate without you having to be wholly focused working in it during the process.

So, the second thing to do to improve your chances of a successful sale is to:

Prepare yourself mentally for a lengthy process.

12.2 When you start a process, what things should you do to improve your chances of success?

Do you want to stay with the business after a sale has completed or would you prefer to leave? Would you be willing to carry on working in the company as part of the larger group?

You need to be clear about this when you enter discussions and be aware that if you intend to leave immediately, it may put off some potential buyers. Any potential purchaser will want comfort that there will be a smooth handover and integration of the business. If that becomes difficult without your involvement, it could dampen their interest.

I would advise agreeing upfront that you are willing to stay on, at least for a limited period. However, you will have to face the facts and get your head around the reality that it won't be the same.

Once you have sold, you will be working for someone else.

It will be different.

There will be plenty of bureaucracy introduced, the culture may be changed, and you may or may not be happy staying.

The new owners may also want to take the business in a different direction or have other synergies in mind to exploit value.

Whether you have indicated you are willing to stick around for a while or not, a buyer will want comfort that a strong management team can run the company after you have left. They will also want you to ensure that you have handed over all the key supplier and client relationships before you go. For most deals, it is usual for a founder or the founder team to stay for at least 6 to 12 months as a minimum to ensure a smooth handover and integration of the business into the buyer group. Though some companies will want you to stay longer, maybe three years, would that be a deal-breaker?

If you state upfront that you are willing to stay on board for a few years to ensure successful integration within the acquiring company, you will increase your chances of a successful outcome. It will also enable you to sort out any immediate problems or issues that might crop up with the business after the deal has completed. What you don't want is for the buyer to let a situation escalate out of control and then try to claim against the warranties in the Sale and Purchase Agreement. With the exclusion of tax warranties, these usually remain in place for a defined period, often a couple of years. If you are still in place, you will be able to nip any potential issues in the bud and defuse them before they become significant problems.

The due diligence process is usually thorough; have a look at the typical starting list in the appendices at the back of this book. Any potential issues impacting the business are typically disclosed upfront and factored into the price. So, it is unusual for a company to claim against the warranties, though it does happen. Staying in place, at least for a year or two, to keep an eye on the business, to ensure the integration goes smoothly, and so everyone on both sides is happy with the deal is undoubtedly beneficial in my view.

From a buyer perspective, they don't want all founders leaving the business when the deal completes. If the company is still relatively small and an area of the firm is still reliant on one of the founders, then there would be a concern. Unless of course, your company is substantial, and you have already transitioned the running of the day- to-day operation to a professional management team. And so, the company can function independently of the founders. Otherwise, the leaders wanting to leave immediately a deal completes may potentially put off any buyers.

A purchaser wants to be sure the business will successfully transition, can be integrated, and that the value is secured. And that the goodwill doesn't disappear if the founder or founders walk out of the door once they have a pocket full of money.

If you do leave, make sure you have a plan and think carefully about what you are going to do next. When Experian acquired ISL in 2004, I stayed with the company for a couple of years. One of my colleagues decided to leave and pursue a completely different career, whilst another main shareholder chose to retire in his early forties. In his words, 'he was going to learn the guitar, grow his hair long and have many holidays', it was no surprise that he was bored out of his mind after a couple of months, and missed working in the business. Make sure you think hard about what you wish for and what you want before you embark on the sales process, and before you leave the firm.

So, the third thing to do to improve your chances of a successful sale is to:

Be willing to stay on after completion, at least for a period. Communicate this to potential buyers as early as possible, so they know where you stand.

Preparation is vital.

Is your company in a 'go to market' ready state? Do you have a strong management team and a succession plan in place?

Do you have a good range of customers where revenue is not highly reliant on just one or two of them?

Are your contracts in place across all areas to protect the business?

Ensure that everything is in order and shipshape before you go to market. Carry out an audit across all areas of the business. Get a lawyer to look at all your contracts including employee agreements, director service level agreements, customer contracts, supplier arrangements, technology, office lease agreements, outstanding legal issues, business plans, forecasts, and growth initiatives. Are they up to date, do they reflect the latest legislation and are they in line with compliance (e.g., GDPR)? Do you have a Human Resources Handbook with your company policies and procedures that all your staff have signed?

I had a meeting with a friend a year ago who wanted some advice on taking his business to market. When I asked a few basic questions, I found out that 50% of his clients were not on contract, and a substantial amount of on-going business is being carried out based on a handshake and an email. To a buyer, this would be an immediate red flag. What are they buying if half of the customers could potentially walk away when the business changes ownership?

Do you have a business continuity plan that you have tested? Do you have sound policies in place to protect your company from cyber-attacks, malware or being hacked by malicious outside third parties? Do you have cyber insurance in place? There has been an increased prevalence of ransomware and malicious cyber-attacks in recent times; this is likely to carry on growing and so having policies in place, and insurance cover is essential.

Garmin recently paid a multi-million -dollar ransom to criminals who encrypted its computer files[3]. I heard of another company that had cancelled its cyber insurance policy, costing only £6000 per annum, before the 2020 pandemic lockdown as the finance director didn't think the company needed it - they were then hit by a ransomware attack!

You need to have agreed processes, procedures, and cost controls in place with documentation to prove that you know how to run a company. Just as vital is ensuring you safeguard the assets with sensible policies and guidelines for your staff to follow, and for example, concerning compliance with current legislation such as GDPR (General Data Protection Regulation), relating to the protection of personal data and policies relating to commercial confidentiality, and the protection of company physical and intellectual property.

Highlight anything that may be problematic or concern buyers and resolve these before going to market. For example, if you have a couple of essential supplier agreements about to renew, it may be advisable to get these contracts renewed before taking the business to market. Are there any outstanding legal disputes, or issues around ownership of your IP? Are there any significant client contracts about to renew? It would be wise to get these tidied up before entering a sales process.

Most buyers will realise that nothing is perfect, and there are always issues that crop up when running a company. The odd issue may not put them off. However, if there are significant problems likely to impact value, you should consider sorting out as many as possible before entering discussions with interested parties.

So, the fourth thing to do to improve your chances of a successful sale is to:

Prepare your business for sale as much as possible before going to market.

Potential buyers are interested in what you have done with the business to date, and they will also be eager to understand what the growth is going to be like in the future. They want to know what synergies between the two businesses might lead to faster growth and what the benefit will be for them to buy your company.

Before you go to market, make sure your growth initiatives are relatively secure and believable to give your plan credibility. Your expansion ideas need to be rock solid, and you should have a robust financial plan ready to back this up before you present to potential buyers. The financial plans and forecast also need to be professionally prepared and reflect local accounting standards.

In the initial meetings with potential buyers be careful presenting 'hockey stick' type growth curves in the forecasts for the business. You will lose credibility if you are not able to substantiate and prove your claims in detail. You need solid proof to back-up the assumptions behind your numbers. Otherwise, you will find it difficult to convince buyers you know what you are doing.

I have been in meetings with companies on the buyer side, and people have proposed numbers that were higher than the total addressable market in the area they were targeting. Not only were they presenting increasing annual sales by several hundred per cent, but they also didn't understand the market, and didn't have a feel for what is realistic.

I remember going to a meeting in Europe to visit the seller of a tech business that had some products we were interested in at the time. They had some impressive technology, though they had a 'hockey stick' growth curve to attempt to substantiate their aspirational price for the company: tens of millions of Euro. They weren't making any profit at the time, and they had not appropriately prepared the growth plans. The financial plan had many holes; it only took a few minutes looking at their numbers to realise it was not credible or believable. We didn't progress the deal.

Corporate buyers are not easily fooled and will have seen it all before. They will be able to see through a plan based on fantasy rather than fact. That said there is no point being too conservative and not showing ambition. Try to find a happy medium that looks plausible, contains no bull****, and doesn't just appear made-up on the back of a bus ticket.

Another point to consider is that the buyer may like your technology, they may also get along with you, and so decide to go along with your plan, though base a large part of the consideration on an earn-out, contingent on hitting the numbers. My advice would be set stretch goals but stay realistic and keep to the art of the possible. You will gain credibility in the initial buyer meetings.

The buyer will want to see proof you have built a sound business to date. However, it is the future story they are paying a premium for, the more believable this is the more they will pay, and the more likely your deal will complete successfully!

So, the fifth thing to do to improve your chances of a successful sale is to:

Ensure your growth initiatives are believable.

So, when timing the sale of your company, you want to make sure that there is plenty of upside for any buyer to stimulate interest.

A buyer will also want to understand whether there are any strong synergies they can exploit through an acquisition. You should research the buyer company and try to find out about their existing products and offerings. People generally like to talk about themselves. You should encourage the buyer into meaningful conversations about the potential synergies with their business and their products. It will increase their level of engagement, help to develop a relationship between both parties, and increase their interest in a deal.

The sixth action to improve the chances of a successful sale is for you to:

Research potential buyers to uncover potential synergies you can highlight in meetings with them. Engage them in meaningful conversations focusing on mutual opportunities to get them excited in a deal.

12.3 What are simple things to do during the sales process to ensure it does not get derailed?

The process, as we have alluded to, is a marathon rather than a sprint. At the same time, you will also have to continue running your existing business. The whole thing can get very wearing, and the due diligence and negotiation phases can be quite prolonged.

During the whole of this don't let your standards drop. Always treat everyone with respect, behave honestly, and with integrity throughout every part of the process.

Build credibility and trust with potential buyers.

Do not get emotionally involved in negotiations.

It may be your 'baby' or your life's work so it can be easy to get emotional during negotiations. It would be best if you keep emotions out of the process wherever possible. That is where professional advisors can help in being neutral about the deal. They can keep to the facts, and so are better placed to negotiate on your behalf.

Remember you may be working with the buyer side people after the deal if you have decided to remain with the business. It would be best if you stayed passive, and ideally not negotiate the deal directly yourself. When a blockage appears in the process, chances are the advisors will have experienced something similar before. They will know how to diffuse any tension, have an idea what a fair resolution is, and more importantly, how to handle it.

So, the seventh thing to do to improve your chances of a successful sale is to:

<u>Always be honest, respectful, and keep emotions out of the process.</u>

It is crucial to maintain trust during the process and not to appear to the buyer to be hiding anything. If any issues could materially impact the business, you need to make sure that the buyer is aware of these as early as possible.

There may be past legal issues, problems not completely fixed, or specific matters that have the potential to resurface. It would be best if you tried to resolve any significant issues as much as you can before taking the business to market. However, there may be something fixed as much as you are able, though which might still worry a buyer. These should be brought onto the table as early as practically possible in the process.

Do not waste months on the process and then table a significant issue late in the due diligence phase. Tabling surprises late may spook the buyer into walking away from the table, or more likely, lead to a renegotiation of the price.

You will also lose credibility if the buyer side thinks that you have been hiding something that could materially impact the business in the future.

When I was working at ISL, and we were in the process of selling the business, we had a potential issue that we needed to get onto the table. One of the products we were providing to the UK personal lines insurance market had a 90% market share. The product compared insurer market prices, and so, in theory, could have been used negatively by companies to coordinate pricing against the interest of consumers.

In practice, though, there was no evidence in the industry of coordination of pricing, in fact, the car insurance market historically had been losing money. Prices for private car insurance were not rising relative to inflation, and there were lots of new insurance companies entering the market offering cheaper cover. The product facilitated competition, and so was of benefit to the consumer.

We tabled this potential concern early in the due diligence phase, and the buyer was able to take advice before moving forward.

Please don't sit on anything that might be a deal-breaker; get it on the table early.

So, the eighth thing to do to improve your chances of a successful sale is to:

Get any potential deal-breakers onto the table as early as possible.

When you engage with potential buyers, particularly during the early stages of the process, ask plenty of questions. Try to find out as much as you can about the culture of the buyer firm,

What are their values? How is it structured?

How do they operate and run their company?

It is important if you intend to stay with the company after completion and remain involved as it grows.

Find out if there is a strong cultural alignment.

One of the main reasons acquisitions often fail to deliver the expected value is due to differences in culture between the buyer and seller companies. The buyer may highlight this during the process; if this happens, you can discuss how you will work together to address it post-completion. Perhaps by considering the differences prior to initiating the integration phase after completion.

Senior management from both parties should devote some time to understand any disparities and plan a transition path for the seller company via a change programme.

You are selling, so why is this important and of interest?

If you agree on a deal structure with a large element of earn-out, you need people to stay at the company post-completion. Things must go well post-completion if you are going to have any chance of achieving earn-out targets. You want to make sure that things go smoothly and large cultural differences with the acquiring firm may encourage some people to leave for employment elsewhere.

In my last business, we allowed people to make the most of technology and to work wherever they wanted, whether that was from home or the office. We also encouraged people to take responsibility for their own development and judged them by the quality of the work, not the hours they were sitting at their desks in the office. We started with this policy as a strategy before large corporates trusted people to work from home.

Reflecting on the current pandemic the world of work is moving more in that direction but ten years ago it was unusual, and so enabled us to hire some great talent, people who were tired of lost hours commuting to and from big cities. Post-completion if we had imposed new conditions requiring staff to return to commuting five days a week people would have started looking for employment elsewhere.

Fortunately, the company that acquired us, were ahead of the curve for a large corporate, and so the staff continued with the same freedoms post-completion.

Just as important, you should also be thinking about what happens to your business and your team post-completion.

Most entrepreneurs that have spent years building up a successful company care deeply about the business and the people who work in it.

They want to make sure that there is an excellent cultural fit with the acquiring company, that their team will be happy, and that the company is in good hands, and will continue to prosper when sold.

So, the ninth thing to do to improve your chances of a successful sale is to:

Make sure there is a strong cultural alignment with the buyer and consider whether any change programme may be necessary to harmonise any differences post-completion.

References / Further reading

[1] https://www.forbes.com/sites/richardparker/2016/10/24/the-business-for-sale-marketplace-why-90-of-listings-never-sell/

[2] https://techcrunch.com/2017/05/17/heres-how-likely-your-startup-is-to-get-acquired-at-any-stage/

[3] https://news.sky.com/story/garmin-paid-multi-million-dollar-ransom-to-criminals-using-arete-ir-say-sources-

[4] Groysberg B, Lee J, Price J, Cheng Y, '*The Leaders Guide to Corporate Culture*' Harvard Business Review 2018

Key takeaways

• To improve your chances of a successful sale completing there are a few things that can help:

• Do a reality check of your price expectations. Listen to your advisors about the likely range of valuations. How does this compare to what you would accept?

• Prepare yourself mentally for a lengthy process. Ensure that you have made provisions in the business so things can progress whilst you are working on the sale.

• Be willing to stay on after the completion of the deal. The buyer will want comfort that the business can run smoothly after completion of the sale, and that it can be successfully integrated.

• Thorough preparation is vital before you go to market. Contracts across all areas should be in place. Do not leave unresolved, outstanding issues that could impact value. A buyer will be switched off if things are in a mess and the business has not been run properly.

• Ensure your growth initiatives are believable, that your financial plan underpinning it has been professionally prepared, and that it is credible.

• Research potential buyers to uncover potential synergies you can highlight in meetings with them. Engage them in meaningful conversations using this conduit to get them excited in doing a deal.

• Always be honest, treat everyone with respect and try to keep emotion out of the process. Get any potential dealbreakers onto the table early.

(Continued)

• Make sure that you get any potential issues that could be dealbreakers onto the table as early as possible in the process. Do not spring a surprise on a buyer late in the due diligence phase, otherwise the deal may fail to close, or the buyer may want to renegotiate the price.

• Make sure there is strong cultural alignment with the buyer and consider any change programme necessary to harmonise any differences post-completion.

HOMEWORK

Now over to you. Preparation is key to a successful sales process. How much work do you need to do to prepare the company for sale? The questions below are not a due diligence checklist but are things that could immediately derail any sale process or give the impression the company is not well run if not in order. Answer the questions and the list will help to flag where some of the holes are and get you started on what work needs to be done prior to taking your company to market.

1. *How many customers do you serve per year? What percentage of your customers are on contract? Are these annual or multi-year recurring contracts (e.g., 3 years duration)? Are the fees fixed or variable, perhaps linked to usage of your product? How many of your existing client contracts have a change of control clause (i.e., if you sell your company and under new ownership the other party has the right to cancel)?*

2. *How many suppliers do you have? Are they all on contract? Are any supplier contracts likely to expire in the next 12 months? Is there a change of control clause in any agreement with any of your suppliers?*

3. *Are all your employees (including Directors, Non-Executive Directors, contractors, and part-time staff) on contract? Is any part of your business completely reliant on one person? Do you have a succession plan in place?*

4. Do you own the Intellectual Property (IP) you use in your company or have licences in place to cover how use? Do you have any protection of your IP (e.g., patents, registered trademarks, exclusive contractual agreements with supplier partners)?

5.What financial reporting do you have in place? You will be expected to have your finger on the pulse of the business and know the numbers inside out. Do you have a monthly management accounts pack provided by your Finance Director or Manager? What aspects doe this cover? For example, it might include expenditure and income tracked against budget and forecast, sales, and the movement in value of the pipeline, the current position of debtors and monies owed, cashflow and an update of the forecast as well as covering the position of the balance sheet and cash in the bank.

6. *Has there been any threatened or actual litigation impacting the business in recent years? Are there any outstanding issues relating to compliance, legal issues, intellectual property rights or anything outstanding that could impact the value of the business?*

7.Do you have a disaster recovery plan in place? Do you have a cyber security policy and has this been tested and kept up to date? Is documentation in place covering all parts of your business? Where are the gaps you know of?

8.What processes and procedures do you have in place, across the whole of your business? Is this documented and where are the gaps?

9.Do you have a staff handbook with policies for health & safety, mobile phone usage, use of personal data and data protection, cyber security, amongst others? Where are the gaps you know of?

CHAPTER 13: WHAT HAPPENS NEXT PROGRESSING THE BUSINESS UNDER CORPORATE OWNERSHIP?

'Love all, trust few, do wrong to none.'

- William Shakespeare

13.1 Closing the deal, what is it like?

The closing of the sale usually takes place at your lawyer's office and can be quite frantic. After months of effort on either side, there are often loose ends still to be tidied up, a few remaining contractual points to be negotiated, and a whole truckload of paperwork to wade through and sign.

You have committed to complete by this date, and excited, though like a weary, untrained participant in your first marathon, you stumble on. Crowds of lawyers and accountants madly rush around you, like headless chickens, urging you forward, towards that elusive finish line.

It's an exhausting finale.

It can take the whole day and go into the night.

Then, when it is finally completed, the ink still drying on the paperwork, and the money wired through to your bank - you feel a real sense of achievement and fulfilment.

It is a great relief when you finally cross the finish line.

Selling a company can be a gruelling ordeal and can drag on for what seems like an eternity. Many businesses fail to sell; a lot of processes fall over at different hurdles. Completing a sale is a significant accomplishment. It is another target reached in your plan, and another milestone on your journey to celebrate.

The popping of champagne corks signifies completion of the transaction and at last, the time to relax. With the deal done, the fizz is passed around, and it somehow tastes better than usual. Maybe it's the joy, perhaps the adrenalin of finally getting over the line, or maybe you are just dog-tired and welcome a drink. It is an exhilarating experience, a moment to share with your principal shareholders, and one that lives long in the memory.

You then go out with your team and advisors for dinner and a few drinks to celebrate. These are fleeting moments, they go by in a flash, so please try to be in the present and don't spend half the night on your phone texting friends and family.

Congratulate and thank the team, including all advisors that worked on the deal for their input and contribution.

Remember that without them all, you would not be here.

Savour and enjoy the moment.

Then you need to go out and buy yourself a present. And buy a gift for your long-suffering wife or partner! After all, they have had to put up with you working long hours on your business for years and years.

I know one guy went out and bought himself a brand-new Ferrari straight away. Another guy in my team went out and bought a new Porsche 911- whatever it is treat yourself; it brings back that feeling of exhilaration. You also want to make sure you have something to show for all that hard work and effort.

Ideally, go on holiday, have a couple of weeks to recharge the batteries, and then return fresh to focus on the new job. Working for the new owner.

In my case, in a large corporate group with thousands of employees.

13.2 Back in the Corporate World - How do you adjust to a new regime?

When you first go back to your office and start work for the new company, back working in the corporate world, it is quite different. You have crossed the bridge from being a business owner to an employee.

My first reaction, when arriving back at the office and sitting at my desk for the first-time post-deal completion was:

'My god, what have I done'.

The feeling was like having sold one of your children. The business was your baby, something you created and built up, something you put your heart and soul into.

You now must get used to doing things differently, following another set of someone else's priorities and to taking direction from elsewhere.

Give yourself a minute or two that first morning back sitting at your desk. Then get over it, put it behind you and move on. You need to get your head around a few things quite quickly. The first is that you are now an employee, the second that there will be new controls put in place you have to adhere to, and the third that the culture may be quite different and something you need to adjust to fast.

On that initial morning back in the office though, the first thing you should do is speak to all the staff. They will be worried about the future and their job security, whether the office will be moved, or whether they soon may be surplus to requirements. For me, in the first deal involving ISL, there was certainly a lot of concern amongst the team. Experian were a major competitor, there was a lot of crossover in product offerings, and there were potential cost savings to be gained through combining resources.

It is important to reassure all your people, calm any nerves, and explain that the reason large companies buy smaller technology firms is to acquire the team, the expertise, and the deep domain knowledge. At ISL we had been winning the lion's share of business in the market; the team were going to be important to future growth.

On the second sale to Verisk, all the staff received something from the deal, so were all aware of what was happening as the process concluded. They knew a trade deal was likely.   When we started Business Insight, from day one, we stated our intent for everyone on the team to share in the success of the company, and that the plan was to exit through a trade sale. We hired talented people and locked them in with shares after an initial qualifying period. For some it enabled them to clear mortgages, for others it resulted in a significant nest egg. Even then, people still need reassuring, particularly when they hear of any founders leaving post-completion.

Once you have informed the staff, clients, and suppliers about the change of ownership, the next major task is sorting out the integration of the business into the group. The integration planning, and implementation, is usually left for local management to lead and deliver. Do not underestimate the amount of time and effort this requires. From different financial systems, processes, and procedures to adopt, to regrading job grades, harmonizing benefits, replacing CRM systems, transitioning to a different culture, accepting new ways of working through to integrating product offerings and brands. It is a long, long list of things to sort out.

Meanwhile, you still have a business to run. And now have numbers to hit with expectations of growth from the group company. Integration can be time consuming and frustrating.

You may have thought you were working crazy hours during the sale process, juggling your time between focusing on the deal, and staying involved managing your business. Guess what, this intensity often continues post-completion.

Something you also need to get used to quickly is the level of bureaucracy; this increases tenfold. You will soon find the weight of countless new processes and procedures make your workload heavier, with layers of boxes to be ticked and signoffs required at each decision-making juncture. There are also endless conference calls and far too many meetings in large organisations. Many are surplus to requirements and interrupt the workflow, dampen innovation, and restrict agility. Consequently, the wheels turn a lot slower, it takes longer to get things done, and you sometimes feel like you are wading through deep mud.

The sheer level and weight of bureaucracy can hinder progress in large companies, and often dampens any competitive advantages. There are sensible reasons for most of this, though it can take a lot of getting used to and can be frustrating for entrepreneurs who want to get stuff done in a hurry.

I remember working with a company acquired whilst I was working for Marsh McLennan (MMC). One of the owners stayed post-completion, though he left after six months. He could never get used to being an employee, the amount of administration, and having to work within the rules. He used to continually complain to me about not being able to buy anything, 'even paperclips', without having to raise a purchase order with Head Office.

It is a different mindset working within a large corporate, and for an entrepreneur, the bureaucracy is probably one of the hardest things to get used to. You need to appreciate that many corporate executives are averse to taking risk and innovating, the rewards often don't compensate enough for the risk of screwing up, so invariably they tend to be slow to act, usually pursue more conservative options, and the path to action is a long one.

The skill set is also different, working on a start-up and then scaling up, compared to working as a senior manager and salaried employee within a large corporate. In a large organization you need diplomacy, strong communication skills, emotional intelligence, and the ability to manage upwards and sideways, as well as down the chain. I was lucky that after both of my exits I got along well with the guys I reported into, we shared the same values.

It also helped that we were all partial to good food and a nice glass of wine.

You need 'softer' skills in being able to get your message across to different personalities, groups, and get accustomed to doing some public speaking. By 'softer', I don't mean easier, less relevant, or less significant than being able to code, create products, multi-task or be a 'one-man-army' as some have likened the start-up skill set to. On the contrary, managing large teams of people, getting your message across to different personalities, and standing up regularly in front of groups of people to give motivational talks, is demanding and tough.

If you want to survive and thrive in a large corporate environment, you need to be aware of this and sharpen these skills.

Try to develop skills so you can influence people to your way of thinking.

You also need to find out how the company works, understand how to get stuff done, and where there are workarounds. You need to work with the system, not against it, or give up when you go down a blind alley. You also need patience, as it takes longer to get things done, and there will be more roadblocks to navigate.

How do you think you will manage?

The corporate environment can be a culture shock for those used to running their own show. It may entail a change in attitude. It certainly necessitates the ability to adapt quickly. Crossing the bridge back from owner to employee can be a difficult path for some after the freedom of being your own boss and doing your own thing.

Having said that, working in large multi-national corporations can bring great opportunities to expand your experience, broaden knowledge, travel to different countries, and enrich your understanding of other cultures. There is more job security, and the time spent working in a large group can be very enjoyable, fulfilling and help you to grow your skills and abilities.

I have worked in a few large organisations and always enjoyed my time. For example, I loved working at Verisk; the people were friendly, extremely talented and the culture was collaborative and inclusive.

Being part of a large group can also really help the expansion of the business, providing access to a wider base of skills, a pathway into foreign markets, and the distribution capabilities that can supercharge sales.

A large corporate trade buyer also tends to be more focused on long term value creation. Not how quickly they can push up profits in the short term at the risk of sacrificing essential spend, losing sight of longer-term growth opportunities, or potentially losing people.

At one of the large corporate companies where I worked, the managing director (MD) of a recent overseas acquisition had died suddenly, not long after completion of the deal. It was a small operation, and the MD had been the leader, the main salesperson, and the key contact with suppliers. Fortunately, there was a natural successor internally and he was promoted into the role. The numbers went backwards, and the business struggled for the next 12 months. Instead of replacing the new leader, the senior management of the group spent time with him, giving significant support and encouragement.

They understood the market, realized it would take time to rebuild and settle into the new role, to recover from a difficult situation. They remained patient.

I think life in a large corporate can also be a lot more palatable if you share the same core values and core business. It makes a difference if you both speak the same language and the top team have a thorough understanding of the value you can add. They will be more empathetic and grasp any ideas you bring to the table a lot quicker. It doesn't mean you will get any additional resources, but they are more likely to listen, and you will probably be further up the priority list.

Contrast that with when the business is a bolt-on, outside the core activities of the group, and that doesn't have much to do with the main day to day 'bread and butter' activities - it is extremely tough getting additional resources.

At the end of the day, it will be a different ride working for a large company, but it can still be rewarding and exciting, especially if there is an earn-out, and you can still share in any upside.

13.3 How do you improve your chances of achieving an earn-out within a large organisation?

Get help with integration and delegate as much as you can.

An earn-out is usually the cherry or icing on the cake, not a significant part of the deal itself. It is a useful way of keeping the management team aligned and motivated post-completion, to keep driving the growth during and after the integration of the business into the group.

It can work very well for both parties though I think a few things can help things run more smoothly. Making sure there is clarity upfront on both sides on a few points will generate more trust, foster a stronger working relationship, and ultimately improve the chances of success.

First, if you are going to stand any chance of growing the business post-completion, and hitting earn-out targets, you need to hand-off as much of the integration process as possible. Ideally, ask the group company for help and resources, such as a full-time project manager, or specialist contractor experienced in integration and change management, to ensure you get on top of the integration ASAP.

It amazes me that large companies acquire smaller businesses for quite large amounts of money, and then frequently don't put in as much effort or provide as much help into planning a smooth integration. Thought and planning need to be put where there are disparities in culture, as well as systems, pay & benefits, and ways of working.

Where there are large differences in culture, for example, some thinking must be put into what needs to change, the period of transition, and the details of how to harmonize and reduce the gaps, otherwise people will leave. It is a reason many acquisitions fail to deliver anticipated value[1].

So, please ask and make your case for help with integration straightaway.

In the first exit I was involved in, we had little help with integration, this made running the business and hitting aggressive sales targets for the earn-out tough going. However, the second time around a project manager and some resources were assigned to help incorporate the firm into the group structure. This made a big difference and made the overall workload more palatable for the team to cope with.

Be crystal clear on the metrics used to trigger earn-out payments.

Ensure you are crystal clear on what the earn-out metrics are from day one. Preferably, these will have been negotiated before you complete the deal and have signed over the company. Earn-outs are sometimes a small part of the overall deal and so details can be overlooked. When negotiating earn-out targets try to make sure they are aligned with a transparent, easily reported metric, such as turnover or sales revenue.

Linking the earn-out to a metric such as operating profit could lead to disagreement later when a range of group costs are assigned to you, and when accounting policies, such as income recognition, are changed. It may also drive cost curbing behaviours not aligned with fast growth.

Make sure you get agreement that indirect corporate cost allocations to the CAPEX/OPEX expense line are excluded for the purpose of calculating your earn-out. As with all the points here, get these agreed early, don't assume anything, and then find out much later you are not aligned with the buyer.

Delegate admin tasks and ask for help if too much time is being wasted.

Assess where you are spending your time and ask the question: Is this task contributing towards growing the company and my earn-out? If the answer is no, delegate the task, or consider whether you need to ask for extra help or kick it into the long grass.

In the drive to reduce costs many big companies cut the number of administrative staff in recent times and pushed the workload back onto managers. It means that too much time is regularly spent by expensive people on low grade tasks. If you are in this position ask for help, ensure you have adequate assistance so you are free to spend more of your time on tasks you should be spending your time on, driving the business forward.

Build credibility, be laser focused on hitting your numbers from day one.

One thing you certainly must do, first and foremost, is to be super focused on hitting your numbers from the start. After working for two large American corporations, I found out that hitting your numbers every time builds credibility internally. And with credibility you start to get a voice in the organization, you will be afforded a little more freedom, and requests for resources are looked on more favourably. With access to more resources, you will generate opportunities to grow faster, create more value, and reach your earn-out targets quicker.

Try to keep control of the sales function.

One of the benefits of joining a large organization can be having access to greater marketing resources, and wider distribution capabilities. This is brilliant in supercharging your sales though you need to be clear with your new owners upfront who will have control of the sales function in your business post-completion. Otherwise, you may find there is a change in reporting lines and be surprised to find the sales team reporting directly into head office.

This may happen when acquired by a company already entrenched in your market sector and where there is a matrix reporting structure. In a matrix structure, core services such as sales, development, operations, and human resources work across the various business units supporting different client offerings. You have shared services and functional leads that work across different business units providing support on such things as sales, human resources or talent management, and research and development (R&D).

Losing control of the sales function is something you need to discuss and prevent if you can. On completion of the deal the last thing you will want is your Sales Director told he has a new boss, and rather than reporting to you, is now reporting into a central team working across the whole group. A new manager will have his own objectives and targets, he almost certainly won't be focused on making sure you hit your earn-out. The sales resources in your business may then be diverted away being completely focused on selling your products, and to make matters worse, you will still be held accountable for making your numbers.

It is critical you don't lose control of the sales function, otherwise the chances of hitting the earn-out targets will diminish. Try to keep the business ring-fenced on the sales side, at least for the period of the earn-out, and ensure you still retain access to the distribution capabilities of the group.

Candidly, when this is debated internally the main gripes that will emanate from the central sales team will be lost commission.

Consequently, you need to think about that in advance and be ready before you go in any meeting to discuss the way forward. Get an attractive commission deal signed off and ready to put in place with the wider sales team in the group. Encourage all the sales guys to open doors to new clients, make introductions to help sell your products and promote your area more widely across the market.

Find out what controls are in place quickly and find a way to remove roadblocks fast.

What controls will be in place? Will you be able to sign contracts? During the time I worked at one large corporation, the CEO was the only person allowed to sign contracts. The process slowed the whole business down, frequently taking weeks to get contracts turned around, and having an impact on the pipeline.

When you experience something similar you need to find ways to remove the blockage. Phone the guy up and explain the situation. Ask if you can sign, given certain criteria. Search for a way around the blockage.

Will new products count towards the earn-out?

If you develop new products post-completion, will you be given credit against your earn out? Or will you only be given recognition for the original products that came with the sale? It's worth clarifying if you are spending significant amounts of your time on new innovative products, will these be acknowledged against your earn-out target, will they count?

For my earn-out, it was initially suggested that only the original product set would count. We argued this would drive the wrong behaviours in the team, that we should be forward looking, and always be thinking about creating new products. Thankfully, common-sense prevailed, and the agreement was changed to also include revenue from all new products we developed.

Finally, stay clear of politics.

There is always a level of politics in large organisations - it is   an inevitable fact.

Some companies seem to be worse than others from what I have heard, compared to what I have experienced. My advice is stay well clear of all such shenanigans, keep negative opinions about people to yourself and don't participate in idle gossip.

Stay neutral, keep close to your product base, your clients, and focus on hitting your numbers.

References / Further Reading

1. https://www.forbes.com/sites/forbestechcouncil/2017/1 0/19/the-three-reasons-why-tech-ma-deals-fail-to-deliver-value

Key takeaways

• Closing of a deal can be frantic, though it goes by in a flash. What will you buy as a present to yourself for all the sacrifices and hard work?

• The corporate world is quite different to what you have been accustomed to. There is a lot of bureaucracy, it requires a different skillset, and you need to adapt quickly.

• The first task to do once you start back under the new owner is to reassure your staff about the immediate future.

• To improve your chances of successfully achieving your earn-out you need to:

- Ask for support and delegate the integration, planning, and implementation of the business into the new group organization. Do not underestimate the amount of work involved in integration. Your chances of hitting any ambitious growth targets will be diminished if you must focus on integration.

- Be crystal clear regarding the metrics used to trigger any earn-out payments.

- Delegate as many administrative tasks as you can. Ask for more resources if too much of your time is being wasted on low grade tasks.

- Build credibility internally with the new owners, be laser focused on hitting your numbers from day one.

- Try to keep control of the sales function, at least for the period of the earn-out.

- Find out what controls are in place and uncover ways of removing roadblocks quickly.

- Check whether new products will count towards the earn-out. If not argue the case to get this changed.

- Stay clear of any politics.

HOMEWORK

Now over to you.

1. *Start by making a bucket list of things you would like to buy as a present to yourself?*

2. *Make a list of personal contacts that have helped you along the way in growing the business. Once the deal has been made public be sure to give each of these people a call, thank them and arrange to take them out for lunch?*

CHAPTER 14: SUMMARY AND PARTING THOUGHTS

'A winner is a dreamer who never gives up'

- *Nelson Mandela*

When you start an entrepreneurial process it's all about the idea, the concept, the opportunity. If you don't have a great product or service, something that solves a problem, something that people want to buy, you won't get very far. Starting a new venture is tough. It is a rollercoaster ride, requiring a vast amount of hard work, determination, and conviction.

Scaling your start-up business into an established company, and then selling it for millions is even more challenging.

It is not for the faint-hearted.

Yet it can be done; take courage from my experiences. And, if I can do it, on more than one occasion, then SO CAN YOU. Yes, you will have to work long hours, be strong-minded, determined and recruit great talent to help make it happen. In my mind, though, the most significant factors, in shaping success beyond a great idea, in being able to scale a business, boils down to three things.

You, the founder, your beliefs and vision, your tenacity to keep moving forward, your resilience to cope with setbacks, your determination to move things forward, that this will be successful and something that will work. You need to be able to communicate the vision effectively and be able to influence others. You must be able to enthuse and energise people to join you on the journey, suppliers to want to work with you, and customers to trust you and buy from you.

And, eventually, for people to buy the company from you.

Secondly, you need a great team that is functionally diverse, with a wide pool of skills, that come together into a cohesive unit all working on a common goal.

Finally, you need a purpose, a reason to be in business, something that is not just self-serving, if you want to motivate and unite others to follow you. To have an emotional attachment, something that binds everyone together and drives a higher performance. Pursuing a goal of just money alone will not be enough.

Look to help others, make a difference, and add value to society.

There are lots of references at the end of each chapter, some are interesting and relevant articles, and some are best-selling business books I have read in the past and found insightful and useful. However, if you read anything further, to help you on your entrepreneurial path, please consider reading the books by Dr Viktor Frankl[1] and Dale Carnegie[2]. Both should be on everyone's compulsory reading list, not only those embarking on a career as an entrepreneur.

Frankl was a psychiatrist who survived four concentration camps during World War II, including Auschwitz. He witnessed and suffered unimaginable atrocities at the hands of the Nazis. In his book, which he wrote in the immediate aftermath of the war, he discusses mindset and meaning considering his own experiences.

Frankl observed a stronger will to live in some of his fellow prisoners, who he believed were more likely to survive, compared to others who often lost hope and gave up. He attributed this mindset to finding a larger purpose, knowing the 'why', having dreams to fulfil in life where they could contribute to the World, conscious of some sense to their existence. He argues that if you want to find meaning and fulfilment in life then pursue a worthwhile cause, success and wealth will follow as a biproduct.

Frankl refers to the German philosopher Friedrich Nietzsche and believes you should search to uncover the 'Why?' in what you do.

As Nietzsche puts it,

'Once you know the 'Why?', you will be able to bear almost any 'How?'.

Dale Carnegie's book is a gem in helping to understand how to communicate more effectively, how to connect with people, and how to influence others towards your way of thinking. Read this and you will discover how to improve these key skills. These are crucial for every entrepreneur as you progress along the path of successfully scaling up your business.

Thank you for reading this book. I sincerely hope it has been of some use to you, that you have picked up a few tips, and perhaps got some inspiration. I wish you all the best of luck in your future business ventures.

When you do eventually sell your business and collect that large cheque (or receive that bank transfer), you will soon understand, and realise, as an entrepreneur, it wasn't all about the money after all.

It was about the freedom and challenge to be your own boss and do your own thing. To compete against much larger and more prominent companies in the market, and win!

It was about creating something of worth that is sustainable, that serves a purpose and that is of value to society.

It was about executing your plan, making it happen and having some fun along the way.

It was all about the journey!

References / Further Reading

1. Frankl E. Victor: 'Man's search for meaning' The classic tribute to hope from the Holocaust. Rider
2. Carnegie Dale: 'How to win friends and influence people' Penguin.

The 'Why' behind this book

I wrote this book during the lockdown of the 2020 pandemic because I want to share some of my career experiences to help others. I am passionate about the value entrepreneurship contributes to society through generating new jobs, innovation and bringing new ideas to market, not to mention the impact of wealth creation on the economy. I have been successful as an entrepreneur, and I want to give something back that may be useful to business owners, prospective entrepreneurs and young people thinking about starting their own firm.

A proportion of the proceeds from this book will be donated to the Prince's Trust (www.princes-trust.org.uk), a charity that helps and supports young people aged 11-30, often from disadvantaged backgrounds, build their confidence, start a business and fulfil their potential. A career as an entrepreneur can be satisfying, exciting and extremely rewarding. I want to help more people, like myself from less well-off backgrounds, to have the courage to do their own thing, follow their passion and start their own company. By purchasing this book, you have contributed.

Thank you for your support.

Next Steps

Please go to the website www.scale-for-sale.com if you would like to download the worksheets included in each chapter. The password for the pdf file is 'START-TO-SCALE'.

You can also connect with me on LinkedIn at https://www.linkedin.com/in/mark-harrison-scale-for-sale/ or send a message to mark.harrison@scale-for-sale.com.

If you enjoyed reading this book, please write a review on Amazon or give the book a mention on social media with a link to my website (www.scale-for-sale.com). I'd love the book to help others and to be useful, so if you have found it to be of any benefit, please spread the word. It will have made writing it worthwhile. Thank you.

APPENDICES

EXAMPLE: KEY COMPONENTS OF A CONFIDENTIAL INFORMATION MEMORANDUM

What are the typical components of a Confidential Information Memorandum?

This is a sales document to showcase your company so make sure you (with support from your advisors) put in the graft to ensure it is a quality document. Some advisors also produce this in the form of a slide deck or pitch deck rather than a report though cutdown a little, it will tend to cover a similar structure. The following list of points are the typical sections usually covered within a sales memorandum for the sale of a technology business (e.g., software/analytics). It may need to be adjusted for other industries (e.g., describing capital assets such as machinery) though many of the sections will be similar.

1. Confidentiality & legal notice, disclaimer, terms of distribution.

2. **Executive summary.** In this initial section cover the purpose of the memorandum (e.g., 'sets out the investment opportunity for potential purchasers wishing to acquire 100% of the share capital of...), the reason for the sale, the proposition, and an overview of the financial performance and future opportunity. Make sure you also highlight the strategic key value drivers, for example, high growth profitable company, blue-chip customer base, experienced management team, trusted & established brand etc. This will grab the attention of potential buyers and arouse an eager interest to continue reading the rest of the document.

3. **Value proposition, your product offering.** Why do you do what you do? What value do you provide for your customers

across your different product offerings and why do people buy from you?

4. **The competitive landscape and current industry trends in your area.** What is happening in your industry now? What are the key trends impacting the market and your company? How might these influence your strategy and growth initiatives? What competition do you currently face and how do you compete? How is the competitive landscape changing?

5. **Your customers and suppliers. What is the total addressable market for each market segment you are targeting?** How many customers do you have and how is the revenue distributed across these? How much of this is repeat income and how much is secured for the next few years ahead? For each of your revenue generating areas what is the total addressable market for each segment.

6. **Your suppliers.** What are the range of suppliers you use and what agreements do you have in place? Are any of these agreements exclusive? Are there any restrictions that might impact any potential growth initiatives?

7. **Operations and your team, including management experience, depth, and strengths.** What technologies do you use to build your products? What is the make-up of the team (management\finance & admin\software development\analytics\production\sales\customer support)? What is the background and experience of the key individuals in the management team? What is the culture and how is the company operated? How is the share ownership structured? What offices do you lease or own and what are the terms of the agreement(s)?

8. **Growth initiatives that make the company an attractive purchase.** What are the future opportunities that are going to feed the growth of the business over the next few years? It must be believable to grab the interest of potential purchasers. There needs to be some potential upside for the buyer to get excited about buying the company. It will also help to justify a higher price.

9. **Potential synergies between your company and the buyer (customize for different buyers where the opportunities may differ).** Would you be able to tap into new markets and customers through the buyer? Do they have resources that could help to supercharge your growth in existing and new markets? Are there significant cross-selling opportunities for the buyer to sell other products and services into your customer base? Are there potentially significant cost savings to be realised through integrating the business into the buyer company? Could the resources of both companies be combined such that the value generated is greater than simply a sum of the parts?

10. **Strengths & opportunities.** What are the existing strengths and value drivers of the business? What are the opportunities in the current and other markets, including overseas, that a buyer with more resources could take advantage of? What are the amazing opportunities that make the purchase of your company such an exciting proposition?

11. **Your financial plan** Include a summary profit and loss account for the last 3 years and the next 3 years ahead. Make sure this is presented in a way that is fair but also shows your business in the most attractive way. For example, if there were any unusual one-off costs in any year, add these back in. If you have several Non-executive Directors salaries included that won't be staying with the company add these

back as well. Make sure you get these professionally prepared and presented clearly. When you get to the presentation stage and due diligence the numbers will be put under the microscope, you will be expected to know them thoroughly.

12. Appendices This should include an organization chart, full audited accounts for the last 3 years and any product diagrams if it aids clarity and understanding of what you do. However, always be mindful of what information you are supplying and protect trade secrets, commercially sensitive information, and your IP as much as you are able.

EXAMPLE LETTER OF INTENT

Mr Richard Splash,
Managing Director,
Ideal Software Limited,
31 Kings Square,
Leeds,
LS3 1UC,
UK.
20th November 2020

Strictly Private & Confidential
Subject to Contract, Due Diligence, and BBS Group Plc board Approval

Dear Richard,

Following the recent discussions this non-binding letter sets out the principal terms of the offer by BBS Group Plc ("BBS") to acquire the entire issued share capital of Ideal Software Limited ("the Company").

The assumption is that the Company is acquired on a debt free basis on completion.

Subject to contract, satisfactory outcome of the due diligence and BBS board approval, BBS is prepared to offer:

1. £18,200,000 payable in cash (subject to £1,000,000 retention to be held in Escrow for 12 months against any claims arising) on completion of the acquisition.

    This payment is made on the basis that there is a minimum of £2,000,000 in cash in the Company's bank account available for the benefit of BBS on completion.

    To the extent that the cash balance exceeds/is less than £2,000,000 then an adjustment will be made, pound for pound, to the consideration paid as appropriate. Additional consideration will be paid where there is an excess and, if there is a shortfall, then a deduction will be made to the consideration.

In any event the Company will have a minimum cash balance of £250,000 at completion; and

2. A further amount of up to £1,800,000 which will be payable in bank guaranteed 6-month loan notes, with a 1% interest rate, issued to shareholders in equal instalments over a three-year period on achievement of agreed financial targets.

The targets, against which the additional payments will be made, will be set as future annual revenue levels to be achieved by the Ideal Software product set.
The revenue targets for each of the three years following completion are to be mutually agreed in writing prior to closure of the transaction.

All cash amounts to be paid would be made available by BBS.
The terms and conditions for the Company staff will be no worse than those which they currently enjoy, subject to due diligence. We value the deep domain expertise of the staff and fully intend to retain the services of all staff involved with the Company. It is our intention to retain the office space in Leeds.

To enable a smooth transition, continuity, and the functional integration of the business post acquisition, we will require Mr Richard Splash, as a key employee and the on-site leader, to remain with the company for a minimum period of 24 months post completion. Mr Richard Splash will be paid an annual salary of £300,000 and will be entitled to a bonus of £100,000 subject to achieving certain agreed performance objectives.

This offer is subject to your agreement to you granting us an initial exclusive sixty-day period to undertake formal due diligence on the Company, which will involve our external advisory team. A lockout agreement is attached with this letter, if you agree please countersign, and return this document to me as soon as possible.

The offer is also subject to the signing of a formal sale and purchase agreement which will include the usual provisions such as warranties, liabilities, restrictive covenants, and retentions. Please send me details of your legal team looking after the negotiation of the transaction for you.

This letter is confidential to you, and us, and our respective advisors, and is subject to the confidentiality agreement already entered into signed on 12th August 2020, which continues in full force and effect despite the signing of this letter.

Each party shall bear all its own costs and expenses in connection with this transaction, whether or not it proceeds. We would be grateful if you would respond in writing to me, confirming your agreement to the terms of this offer, together with the signed lock-out agreement at your earliest opportunity.

I look forward to progressing this to a satisfactory conclusion and welcoming you into the BBS Group soon.

Yours sincerely

William Biggleswade
Director
For and on behalf of
BBS GROUP PLC

EXAMPLE DUE DILIGENCE CHECKLIST (INITIAL)
(Not exhaustive and pre-Legal Diligence & Disclosures)

General business information

- Corporate structure, with details of any subsidiary companies or holding companies, share ownership structure and share class rights.
- Articles of Association and Shareholders Agreement
- Brief history of the development of the business.
- Sight of statutory records for all companies in the Group.
- General background information as available, including marketing brochures, advertising literature, strategy papers and plans.
- Copies of board minutes.
- Copy of disaster recovery\business continuity plan.
- Copies of business insurance coverages by type and level of cover.

Finances

- Copies of last three years audited accounts with full trading account and detailed balance sheet, and auditors' reports to management for the last three years.
- Detailed profit and loss statements for the last three years with explanations for any significant fluctuations in performance.
- Monthly management accounts for the last two years and the Budget/Forecast for the current year.
- Details of the Dividend policy.
- Notes on accounting policies used (e.g., revenue recognition, depreciation and research and development). Have any policies changed over the last five years?

- Highlight any exceptional or non-recurring expenditure.
- Details of Borrowings including hp/lease finance; Detailed analysis of all overheads, fixed vs variables costs, and reasoning for any fluctuations from year to year.
- Aged list of Debtors with summary of bad debt provisions, and details of all historical bad debts incurred over the last three years.
- Aged list of Creditors; an analysis of all accruals and committed future costs.
- Details of tangible fixed assets (fixed asset register and any property owned or leased) and intangible fixed assets (trademarks, patents, licences, capitalized goodwill) with historical cost, amortization, and related income stream.
- Detail all existing loan agreements, bank facilities and outstanding finance.
- Copies of all tax computations (Corporation Tax, VAT, PAYE/NIC) and relevant paperwork, including correspondence with HMRC for the last 7 years.

Management and Staff

- Details relating to Directors and Senior Management, covering roles & responsibilities, reporting structure, and remuneration. Include example Director's Service level agreement and employee contract (anonymized).
- Schedule of anonymised employees by; role, service length, notice period and remuneration & benefits.
- Details of pension scheme provided.

Products/Customers/Suppliers

- Schedule of largest ten customers in the current year and previous two years.

- Schedule of ten largest suppliers/contractors. Details of any exclusive agreements.
- Details of commercial terms by customer and suppliers (redacted where necessary to protect confidential information), i.e., length of contract, value, renewal date, products licenced etc.
- Technical specifications of products.
- Pricing policy and any changes made recently.
- Analysis of turnover by product and country.

IT/Operations

- Software Architecture, methods, development tools.
- Programming languages used and depth of expertise, knowledge of staff.
- Hardware and operating systems.
- Security of systems, controls, and policies in place.
- Use of any unlicenced software.
- Inventory of databases.
- Inventory of all internal support systems.
- Documentation of products, systems, software, procedures & processes.

Market Dynamics

- List of main competitors with estimated market share of relevant markets.
- Trends in the market (past, present, and future).
- Analysis of Total Addressable Market (by applicable market segment)

Legal

- Litigation actual/pending/threatened and disputes. Identify the status of each action, the likely outcome and expected costs.

- Copy of standard contractual template used with customers and suppliers.
- Schedule of contracts where terms of agreement have deviated from standard terms.

Office/Property

- Summary of premises with details of tenure, addresses, size with lease agreements and rent details, rent reviews, break dates, or estimated value (if owned).

Acknowledgements

I feel extremely lucky and fortunate to have had the free time to focus on writing this book. It is an indulgence, spending six months or more absorbed on putting a manuscript together, and I wouldn't have been able to do this without the support of my long-suffering wife Alison.

Alison, I love you, and thank-you for everything you do. You have always been incredibly supportive of my entrepreneurial ventures over the years and have done an amazing job of looking after our family, whilst I focused on business. I am lucky to have you and our three wonderful children Abby, Josh, and Jonathan.

To my kids, you mean the world to me and I am immensely proud of all three of you. If you get around to reading this one day, remember; follow your passion, be courageous, work hard and grasp all opportunities that present themselves to you in life.

To my Mum and Dad, thank-you for your love, support, and the main advice you gave me as a child; work hard, get as much as you can from education and treat everyone fairly and with respect.

In writing this book a big thank-you is due to my friends and fellow authors, Maroun Mourad and Siddharth Bhaskar, for providing encouragement at the start of this project, and for giving your support as well as constructive feedback on early drafts throughout the writing process.

I would also like to thank Martin Davies, Rob Archer, Mike Prentice, Jas Awla, Dr Maria Wishart, Dr Paul Beven, Alan Strange, Will Jackson-Moore, Nick Phelps, Felicity Jones, Mike Bright, Steve Allen and Paul O'Dea for your comments and constructive advice on the manuscript. I am fortunate to know such an esteemed group of smart people and grateful for all your advice and input.

I need to say thank-you to all my business partners and colleagues who I have been blessed to work with over the years. I have never stopped learning from you. It has been a privilege and a lot of fun to work with you all. The business successes described in this book are as much down to you as to my efforts. They are the result of great teamwork. I have been successful mainly because I have been privileged in meeting and being able to surround myself with great people and amazing talent. It has often been said there is no 'I' in team and I have been extremely lucky to be part of some fantastic outfits.

To my mentors and friends Mike Prentice and Tony McCallum, thank-you for all your advice and support over the years, it was fun working with you.

Thank you also to all the clients and suppliers that I have worked with, those early adopters taking a chance on a new entrant and all those that have helped to promote technology start-ups in the Insurance market, or 'insurtechs' as they are now more commonly referred to.

To anyone reading this far that I failed to mention and to who I owe a debt of gratitude, my apologies. I'll buy you a pint when I next see you, perhaps at the start of the next adventure.

Printed in Great Britain
by Amazon

62016635R00210